WORLD WAR II
IN THEIR OWN WORDS

WORLD WAR II
IN THEIR OWN WORDS

AN ORAL HISTORY OF PENNSYLVANIA'S VETERANS

BRIAN LOCKMAN

With additional text by Dan Cupper

STACKPOLE
BOOKS

PCN

Published by
STACKPOLE BOOKS
5067 Ritter Road
Mechanicsburg, PA 17055
www.stackpolebooks.com

Printed in the United States of America

10 9 8 7 6 5 4 3 2

FIRST EDITION

Cover design by Wendy Reynolds

Library of Congress Cataloging-in-Publication Data

World War II in their own words : an oral history of Pennsylvania's veterans / [edited by]
Brian Lockman ; with additional text by Dan Cupper.— 1st ed.
    p.   cm.
Includes bibliographical references and index.
ISBN 0-8117-3209-6
    1. World War, 1939–1945—Personal narratives, American. 2. World War,
1939–1945 —Veterans—Pennsylvania—Biography. 3. Oral history. I. Title: World War
Two in their own words. II. Title: World War 2 in their own words. III. Lockman, Brian.
IV. Cupper, Dan. V. Title.
D811.A2W619 2005
940.54'8173'0922748—dc22
                              2004023521

ISBN 978-0-8117-3209-3

☆ CONTENTS ☆

☆ MAPS ☆

☆ FOREWORD ☆

As a veteran of another era, I am honored to have been asked by Pennsylvania Cable Network to offer a foreword for this book reflecting the magnificent television series "World War II: In Their Own Words."

This was an extremely professional venture that permitted some of our "greatest generation" of Pennsylvanians the opportunity to express, without prompting or coaching, their service to our great nation during World War II. Many of these veterans were heroes—but not in their own eyes. Their attitude was "We had a job to do and we did it." And that was the attitude of the majority of these patriots. Dialogue by these great Americans concerned their duties and that of others in their units or aboard their ships. They did not seek fanfare or accolades. The atmosphere was humorous at times and highly emotional at others.

AMVETS recognized PCN for this fantastic series, and the book is of equal value. "World War II: In Their Own Words" is a superb example of PCN's tasteful and ethical programming.

> Kenneth F. Cahill, Executive Director
> AMVETS Department of Pennsylvania

☆ PREFACE ☆

When he came to the front door, he smiled warmly at me, but I could see some apprehension in his eyes. He opened the screen door as wide as it could go as my camera operator, Josh, and I spilled into his living room, armed with heavy bags containing cameras, lights, cables, and audio equipment. "My goodness," he said. "I didn't realize you would be bringing so much equipment with you! Now I'm really getting nervous." He chuckled.

"There's nothing to be nervous about," I reassured him. "I promise you that I won't ask any difficult questions. This interview will be just like having a conversation with someone about your experiences in the war. I just want to hear your story: Hank Heim's story." Hank smiled and said, "Well, I hope I give you a good enough story." Boy, did he give me a good one!

After the equipment was set up and Hank and I were seated across from each other, Josh cued me to start the interview. The apprehension left Hank's eyes as he heard my first question and realized how easy this was going to be. My first question always sets the stage for the story. I like to know what a veteran was doing before he or she joined the service, and whether he or she was drafted or enlisted. Hank had been working in the coal mines and had a terrible accident, and his father decided that Hank would never go back to the mines. So Hank enlisted in the U.S. Army. Thus began Hank's tale of his fascinating and heroic experiences during World War II.

Within minutes, I was whisked away to the early hours of December 7, 1941, on a base in Pearl Harbor, where Hank was writing a letter to his brother while his roommates slept. He didn't get any further than "Dear

Bob" when the first attack began. He looked outside his window to see the USS *Arizona* blow up right in front of him.

Hank proceeded to describe his incredible journey from the attacks on Pearl Harbor to the desert in North Africa, where he would eat his K rations while sitting in the sand, to his missions over Europe as a bomber pilot. He even recounted his continued service in the Korean War. I was spellbound throughout his entire story. I laughed, I cried, I felt exhilarated . . . and I was extremely humbled.

Since I began interviewing World War II veterans of Pennsylvania in April 2002, one word has crept into my vocabulary that I invariably say when I describe my project: humbling. Sure, I had seen Steven Spielberg's movie *Saving Private Ryan* and Tom Hanks's series *Band of Brothers,* and I was certainly aware of the great sacrifices of the incredible generation that fought and worked for my freedom, but it was not until I sat across from veterans and heard them tell their stories that I had a real sense of all that they had sacrificed and how truly brave they were. These men and women, hailing from little towns in Pennsylvania such as Fayetteville, Duncannon, New Bethlehem, and Pen Argyl, grew up experiencing the hardships of the Great Depression. Most of them had rarely left their county, let alone their country. Some of them were so eager to join the services to fight for their country that they went so far as to lie about their age or forge their parents' signatures so that they could enlist. They left behind their parents, their betrothed or spouses, and sometimes even their children.

At the time I started the project, I had just turned twenty-three. I could not fathom the heartbreak of parting with my loved one and the uncertainty of his return. Even the thought of knowing that someone close to me would flirt with death on the ground, in the ocean, or in the air put a lump in my throat. My generation has had the luxury of air-conditioned homes and automobiles, convenient air travel, plenty of food and clothing, and an inevitable college education followed by immediate employment. How vastly different and easy my life has been compared with the lives of the men and women whom I have interviewed! I am in awe of the bravery, resilience, work ethic, and true patriotism of this generation, and I am honored to have been in their presence.

Pennsylvania Cable Network's World War II series began with a meeting of the Programming Department in December 2001. America had just commemorated the sixty-year anniversary of the attack on Pearl Harbor. The PCN staff of four producers and Bill Bova, the vice president of programming, got together and tried to think of a way to showcase the many World War II veterans living in Pennsylvania. Somehow the group determined that I would produce a couple of interviews with veterans using one camera. I was instructed not to edit their words. I knew very little about the war, so I was intimidated by the task ahead of me. I armed myself with phone books from all over the state to look for Veterans of Foreign Wars (VFW) posts and American Legions that might be able to supply me with the names of a couple of veterans. I also bought a few history books to educate myself about World War II. My first few phone calls to veterans were a little awkward. In fact, many veterans heard my young, pleasant voice on the line and promptly hung up, thinking I was trying to sell them something. Eventually I was able to schedule some interviews and quickly learned that most veterans were eager to talk about their experiences and recalled their time overseas in vivid detail.

I am not sure how it happened, but word of PCN's World War II series quickly spread to the far corners of Pennsylvania, and instead of my having to solicit interviews for my project, veterans began contacting me, asking me to interview them. My small project turned into a twenty-four-hour television event, which led to three additional installments of the series. Now, nearly three years after the project's inception, PCN is interviewing veterans for part five of the series. To date, we have interviewed more than 150 veterans, and every story has been unique and a learning experience for me.

The veterans in this book are from the television series, and the stories you will read are taken directly from their interviews. These are the words of ordinary men and women who lived out of their helmets, slept in foxholes, parachuted out of planes into combat, and narrowly escaped death. Both the television series and this book allow you to experience World War II through the words of the people who were there.

My hope is that the stories in this book compel you to find World War II veterans in your community and ask them to tell you their stories. Ask them what it was like to leave home at a young age to fight for their country. Ask them what they saw and what they did overseas. But most important, reach out and shake their hands, and thank them for their sacrifice for your freedom.

Jolene Risser
PCN Producer, "World War II: In Their Own Words"
June 21, 2004

☆ ACKNOWLEDGMENTS ☆

This book is the work of many hands. It never would have come into being if it had not first been a successful television series on the Pennsylvania Cable Network (PCN), a nonprofit, public-affairs cable television network that focuses on the people, politics, history, business, and culture of the Keystone State. PCN was created by and receives its funding from Pennsylvania's cable television companies as a public service.

The television series, comprising to date more than 150 full-length interviews with Pennsylvanians who served in World War II, was produced by Jolene Risser, who located the veterans, persuaded them to sit down for PCN's cameras, conducted nearly all of the interviews, and shepherded the project from concept to air, under the supervision of Bill Bova, PCN's vice president of programming.

Risser received assistance from many people along the way, including PCN camera operators and field producers Corey Clarke, Dave Emenheiser, Matt Hall, Tony Hooper, Robert Krout, Kevin Love, Josh Mackley, and Katie Petrachonis. Larry Kaspar, Bill Bova, and Brian Lockman helped out by conducting additional interviews.

Postproduction work was provided by PCN staffers Kris Hiller, Natalie Hladio, Dave Koch, Nate Kresge, and Brian McCarty. Jennifer Rogers produced the graphics for the television series. Technical assistance was provided by Debra Kohr Sheppard, John Fox, Mark Kendall, Shawn McLain, and Kurt Beadle, with additional assistance coming from Francine Cesari and Theresa Elliot.

Thanks to Nicki Lefever, a staff writer for the *Lancaster Intelligencer Journal,* who featured our project in an article that jump-started a huge interest in the Lancaster area. The *Citizen Standard* gave the project a big boost in its early stages by recruiting World War II vets in Schuylkill, Dauphin, and Northumberland Counties.

Deb Phillips coordinated interviews at Masonic homes, and Mary Ugoletti of Atlantic Broadband Cable set up interviews in Johnstown and Uniontown.

Dick Tyler, Military Order of the Purple Heart, Chalfont, organized the first set of interviews with the cooperation of the Willow Grove Naval Air Station, and Kevin Craft of the Columbia, Pennsylvania, VFW got the ball rolling in Lancaster. Joe Mutzabaugh coordinated several interviews in Duncannon, Lianna Stewart made arrangements for several interviews at Millersville University, and Vince Vicari helped arrange a series of interviews in the Lehigh Valley.

Turning the television series into a book was an entirely different challenge. This project never would have been completed if not for the tireless efforts of PCN's director of corporate communications, Rick Cochran, whose attention to detail, follow-up, good suggestions, and patience were integral parts of the final product. Rick was assisted by Roseann Mazzella, along with Debbie Eckstine and Pam Wert.

The good people at Stackpole Books are a pleasure to work with. Thanks especially to Kyle Weaver for acquiring and developing the project, to David Reisch for his work on production, and to Joyce Bond for copyediting.

Dan Cupper was responsible for the informational "sidebars" that appear throughout the book. These pieces provide background information that should help the viewer gain a better understanding of the veterans' stories. Dan is a first-class writer and researcher, and his work is a welcome addition to this book.

Chris Anderson, editor of *World War II* magazine, helped verify the historical accuracy of the veterans' stories. Chris regularly leads battlefield tours to Europe and is the editor of *Fighting With the Screaming Eagles* by Robert Bowen.

Thanks to the members of PCN's board of directors for all their support and encouragement: David R. Breidinger of Comcast; James D. Munchel of Susquehanna Media Company; David Dane of Atlantic Broadband; Michael Doyle of Comcast; James J. Duratz of Meadville, Pennsylvania; Joseph S. Gans of Gans Multimedia Partnership; Steve Makowski of Adelphia; Fred A.

Reinhard of Pencor Services, Inc.; William C. Stewart of the Armstrong Group of Companies; Robert J. Tarlton of Lansford, Pennsylvania; and Hoyt D. Walter of Service Electric Cablevision.

And special thanks to Pennsylvania's cable television companies for creating and supporting PCN and its public service mission, which enables the network to bring Pennsylvanians closer to their government, history, culture, and fellow citizens.

☆ Henry Heim ☆
New Cumberland, Pennsylvania

Henry Heim enlisted in the Army Air Corps in 1940 as a machine gunner and was wounded at Pearl Harbor. He went on to fly a B-17 Flying Fortress as a member of the 2nd Bomb Group, 20th Squadron. He flew more than seventy-five missions over North Africa, Germany, and the Balkans.

I was a miner working part-time with my father until I was in a cave-in one day. He dug me out and assured me that it was the last day I would ever work in the mines, that I should join the service. I did that about a week later, July 2, 1940.

I went into the Army Air Corps and was sent to Fort Dix for my boot training. After completing that, I was sent to New York, got on a boat, and went to Hawaii, where I was assigned to the 31st Bomb Squadron, Hickam Field. After some schooling, I became an armored gunner—that's a machine gunner. I was a gunner when the Japanese struck on December 7, 1941.

There were about forty men in the barracks wing I was assigned to. I was the only one up. I had my breakfast and was sitting on my cot writing a letter to my brother when I heard a lot of fighter planes. It got real

1

noisy, and some of the guys who were trying to sleep stuck their head up out of bed and cussed out the navy, because they thought our navy was on maneuvers.

Then I heard a roar like a plane diving, and then an awful explosion rocked the barracks. I ran over and looked out the window. I could see the boats in Pearl Harbor on Battleship Row, and I saw what looked like fire. Then another airplane came down, and something dropped out from under it. It hit the boat and the boat exploded. It [the boat] came up out of the water, went back down, and rolled over. It was the *Arizona*.

I had a classmate from high school on the *Arizona*. I had dinner with him on the *Arizona* the Sunday before the raid. We walked around the ship, had a good lunch, and I invited him to come over the next Sunday. He said okay, he would be over about 10:00 A.M. Well the boat was underwater by 7:00 or 8:00. He's still in it.

I knew then that somebody was attacking, but I did not know who. About that time, here comes an airplane right by the window, and it had a pilot shooting straight ahead and a gunner on the plane shooting to the side. I looked up and saw this big rising sun, and I let out a bellow, "Japs!" and hit the floor. Bullets cut through the window screen and shot off a chandelier in the room. When it hit the floor, it crashed, and you should have seen those forty guys jumping out of bed trying to get out of there.

I tried to get out of the barracks two different times, and both times I ran out the door, the Japs were circling, and they dove down and strafed me. The first time I dove back in, the bullets struck the marble floors, so I thought I would find another door. I found a second door, the same thing. Finally I went out the back way, and I did get through. I went over to the hangar where my duty post was and saw a friend of mine, who was a gunner. He was running into the hangar, and I remember I was yelling something at him, and that's the last I remember. They dropped a 500-pounder through the roof of the hangar.

When I came to, I was bleeding pretty badly out of my mouth and my nose. The concussion must have popped my jaws so hard that it split two of my molars and drove them like little razor blades up through my gums and cut my mouth to ribbons.

I kept going after I found out I wasn't dying. I got a machine gun and put it in my airplane, which was shot to pieces, but I still got it in the nose of the plane and started to hammer away at the Japs. They were very low, and one of the Japs came down through there shooting. I felt some bullets

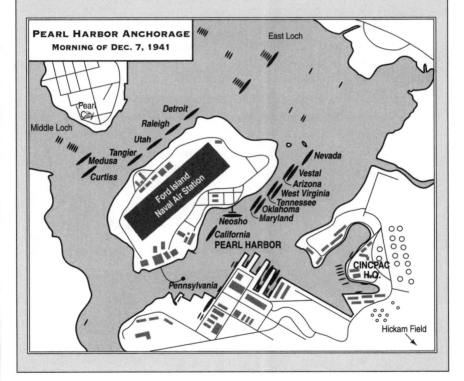

Pearl Harbor Facts

Military facilities damaged

Hickam Field	Ford Island Naval Air Station
Wheeler Field	Kaneohe Bay Naval Air Station
Bellows Field	Ewa Marine Corps Air Station
	Schofield Barracks

PEARL HARBOR ANCHORAGE
MORNING OF DEC. 7, 1941

East Loch

Pearl City

Middle Loch

Detroit
Raleigh
Utah
Tangier
Medusa
Curtiss

Ford Island Naval Air Station

Nevada
Vestal
Arizona
West Virginia
Tennessee
Oklahoma
Maryland
Neosho
California
PEARL HARBOR

Pennsylvania

CINCPAC H.Q.

Hickam Field

striking the plexiglass all around me, and then I smelled smoke. The plane had caught on fire.

I got out of there, and from then on, I was trying to outrun the Japs until the raid ended. I went over to the hospital to get something for my mouth, and when I stepped in the corridor of the hospital, there were navy people, marines, Army Air Corps, and I looked up the hall and all I saw—it's a lit-

Pearl Harbor Facts

Battleships at Pearl Harbor

The first seven ships below were moored together in Battleship Row.

USS *Arizona*: destroyed; became a memorial.

USS *Oklahoma*: hit by five torpedoes and capsized; raised in 1943, but being an older ship (launched in 1914), it was not returned to service.

USS *California*: sank in shallow water; refloated in 1942; returned to service.

USS *Nevada*: deliberately beached to prevent channel blockage; refloated in 1942 and returned to service.

USS *West Virginia*: sank in shallow water; refloated in 1942; returned to service.

USS *Maryland*: hit but not sunk; returned to service in 1942.

USS *Tennessee*: hit but not sunk; incurred lightest damage; returned to service in 1942.

USS *Utah*: ex-battleship, converted to a training ship (bombing target), sank in shallow water; launched in 1909, it was considered to be obsolete and was not returned to service; became a memorial.

USS *Pennsylvania*: damaged in dry dock; returned to service.

tle morbid—was blood and men yelling and carrying on with pain. I thought I wasn't that bad off, so I turned around and went back out, and all night I washed my mouth out with cold water.

That was my Pearl Harbor.

After that they sent me to the States. I wanted to be an Air Corps pilot. I knew I didn't have the smarts, but when the war started, I guess they lowered the requirements. You could have knocked me over with a feather when I found out that I passed the written test. Then I took the physical, and they flunked me because I had two teeth missing in my mouth. They wouldn't take me until I told the board that I lost those two teeth at Pearl Harbor.

Pearl Harbor Facts

Pearl Harbor Casualties and Losses

American military personnel killed

Navy	1,998
Marine Corps	109
Army and Army Air Corps	236
Total, military	2,343
Fatalities on USS *Arizona* alone	1,177
American civilians killed	48
Americans wounded	1,178
Japanese killed	64
American planes destroyed in attack	164
American planes damaged in attack	159
Japanese planes involved in attack	350
Japanese planes destroyed	29
Japanese planes damaged	74
Battleships sunk	6
American ships sunk or beached	12
Japanese ships (minisubs) sunk or beached	5

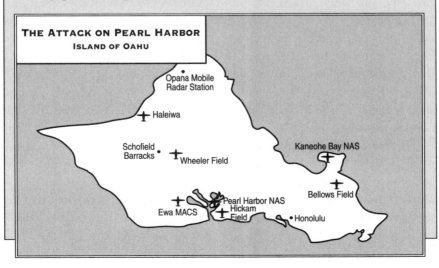

THE ATTACK ON PEARL HARBOR
ISLAND OF OAHU

Opana Mobile Radar Station
Haleiwa
Schofield Barracks
Wheeler Field
Kaneohe Bay NAS
Bellows Field
Pearl Harbor NAS
Hickam Field
Ewa MACS
Honolulu

Then I went to flying school. It took nine months in flying school to become a pilot. Nowadays, I think it takes two and a half years or more, but they couldn't wait that long. Because of the short training time, there were a lot of guys who made mistakes the first week or two they were in combat. You didn't get the training that you should have, but they didn't have the time to give it to you.

I flew my own airplane over to Europe. We took the northern route at night, solid instruments. Couldn't see the land or lights or anything, and my poor navigator couldn't get a celestial fix. We were heading for Prestwick, Scotland, and when we broke out of the overcast sky, we were only 300 feet off the ground and we landed. Out of thirteen bombers that started over, only eight of us made it. We don't know where the other five got to.

After I landed, I looked out of the cockpit and saw this civilian—he looked like a spy, you know, the collar up and walking around. I wondered, what was this civilian doing?

I jumped out of the cockpit and started to walk away when this guy turned toward me and put his hand out, and it was Bob Hope. He was there on tour. He came over and shook my hand and said, "Where are you going?" I said, "I'm going in to get a room." The room was in a hotel the army had taken over. So when I got in there, I went up to the room and slept. Then I took a good hot shower and dressed. When I came out, I locked my door and heard a door slam down the hall. I looked up and there was Bob Hope again. "Come on, buddy," he said, "I'll walk down with you," and we went down to the dining room. Bob Hope went over to one end of the restaurant where it was all plush. I went over to sit with the other GIs.

The next day I took off and went down to England. From England I flew down the coast into French Morocco, up to Oran, Algeria, and into Tunis, Tunisia, where I joined my group. In Africa it was very, very hot during the day and it got cold at night. We had a tent that had no floor except the sand. We had a canvas cot, one blanket, no pillow. We had no sheets or mattresses, and we had no shower. When the shower finally arrived, we were allowed one shower a week.

That's where I learned to drink coffee, because you couldn't drink the water. When I came back from a mission, everybody got a two-ounce shot of whiskey in a little paper cup—100 proof. I wasn't a drinking man; I didn't even touch coffee. The major came over and poured something in a little paper cup and set it down in front of me. I said, "Oh no, sir, I don't drink," and I pushed it back. Well that's the last time I said anything like that to a major. He put his nose right up to me and said, "I'm not asking you, I'm telling you to drink it. You can drink it in coffee, water . . ." They did have big cans of grapefruit juice that I swear they must have drained the acid out of batteries—so I had to use it in coffee. Well I gagged and gagged until I got it down. But after about twenty missions, if you made twenty missions, you were looking forward to it.

The meals were terrible. The mashed potatoes, for instance, were so gummy you could hold a spoon upside down and it wouldn't fall off. If you had meat you didn't get much, and it was very coarse and very fatty. I swear it was horsemeat. They put that on your mashed potatoes, and then you would go down the line to the next guy, and he had a big kettle that was supposed to be gravy—I swear it was nothing more than brown water. He would pour that all over. Then came dessert. It was always the same: fruit cocktail. And guess where they would put it—on top of your gravy, on top of your meat, on top of everything. Then you got your coffee, boiling hot. If you wanted to take a drink of that coffee and you put the cup to your mouth, you would burn your lips, the cup was that hot. When the cup got cold enough to touch your lips, the coffee was cold. That's how the meals were all the time.

When I first got to Italy, the colonel called us in, he must have been forty years old. He scared me just looking at him—I was just a shavetail, you know. I walked in and there he was chomping on a cigar, and the juice was running down his chin. He looks us over, and the first thing that pops out of his mouth is, "If you SOBs think you're going to come over here for some medals, think again. If you get wounded we'll give you a Purple Heart, and if you get killed we'll send it back to your people. The good news is the life span of an aircrew member is nine missions." I looked at the navigator and I said, "Well, it doesn't take a mathematician to know that we are not going to make it. We are supposed to fly fifty missions. The life span is nine."

He was right; a lot of the guys didn't make nine. A copilot of mine—I don't think he was in combat more than two minutes, he was dead. That was my start in combat in Europe.

German fighter pilots were tremendous, and the accuracy of their anti-aircraft fire was out of this world. We were bombing Munich, and they set a wall of flak as antiaircraft fire. There were so many exploding shells that you couldn't see the sun, the sky, or anything. There were times I would say to myself, "Oh my God, I've only got a few seconds to live." If you were trailing another squadron and they went through it first, it was nothing to see explosions and see planes that were burning going down. There was no way you could get through it. It was terrible. Their antiaircraft fire was accurate—oh, was it accurate.

I had a few close ones. When I bombed Vienna, Austria, I came home on two engines. Two out of the four were still turning, and my plane was shot to pieces. Two different ground crews counted the holes. They counted 437 holes shot through my airplane. I only had one man who was killed. I didn't have any wounded, just one man killed. I had a good airplane. A good airplane and good crews. I think that's what got me through it.

The Germans had antiaircraft shells that were set on altitude, so they would explode at 500 feet. On a bombing run one day, a shell came through the cockpit. It came in one end and went out the other. It went off above the tail and, I won't say it was completely blown off, it was just in shreds, just over the tail gunner. I lost about three and a half feet of the wingtip on that mission. And holes—there was a hole in the gas tank that you could stick a football through, with gas pouring out of it.

I thought I was going to have to be interred in Switzerland, because I was above the Alps, I had flown out of formation and couldn't get enough altitude to get over the mountains. So I got a course from my navigator for the Brenner Pass, and I went down through the pass. It was a chore, I'll tell you. I could look out and see mountains on both sides. I came around a turn and eased up, and saw jutting out in front of me a beautiful little red chalet house. Ah, it was pretty.

Another time I had a little turret gunner, about five foot two, 110 pounds. He called me one day in the cockpit and said, "Sir, I'm hit and I can't see." I turned the plane over to the copilot and walked back. The other enlisted men didn't want any part of this. They were a little shy. So I unlocked the door and looked down in. He was hunched down and I pulled him out. He had an oxygen mask on, and I laid him up in my arm; he was almost like a little boy.

I said, "Hang in, Sarge. You are going to be okay." He mumbled something, so I knew he was alive. I unhooked his mask, and when I pulled it off, his eyeballs were laying in the mask. The bullet had gone right behind the bridge of his nose and out the other side. He said something, or tried to say something, and swung his head up to try to look at me. He died right there in my arms.

I have one more story, and then I'll shut up. I was coming home, shot to pieces, going through North Africa. Engine out. All alone. I fell out of formation and I'm still near enemy territory. All a German fighter had to do was sweep up underneath me, and he'd have shot me down over the water.

I heard my left waist gunner say, "Sir, we got a bogey coming in at 9:00." He said, "He's only sliding in, he's not coming head-on." I said, "Don't shoot." So pretty soon, here he came right up alongside of my wing. It was a Focke-Wulf 190, and he was looking at me and I was looking at him.

Now this is not a movie; this is the real McCoy. He sat there escorting me out over the water. There was a spot over the ocean that the Germans didn't go beyond, because if they did, they wouldn't be able to get back. Just before we got there, he slid up to where I could look him right in the eye. He looked at me, saluted me, and I saluted him back. He nodded and went on home. That happened to me, and that happened to other people too. I heard it said they got no joy in killing a man who was already dead, in a sense. You know what I mean. Like I couldn't hurt him, but he could hurt me. I was out of it.

One thing that helped me get through was teamwork. I still say you must have teamwork and surround yourself with good people, and you will be successful. I have the sneaking suspicion it's one of the reasons I'm here.

And you have to have a heck of a lot of luck. My planes had holes all around. I would see a hole and think, "If I had been that far forward or that much farther up, I would have been hit." You had to have a lot of luck and good crew. I think you had to have a lot of confidence in yourself, too.

But I just resigned myself to the fact that I was going to get killed. There was nothing I could do about it. It may sound silly, but I believe that helped. I would take off in the morning when it was dark, and as it got to be daylight I often said to myself, "Well, there's the sun coming up. I wonder if I'm going to see it set today." I had just resigned myself to that. Some guys couldn't. And it was nothing to lay in your tent at night and hear the combat people screaming their heads off. Boy, it was tough to take, I'll tell you.

Everybody was happy to get their fifty missions, but very few people did. I was only the ninth pilot to ever make fifty missions. But they needed lead pilots so badly, they asked three of us—another captain and a major—if we would mind volunteering. We could quit anytime. They couldn't promise us anything, no promotions or anything. The only thing they would promise is that they would have us home in three days after we quit. So the three of us agreed. In six or seven missions, the one captain was killed, and on the thirteenth mission, the major was killed. So out of the three of us that volunteered, I was the only guy left.

So I made my fifty missions, and I made twenty-five more. At first I thought maybe I could get in a hundred—another fifty—but I burned out. I was 23 years old in age and 123 in body. I had given everything. I didn't have any more to give. That's a terrible feeling. Thank God I quit, because I didn't want to kill any of my own men. So I quit. And they were true to their word. I was home in three days.

A lot of people had it tougher, but there were times I would have given six months' pay for a six-inch rut to lay down in. Up there you don't have any rut to lie down in. You're sticking right out there. You can't lie down and you can't run. But there were times I would have given six months just for a little time back in the coal mine. I often thought, "Oh, why did I leave the coal mines?" I wouldn't trade the experience for all the money in the world, but I would never want to go through it again, and I hope no one's children would have to go through it.

Someone asked me this past week, "Didn't you cry, weren't you scared?" Well, I want to tell you something. A commander—I don't care if you only command two men, three men, or four men, you are a commander—is not allowed to show fear. He is not allowed to cry. He has got to be calm all the time when his guts are just tearing to pieces. Because your men are looking at you, and if you are going to start screaming, they are going to do the same.

As hard as it was, I tried not to show these things. I tried to be a commander. Cry? I waited until I got back to the bunk where I could put a blanket over my head, and then they couldn't see it. Like I said, I don't want anybody to go through that anymore. No one. There has got to be a better way.

AFTER THE WAR . . .

Hank Heim served in the reserves and worked for Bell Telephone. His unit was reactivated at the start of the Korean War. After that tour, Heim went back to Bell Telephone as a construction foreman and a teacher for the company. He retired at the age of fifty-seven, and then worked as a tradesman supervisor for the Camp Hill Correctional Institution and as a security manager for Capitol Blue Shield. Heim has been married for sixty-one years and has two children.

☆ Irvin R. Friedman ☆
Philadelphia

• •

Irvin Friedman grew up in Philadelphia. He was living in
Washington, D.C., and working for the government when
he was drafted into the army in September 1941. Friedman
served as an assistant to Gen. George Patton early in his
service. His Transportation Corps landed at Normandy.

• •

I went to boot camp in Fort Knox, Kentucky, where I was trained in the
Armored Force. It was there I first met Gen. George S. Patton, who was
commanding general of the Headquarters, 1st Armored Corps. As a matter
of fact, it was on Pearl Harbor Day that I was assigned to General Patton's
headquarters staff as his runner and general aide.

Pearl Harbor Day was a very interesting day. I had received a weekend
pass that Saturday and Sunday, and I was, like all soldiers, roaming around
the streets of Louisville, Kentucky, when the MP trucks pulled up and they
said, "All GIs back to camp." When we went back to Fort Knox, we discovered that the Japanese had struck Pearl Harbor.

That day was hectic. The troops that I had trained with were sent to Seattle, Washington. Evidently they thought the Japanese would come down the

West Coast. I was told to report back to General Patton's headquarters and was assigned to him permanently. I stayed with the general for the next year and a half. From Fort Knox we went to Fort Benning, Georgia, for training with the 82nd Airborne, and then we moved to the desert training center. The American tank troops had never had any training in desert warfare, so the general had established this training center in the Mojave Desert in California. General Patton was named the commanding general of the desert training center.

We went by train from Fort Benning to Indio, California. Then we loaded onto trucks and headed for the desert. We drove miles and miles for countless hours, until civilization disappeared and it was just barren desert all around. They stopped the trucks and said, "All right, all you guys, get off." There was nothing there but sand hills and dunes. This was camp. We threw our bags down on the ground, and that's where we slept.

There was no water, no electricity, no barracks, and no tents. Then gradually, as more and more troops moved into the camp, they brought in tents. We had a water line and an electric line put in, and things improved quite a bit, but it was still pretty primitive living. Before you know it, we had over 100,000 troops assembled in the desert, training in tank warfare.

I was Patton's runner for a while when I first got assigned to him after I had finished my basic training. I was stationed outside his tent, waiting for his orders whenever he needed me to get messages to other generals or other officers. One assignment that I didn't particularly like was to guard Patton's little Piper Cub. Some rancher had put him up at his house for the time being, so the general would leave camp and fly out on this little Piper Cub. And the Piper Cub was there when he stayed in camp; I had to guard it. He said, "That's your baby, to guard my plane." It was really a pain in the neck out in the desert, guarding this tiny little Piper Cub. That was an interesting experience.

I was working in the general's headquarters staff at that time. I was selected for officer candidate school and was sent to Fort Lee, Virginia, for training. I became what they humorously referred to at that time as the "ninety-day wonder." They tried to push four years of West Point into three months, which is impossible. Then I was assigned to an outfit going to Fort Custer, Michigan, for snow and ice training. I had just come out of a year and a half in the desert, and my first assignment is in Fort Custer, Michigan, for snow and ice training!

I was sent over to England as an advance party for my regiment. My assignment was to make arrangements for the company, which was split up into three different areas of the southern base of England. I went alone and had to do all the preparation for the entire regiment: supplies, logistics, the arrangements with the British government, and contracts for where we were to live and the things that we were to get. It was quite a job. Then our regiment came over, and we spent about a year in England waiting for the invasion.

Then the big day came—June 6. You have seen a lot of movies about the invasion, and it was a tremendous event. But the movies kind of spoil you. You think only of that beach landing, with all the terrible deaths and destruction and casualties that occurred in those first forty-eight hours. About 175,000 troops landed in the first forty-eight hours, but we had about another million to come in. Beach landings were occurring for the next two months, till the end of July, so even though the first two days made the big headlines, these beach landings went on for two months.

I had a heavy truck company at that time, and my truck company couldn't land until the army had moved forward and captured some land. We needed to capture the port of Cherbourg and the port of La Havre so our ships could land with the heavy supplies. You couldn't get a lot of big heavy trucks running around there when we were stuck on the Normandy peninsula, and Patton and his tanks were unfortunately stuck there for a little while.

They had forgotten one simple little thing, the smallest item. You think they would have thought of everything, but the littlest thing caused a delay of a couple of weeks. French farms don't have fences around them like American farms. They have hedgerows that are vines as thick as my arm and have grown for hundreds of years. They are about ten feet high and ten feet wide. Patton's tanks couldn't push them down and run through them. He thought he would spread out over the fields and move en masse. Instead, he was stuck going down secondary country roads, and sure enough, you get to the end of a section and there would be a German Tiger tank waiting.

That held up the campaign for a couple of weeks, and everything back-fired. I was sitting out in the English Channel on the landing craft for four days waiting to land, to get on the beach and then move inland. By that time we had captured enough ground for heavy truck companies and heavy artillery pieces to land ashore. But we still landed on the beach, and I drove up onto the beach in my jeep.

There was still a lot of artillery firing and bombing at night. The Luft-waffe was very active, and I made such a great target. When I lined up in full array with my whole company, I spread out to about two miles on the

Gen. George S. Patton Jr.

Equally revered and reviled, Gen. George S. Patton Jr. was one of the most effective, profane, and outspoken military leaders in U.S. history. He proudly wore the nickname "Old Blood and Guts."

Born in 1885, he was a California native who graduated from West Point in 1909. He represented the United States in the pentathlon at the Olympic Games of 1912 in Stockholm, finishing fifth. Fighting in World War I, he developed a deep interest in, and mastery of, tank warfare.

During World War II, he earned praise for leadership in three campaigns: the Operation Torch invasion of North Africa in 1942; the capture of Sicily in 1943; and his 3rd Army's role in the 1944–45 liberation of Europe and rout of Germany. He also participated in the Battle of the Bulge. Patton was the first commander to institute the practice of forcing local German civilians to tour Nazi death camps that had been liberated.

With equal ease, he could deliver one-liners at a party or a blistering motivational speech to soldiers going into battle. Among his lines were the following: "Better to fight for something than live for nothing," "Success is how high you bounce when you hit bottom," and "Do your damnedest in an ostentatious manner all the time." His tight discipline and insistence that men give their best—all the time, every time—won respect and boosted morale. Patton could fine a soldier for a uniform infraction one day and expect him to fight to the death for him the next. He always wore an ivory-handled revolver, partly because of his flamboyance, but also to remind his troops that he was no armchair general.

His bullying style also got him into trouble. Visiting military evacuation hospitals in August 1943, Patton slapped two men who were suffering from combat fatigue, accusing them of being soft. Gen. Dwight D. Eisenhower almost dismissed him, but instead reprimanded him and ordered him to apologize, which he did.

After VE Day Eisenhower appointed Patton military governor of the Bavarian section of Germany, but his outspokenness was his

Gen. Dwight D. Eisenhower, accompanied by Gen. Omar N. Bradley and Lt. Gen. George S. Patton Jr., inspects art treasures stolen by Germans and hidden in salt mines in Germany, April 1945. NATIONAL ARCHIVES

undoing. He was reassigned after defending the idea of using ex-Nazis in administrative posts and skilled jobs; he also advocated rearming Germany to join the United States and Britain in opposing Soviet Russia.

Patton died not in combat, but as a result of an auto accident on Germany's Autobahn in December 1945. He was buried in Luxembourg. ★

highway, loaded with ammunition and explosives. The Luftwaffe were look-ing for us. That was one of the big problems, getting your convoy through alive. As the war progressed and we got further inland into France, the Luft-waffe were being shot down, so they were less of a problem.

The Transportation Corps started what was called the "Red Ball Express." This was an amazing convoy run. We blocked off a road from Paris to Cher-bourg, the port on the Normandy peninsula, and no civilian traffic was allowed. We had big red balls painted on every truck—the Red Ball Express. We had the road to ourselves, which was beautiful, because at that time France did not have a superhighway like Germany had with the Autobahn.

We had one main highway leading all the way down the peninsula. This was about 600 miles round-trip, and no other vehicles were allowed except military trucks. We ran this from the port to the areas where they had depots, and this went on twenty-four hours a day, seven days a week, non-stop. We ran loaded to the gills, and of course we still had to worry about strafing from the Luftwaffe. The Red Ball Express was an amazing feat set up by the Transportation Corps. You see, war is all about supplying the troops; the poor guy that is running the gun on the front can't fire that weapon unless he has the bullets and the ammo to fire. The tanks can't run unless they have the gasoline to make them run.

In the Transportation Corps, I saw the war as very few enlisted men or officers did, because we were on the move constantly. I could be in Paris in the morning and then Brussels, Belgium, in the afternoon. Sometimes it got me into a little trouble. I was used to operating in the 3rd Army area, which I was a part of. They had a password for traveling at night, and if a guard stopped you, you gave him the password. A couple of times, without real-izing it, I drifted into 1st Army area, which was up in Belgium and north-ern France, and the guards stopped me and asked me for the password. I didn't realize I had passed into the 1st Army area, and I didn't know the 1st Army area password.

This was the winter of 1944–45, and Germany had put a lot of its sol-diers in American uniforms. The Germans who had been raised or educated in the United States spoke perfect American English. They had captured American uniforms and were infiltrating our outer lines and knocking off some of our platoons and squads because they thought it was an American squad, since they knew all the baseball lingo, but they were Germans. So when I would stop with my convoy and I didn't know the password, man, I could hear twenty rifles clicking. They thought they had one. And then they would hustle me off to headquarters, and I had to prove who I was and what I was doing and why I didn't know the password.

The Battle of the Bulge was an interesting event. My company was bivouacked about thirty miles south of Paris, and I got orders to proceed to Rheims, France, to pick up the 101st Airborne. They were on R and R, rest and recreation, in the area. My orders were to get them to a place called Bastogne in Belgium, where the Battle of the Bulge was taking place. They were almost totally surrounded at the time. The airplanes couldn't fly because of the overcast skies and cloud formations. So for the first time in their history, the 101st Airborne was not parachuted into a battle; they were driven into a battle with trucks.

After the Battle of the Bulge, the war settled down. I got an assignment to help a combat engineer company put a bridge over the Rhine River. Patton and all the 3rd Army tanks were lined up on the west side of the Rhine, and they couldn't cross over. We were trying to get into Berlin before the Russians, but Patton was stuck because our Air Force had bombed the bridge over the Rhine River. We got orders to build a pontoon bridge, and I was assigned to work with this engineer company to bring up all the pontoons and everything that was needed and help them put up that bridge. They built it in less than forty-eight hours. It was a magnificent thing.

That next morning Patton and his crew showed up to cross the bridge with his tanks. He was in the lead tank, and as he went over the bridge, I gave him a salute and he returned the salute. That was the last time I saw him.

I'll finish out by telling you about my saddest day in the army, and that was the day I came home, the day I was discharged. I left from Liege, Belgium, and we were loaded onto an old, beat-up, rusty Liberty ship full of officers. We arrived in Boston at twilight. It was getting dark when we pulled in, and there was nobody there. Silence. We were used to seeing the news, as the soldiers came home, the parades and the raising flags and kissing of the relatives and family, and crowds greeting the homecomings. But we were coming home long after that occurred. We pulled into this dreary port in Boston. There was nobody there, not a soul. We all walked down the plank, carrying our little duffle bags, looked around, shook hands, and said, "See you, guys."

I put my bag down, looked around, and said to myself, "Here it is, five years later. I'm in Boston, no money, no job, no education, 500 miles from home." And that's the day I came home.

I don't particularly like to talk to civilians about the things that happened in the army, because they don't understand. It's very hard to explain to a civilian what you went through—the sounds, the smells of battle, or the fears that you went through in the war. They just don't understand it. It bores them. But they should hear it. It was an amazing part of American history. I am glad I was part of it.

AFTER THE WAR . . .

Irvin Friedman returned home to Philadelphia following five years with the army. He took advantage of the GI Bill and received his doctor of medical dentistry degree. Dr. Friedman ran a practice in Philadelphia for forty-two years and also spent twenty-two years as an assistant professor of oral medicine at Temple University Dental College. He and his wife, Dorothy, have a son and a daughter.

☆ Chuck Bednarik ☆

Bethlehem, Pennsylvania

Chuck Bednarik served in the U.S. Army Air Forces during World War II. He was an aerial gunner who flew thirty missions over Europe. He played professional football for the Philadelphia Eagles and is a member of the Pro Football Hall of Fame.

I was brought up during the Depression. It was a tough time and I lived in a tough neighborhood. We'd have fistfights every day. You'd put something on your shoulder and say, "Go ahead, knock it off." If the guy knocked it off, boom, boom, boom. Fighting every day, bloody noses over anything.

I was in high school and still had a year to go when I turned eighteen. All my buddies were leaving to go into service, and I thought it was something great to do. I couldn't wait until I was drafted. Lo and behold, two or three months after I turned eighteen, I was drafted.

I was assigned to the Army Air Forces. When they told me, "Maybe you could be a pilot," I got all excited. But I flunked my test. I could pass the one portion of it, but when it got to the mechanics, I didn't know what the heck was going on, and I completely blew it. They asked me if I would like to still be in the air force and go to gunnery school. I said yes, because I would do anything to be in the air force. So I became an aerial gunner and flew thirty combat missions all over Germany.

I had never flown in my life. I'll never forget the first time I got in a plane. It was at Tyndall Field, Florida, where I went for gunnery training. We were assigned a crew and completed training in Boise, Idaho. Training involved flying combat missions and dropping some bombs—but not real ones. That training only took about two months, and then it was time to go.

We picked up a brand new B-24 Liberator bomber and flew it overseas. We were assigned to a place in England that was called Rackheath. It was not too far away from the English Channel, and of course, you had France right across the channel, so we were close enough to get to Europe.

All thirty of my missions were over Germany. We went to Berlin one time—the whole 8th Air Force. There were about 1,500 to 2,000 bombers going over Berlin and dropping bombs on them. But most of our targets were for industrial purposes—places like oil fields or where they made army tanks. It wasn't just a matter of killing people, going over a big city and dropping bombs on them. It was targets that were involved with industry.

On a B-24 or a B-17, you had a nose gunner, you had one in the tail, you had one up in the top turret, one in the belly, and then in the back, you had one on each side. I was in the back in the waist with a .50-caliber machine gun. I only had to fire it on a couple of missions.

It's amazing: We were pushing through France and knocking the Germans as they were going. Our air force was establishing air bases, and when we would get there, they would escort us fighters. So when the Luftwaffe came, our escort planes would go after them. The Germans, of course, had to run. But if you were a straggler and there was a German plane in the area, they'd go right after you, and normally they'd shoot you down. Most of the problem was the antiaircraft fire. They were pretty accurate, and most of the planes I saw go down were as a result of antiaircraft.

The scariest one of my missions over Germany was after General Patton broke through St. Lô. Patton really moved those tanks, and he was pushing the Nazis back. He was going so fast that his 500 tanks ran out of gas, so they called us. My crew was assigned to deliver gas ten miles behind enemy lines, landing on a field that they patched up so we could land. We had no bombs in the bomb bay; we had nothing but gasoline—thousands of gallons of gasoline. Picture taking off or landing with a plane full of gasoline. If we had crashed, I would be dust. That mission scared the hell out of us. We went over and landed, and I could hear some *boom, boom* from where the fighting was going on. We dumped that gas off to them and got the hell out of there real fast. I was scared on missions, but I was still proud, and I was happy to serve my country.

It took nine or ten months to complete thirty missions. You wouldn't go up every day, because most of the time the weather was bad, so you may not fly for ten days, so there was pretty much time in between, and you were happy to be alive for another ten days.

There was a bulletin board that listed crew numbers that were going to fly that day. That was how we knew we were going to fly. If your crew number was on there, that meant you got up at 5:00 A.M., you got a 6:00 A.M. breakfast, you were briefed at 7:00, and at 8:00 you took off for Europe. The trip to Berlin was about seven or eight hours, so by the time we got back, it was 4:00 in the afternoon. For the other missions, we were back at 2:00 or 3:00 in the afternoon.

After that thirtieth mission, when I landed, I'll never forget, I landed and said, "I made it." I kissed the ground and said, "I never want to fly again." I was a kid, only eighteen, nineteen years old, and I was frightened, but so was everybody else. The Nazis were frightened. Those guys were as scared as we were. It's a war. You're killing. It's terrible.

If a young person today wants to go enlist, I admire him. I would want to tell him, "You're a hero of mine. You're a gutty, tough kid, and I'll pray for you."

AFTER THE WAR . . .

Upon his discharge, Chuck Bednarik contacted his high school football coach to inform him that he was eligible to attend college under the GI Bill. Bednarik eventually went on to become a two-time All-American for the University of Pennsylvania and led the Philadelphia Eagles to a 1960 NFL title.

☆ Nick Gazibara ☆

Export, Pennsylvania

Nick Gazibara was a tail gunner in the Army Air Forces.
He was a prisoner of war in Japan and was
interrogated at the Kampei-tai Military Prison in Tokyo.

I went to gunnery school at Buckingham Air Force Base in Fort Myers, Florida. Then I went to Holloman Air Force Base in Alamogordo, New Mexico, where we trained for three or four months in the B-29.

Our first mission was Kawasaki, Japan, near Tokyo, where we were the last plane in the group. When you are last, the chances are the enemy knows where you are. The first thing we saw was one searchlight, then two, then three. We got flak and caught on fire. One of the engines was burning on one side, and then another engine was burning. Then we got a hit in the center of the plane, and the order came to bail out.

The funniest thing about it is, I had a parachute on, and that's the first time I had it on. Most of the time I didn't have a parachute. They told us if we were ever in trouble, pull the lever and the parachute pops out. Well, once I was out in midair, they said count to ten and I did, and I pulled the ripcord and the chute opened.

It was nighttime and I landed in a wooded area. The thing is, when you land with a parachute, what do you do with the parachute? You try to hide it. How was I going to hide a parachute? I tried to fold it, but because it was dark, I couldn't do it. I just threw it down and ran away. Only eight of the eleven guys on the plane that night jumped.

For about the next two weeks, I was going around in circles in the woods. The Japanese knew I was there, but they could never catch me, because I had a little bit of experience in the woods. Not that I was good at it, but I knew how to hide. What was I going to do? There was nobody else. I had no help. I thought I could escape, but I didn't know where I was; I knew I was in Japan, that's all.

By the end of the thirteenth or fourteenth day, I started to run out of food. I didn't have any food other than two sandwiches and a chocolate bar. I came across a rice paddy where there were three women working. I walked up to them, put my hands up, and said, "I want to surrender." They ran away, so I ran in the other direction, figuring, "Boy they are going to catch me now." I took a branch and some limbs and covered myself for the night. The next morning, I could hear them. When they finally found me, they made me hold my hands up and tied my hands to a bamboo pole. They walked me up over the ridge and down for two hours. It was a long way. Then we went into a courtyard of a school, and a man there said he would interrogate me.

They asked me my name and questioned me as much as they could. They weren't brutal or anything. Then they took me back outside, blindfolded me, and led me to a railroad station. I waited a while, and then a train came. We jumped on the train and rode to the next station. When they took me off the train, I was still blindfolded, but I could tell they had tied me to a park bench. There was a bunch of kids there who were all taking chances taking swings at me, punching me a little bit.

Soon I heard a train coming. One guy took me over to the train track and put my head down. I was handcuffed; there was nothing I could do. Here comes that train. I figured, "Oh man, this is the end of it." It turned out the train was coming on the other track, but I didn't know it. The train passed. Then they brought me back, and the kids worked me over again pretty good. That night they put me in this jail and interrogated me again, but nothing brutal; I mean they weren't beating me. The next morning they blindfolded me again, and every time they moved me I was blindfolded and handcuffed.

Tokyo's Kampei-tai Military Prison

In Japan, the Kampei-tai military prison in Tokyo was one of more than 200 places where prisoners of war were interned. It was part of the headquarters building for the Kampei-tai, who were the dreaded and brutal secret military police—technically only the MPs of the Imperial Japanese Army, but in fact a 70,000-member rogue force that spied on the citizenry.

Its personnel were veterans of at least six years' military service. They monitored all publications and radio broadcasts, and had the power to arrest and secretly jail or execute anyone on suspicion of espionage. They were sometimes called the Thought Police.

Kampei-tai agents were known for carrying out torture or beatings, or summarily executing prisoners by gunshot, machine gun, bayoneting, or beheading. During interrogation, they beat prisoners with bamboo sticks or rifle butts. Japanese military personnel treated American POWs with disdain because their culture viewed surrender as supremely disgraceful. After the development of the B-29, whose long flying range allowed routine bombing of the Japanese mainland, military officials began to separate captured Allied airmen from other POWs, deeming them to be "special prisoners" who earned even more cruel treatment and deprivation. Most "special prisoners" were held for mock trials on charges of killing innocent women and children; many also were executed.

Starvation, lack of water and sanitation, and assignment to slave

They transferred me to the Kampei-tai military prison in Tokyo, right near the Imperial Palace. When I got there, it was around May 1 or 2. I was there for only one day, and the next day they had a roll call and moved fifty-two men to another prison in Tokyo. There were seven of my crew members on that move list. On May 25 there was a fire raid on Tokyo. The fire raid hit the prison that these men were in, so they tried to escape. When they tried, they were shot or beheaded. So I lost all of those men.

But I was still held by the Kampei-tai, the only one left out of my crew.

labor were the daily lot of many Allied POWs. Diseases such as scurvy, pellagra, beriberi, enteritis, malaria, and pneumonia were rife. Losing a third to half of one's body weight was not uncommon, and thousands of POWs died of malnutrition.

The Kempei-tai prison in Tokyo stood next to Japan's Imperial Palace. There, POWs were confined to what many survivors described as a dungeon, with thirteen men crowded into flea- and lice-infested cages measuring nine by ten feet. POWs were given little food: three rice balls a day, sometimes with seaweed or a fish head—unless the ration was cut as a reprisal. They were denied medical attention and the opportunity to shave or bathe. The latrine was a hole in the floor with a wooden cover.

Prisoners lived in daily fear that American bombing raids would hit the prison. That never occurred at Kampei-tai headquarters, but it did happen at Tokyo Military Prison, where the building was fire-bombed; when Americans attempted to flee the burning flames, they were machine-gunned.

When the Japanese cause was lost after the nuclear bombing of Hiroshima and Nagasaki, officials ordered all American POWs immediately executed. Five days after Nagasaki, the Kempei-tai headquarters commander ordered a deputy to carry out that order, then committed suicide. The deputy refused to obey the order, knowing that the conquering Allies would soon be in control, and that he would stand a greater chance for leniency if he did not have such an atrocity on his record. Many other captors did the same, but some carried out the order to kill Americans under their control rather than allow them to be liberated. ★

Well, whenever you are held by the Kampei-tai, you are interrogated. They don't interrogate you like you and I are talking; they interrogate you with a bamboo pole. You are handcuffed and you kneel in front of a table. The interrogator—I know his name, Kobyashi—he worked me over. I mean he really beat me three times pretty hard.

To give you an idea how he could beat you: He asked me, "Did you see where your bombs dropped? Did you see them?" I said, "Yes, I saw them, but I didn't know where they fell. I saw them drop." "Just show me where they fell," he said, like a nut. He had a bunch of flag pins and said, "Show me where your bombs dropped." What was I going to do? He's punching the heck out of me. So I take a pin, put one here, put one there. I didn't know where I was putting them. I couldn't read the map; it was all in Japanese, so how was I going to tell what he wanted?

The funniest thing about it is that I put one pin in and *wham!*—he rapped his bamboo pole. He said, "You bombed a hospital!" So that gives you an idea. I didn't have any choice. He was the boss.

The prison was built out of a horse barn—most people know what a horse barn is—and the cells were made out of the horse stalls. We always had fourteen to sixteen men in these stalls. And as far as the food goes, they didn't give you much. They gave you a bowl of rice twice a day and one cup of water. There was nothing to do all day. You just sat. They had guards going back and forth all the time, and if they weren't interrogating you, you sat there. There was nothing you could do. And you were always scared.

On August 17 or 19 of 1945, about 2:00 or 3:00 in the morning, they roused us up. Six of us were handcuffed and blindfolded, tied together, and put on a truck. I'll always remember the truck. They were running out of gasoline, so they used charcoal to make something like gasoline. So it went chugging along until we reached the Bay of Yokohama, where they made us take our clothes off and walk into the bay. Then they gave us soap, one cake of soap to two men, and told us to wash each other.

While we were there, there was a problem with a change in command. There was one officer who had two machine guns, and he wanted to get rid of us, but the other man said, "No, you can't do it." They were arguing while we were in the water. They finally brought us out, and we walked across a bridge into a genuine prison-of-war camp. This camp had—well, it didn't have cots, you laid on a mat, and they had a latrine right outside.

And the food. One of the ironic things is that we had not been eating good food, and the first thing they gave us was cucumbers. Holy cats! On an empty or bad stomach, if you eat cucumbers—boy, I'll tell you it didn't go over too well.

We were there for about a week when, all of a sudden, a bunch of marines came in and picked us up out of the prison and took us to a hospital ship. They used what they called Higgins boats to take us out to the USS *Benevolence,* a hospital ship. First they deloused us, because we were infested with lice. We really wanted to eat, and they said, "Don't overdo it, just take something light; there's broth or other foods." But then this navy guy said, "Don't worry about it. You go over and sit down, and I'll fix you up." He brought a big plate of food, but you know, it was a dumb thing. We thought we could eat, but the first thing we knew, it was coming back up.

From there they sent me to Guam. They checked me out and sent me on to Hawaii, and then to a hospital at the Presidio in San Francisco. I was there for about a week. When I was released, I went to Cambridge, Ohio, right over the Pennsylvania border. They gave me what they call a one-year convalescent furlough. In other words, I was in the service, but I was allowed to go home. So in late '46 I went to Fort Dix, New Jersey, and got my discharge.

People ask if I am able to forget it all. Well, some people do, some people don't. You try to put it out of your mind, but you never forget. For a while I didn't tell my story to anybody. You know, you figure nobody is going to listen. And then ten or twelve years ago, I got involved with the VA, and we had sessions where they put you through a program to try to help you out. They tell you that if you don't keep it in, you are better off than if you try to keep it in.

That's quite a few years ago that this happened. God's taking care of me, that's all I can say. He's helped me out.

AFTER THE WAR . . .

• •

Nick Gazibara went into the construction business and started to build homes. He also worked for twenty years as an agent for the Prudential Insurance Company, until he retired at age sixty-two. Gazibara and his wife of sixty years had three children.

• •

☆ Jack Price ☆

Pen Argyl, Pennsylvania

Jack Price spent thirty months aboard the USS *Coghlan*
as a radioman second class. His primary responsibility
was to receive communications through Morse code.

I graduated from Easton High School in 1942 at the age of seventeen and wanted to join the navy, but my parents said I had to be eighteen. So when I turned eighteen in December, I joined. They sent me to the U.S. Naval Training Base in Sampson, New York, for basic training, which was drilling for the action we might face during the war, physical examination, physical testing, and of course, the gas mask tour. You basically become navy-oriented.

After eight weeks of training, I was sent to California aboard a troop train with many other sailors. We landed in San Francisco, where in August 1943 I was assigned to the USS *Coghlan*, DD606. My entire navy life in World War II was aboard that ship.

When I got aboard the USS *Coghlan*, they were looking for someone who wanted to become a radioman. One qualification was that you had to be able to type. Fortunately I could type and was taken into C Division—

which was the Communication Division aboard the *Coghlan*—and became a radioman striker. From then on I advanced through training, learned Morse code—could take an average of thirty-five words a minute—and rose to the rank of radioman second class.

The first day on the USS *Coghlan* was strange. I didn't know anything about the ship. In fact, I didn't even know the name of it until I arrived there. I found the person who was in charge. He took us downstairs, assigned bunks, and said, "We'll talk to you later on. You'll be oriented aboard the ship."

The *Coghlan* had 250 men. During the three years I was on it, 70 percent of the crew was the same men, so we became very close. At that time a lot of us were deck hands, which involved all kinds of duties like swabbing the deck and washing dishes. But because I could type and was taken into C Division, I never had a day of KP aboard the *Coghlan*. So being in the Communication Division was a little special, but you had your duties at the radio shack all the time.

As a radio striker, you were the gofer. You made the coffee for the men on duty, and you learned to take Morse code. You would sit down and listen to the dit-dots and try to learn them, then when you became a full classified radioman third class, you had your duty watch. You sat at the desk for four hours and copied the scan code, what we called the regular code, which was constantly coming through.

Every ship had its own designated code. If something would come through with that code, you would take the message in code, and then you'd wake up the decoding officer, who would decode the message. They were messages like where to go, what our next operation was going to be, who we were going to rendezvous with, what ship and where, and general information about what battle our ship was going to be involved in.

The usual duty of a radio operator was four hours on and eight hours off, and then you'd swing the shift once a week. So it would be from 4:00 to 12:00, and then 12:00 to 4:00. The best shift was 4:00 to 8:00 in the morning, because at least you got some sleep at night. But someone was always moving on the ship, waking somebody up to go on watch. If you had the 12:00 midnight shift, you'd be relieved at 4:00 A.M. and you would go down to hit the sack. But every morning, one hour prior to sunrise, and every evening, one hour prior to sunset, you were at battle stations.

During battle stations, if you were there for any length of time, the only thing you ever received was a cup of coffee and maybe a sandwich. No regular meals, because the cooks were at their battle stations. You would stay at battle stations sometimes ten, twelve hours at a time, and you would end up with a cup of coffee. So your sleep was always interrupted. If you went to bed at 4:00 A.M., you were up again at 5:00. By that time, morning breakfast would be served, you'd go to chow, then you'd go back to bed and sleep for a while.

Friendships were very thick, very close. We were young kids. I don't know if we could put up with today what we did then, but it was thrilling. We had a lot of fun, we did a lot of kidding. It was close because you were constantly on a routine.

Sometimes we would have to ride out typhoons at sea. The radiomen who were on duty—fortunately I was one of them—were strapped into a chair, and we sat in that chair and took our duty for a period of twelve to fourteen hours instead of the usual four.

I never felt better in my life, physically, because I had three meals a day, I was getting my regular sleep, it was a routine, and everybody was in top shape. During free time we would write letters, do crossword puzzles, and read novels. We had movies on board. Every ship had a movie projector, and if you came alongside another ship, you'd yell, "What movie do you have? We'll swap you." At night, of course, everything was dark. There was no smoking topside. Every time a door opened, the light in the room would go out until the door was shut.

After a tour of duty, we'd come back into Pearl Harbor to get resupplied. We'd go alongside a destroyer tender or in the yard for some quick service, whatever needed to be done. Many of the battleships in Pearl Harbor were still on rock bottom from the Japanese attack. When we went into Pearl, they were still removing the battleship row, and some of the destruction was still there. That made you realize, hey, it's not fun anymore.

Aboard a small ship like the *Coghlan,* we were close to the officers. The captain knew everybody. When you get aboard an aircraft carrier or a battleship, where you've got 4,000 or 5,000 men, is the captain going to know little Jack Price, the radioman? But aboard the *Coghlan,* everybody knew everybody.

We went from San Francisco to the Aleutian Islands, where we participated in the landing of Attu and Kiska. It was cold up in the Aleutian Islands. The seas were rough and it was a real experience.

Our first battle started with the bombarding of Wake Island. The task force consisted of four carriers, eight cruisers, and sixteen destroyers, sailing out of Pearl Harbor. As the planes flew over Wake Island, we went on each side of the island with two cruisers and four destroyers and bombarded the island. We really put Wake Island out of commission. It was thrilling, because we weren't being fired back at; we were just bombarding. But it was a sensation that you were actually taking part in action. Up in Alaska we didn't fire anything. The Japanese evacuated Attu and Kiska, so there wasn't much action up there, but Wake Island was something different.

From there we went to Tarawa, where the marines landed. Unfortunately it was a little different situation there. We were being fired at. The marines took a beating in landing, because the tide went out on them. We picked up dead marines floating in the water and buried them at sea. That has an emotional effect, which still makes you think a lot how lucky you are that you're still alive today to talk about it.

From Tarawa we went to Kwajalein, Saipan, Tinian, and then into Leyte Gulf in the Philippines. There was a battle of what we call Ormoc Bay. Six destroyers went in with supply ships, and only three of us came back out in one piece. We knew something was going on, because before we went in, they came aboard ship and took all the decoding material and all the personal records off the ship. So we knew it could be a suicide run.

It was a close battle, because the marines were in trouble inside Ormoc Bay, and we had to get in and give them some power supply for guns and support. The Japanese had searchlights on shore, and we were lit up like we were on stage, so the first job was to knock out the searchlights. That's when we tangled with a cruiser. We were able to sink the one Japanese transport coming in; we had confirmation of that. I saw the *Abner Read* go down. It took a suicide plane midship and sank within a minute and a half. I was the spotter in gun turret three, so I was topside, observing what was going on.

So it was quite a night. And coming back out, we were attacked by Japanese suicide planes, but fortunately six marine fighters flying corsairs intercepted those guys. If you want to see something thrilling but yet scary to watch, it's an air battle of planes dueling, what they call a dogfight.

That night we also credit our skipper, Capt. [Benjamin Ballard] Cheatham, for saving our lives. The Japanese suicide planes were following wakes of ships so they could dive into the ships. Our captain, realizing what was going on, stopped us dead in the water. Two suicide planes coming after us went over and never touched us. We were wondering what we were doing stopping in the middle of the bay; the captain knew what he was doing. Captain Cheatham was a man I admired most next to my father, who I really admired. Captain Cheatham was a father to all of us young whippersnappers on the *Coghlan*. He was a graduate of Annapolis, class of 1933. He was proud of us and we were proud of him.

During the Leyte operation, believe it or not, we were escorting the USS *Boise*, which had General MacArthur on board. Our orders were that if a torpedo was shot at the USS *Boise*, we were to take it instead. So everybody was protecting MacArthur going into the Philippines.

When the war was over, we were one of the first ships to escort troops into Nagasaki, the city which was bombed by the atomic bomb. It was disastrous. You could not believe the devastation that was done to that city. It looked like flat rubbish land. If you've seen an area after a hurricane or a typhoon, that is what it was like, but it was all flat. We were there for two days and were fortunate to get a tour. They put us on a truck, and we drove around Nagasaki to see what was going on. It was really an experience.

After we left the States in 1943, we were out of the country for twenty-one months. We did not return till 1945. For the last seven months of that tour, nobody put foot on land. The battles were heavy, the destroyers which were out on the picket line were being hit hard. Fortunately we were not hit hard, we were not damaged, so they kept us out there. But being out twenty-one months, we were really tense. One day a doctor came aboard. He talked to the skipper, he talked to the executive officer, and he talked to the doctor we had onboard. And within twenty-four hours, we were headed back to the States, because I guess he could see that we had had it after twenty-one months out of home. I left my home, my mother and dad, in May of '43 and never saw them again until May of '45. So I was away from the city of Easton for two years.

The *Coghlan* ended up with eight battle stars. I don't exactly know how many Japanese aircraft we shot down. After the war, we came back to San Diego, went down through the Panama Canal, and came up to the destroyer base on the East Coast in Charleston, South Carolina, which was for destroyers that were going to be decommissioned.

I am very proud of my ship, the USS *Coghlan*, DD606. It was the main part of my life for three years. Unfortunately the last time I saw the ship was in Philadelphia in 1972, tied up at dry dock. It was scrapped in 1974.

AFTER THE WAR . . .

Between his 1946 discharge from World War II service and when he rejoined the navy in 1951, Jack Price worked for the Mack Printing Company in Easton. In 1953 he returned to the company, where he worked until his retirement in 1985. Price married in 1949 and raised two daughters and one son. He remarried in 1985 and became an emergency medical technician with the Wind Gap Ambulance Squad and has served as a councilman for the borough of Pen Argyl for more than eleven years. He and his wife also deliver Meals on Wheels.

☆ Walter R. Kuczma ☆

West Mifflin, Pennsylvania

....

Walter R. Kuczma was just seventeen, and a tenth-grader,
when he joined the U.S. Navy. He was assigned
to serve as a crew member on the USS *Intrepid*.

....

I was born and raised on the South Side of Pittsburgh, and I wanted to
serve my country. I decided to join the navy on my seventeenth birthday,
and the navy welcomed me but told me I had to go through strict physical
tests and paperwork tests for three days, which I did, and I passed with high
honors. I was in the tenth grade, but they still accepted men at that age when
the country needed people to defend this great nation.

I went to boot camp at a navy training station in Great Lakes, Illinois. On
the way to the training station, I cried like a baby. I said, "What am I doing
here?" But eventually I realized that you have good days and you have bad
days, and you've got to face every day of your life as if it's your last. So I
wiped the tears out of my eyes and went to boot camp.

They gave me a uniform and a big white bag called a duffel bag or overseas bag, and I put everything I owned in that bag. I was put aboard a troop

train, and I asked, "Where am I going?" The navy chief said to me, "You'll know when you get there, mate."

For four nights and three days, I was on the train, heading for San Francisco. We pulled up to a dock where the ships were anchored, loading supplies, and my navy chief said, "This is your new home, mate." I said, "What do you mean? That's a warehouse." He said, "This isn't a warehouse, sonny, this is an aircraft carrier, the USS *Intrepid* CV11." Boy, my chest stuck out. I was so proud to be on a class A fighting ship.

The ship was in San Francisco for repairs, because it had been torpedoed off of Truk Island in the South Pacific. The aircraft carriers were all there fighting the Japanese, but they had to go for supplies, so they were in the Marshall Islands loading when a lone Japanese pilot came down and dropped a torpedo that hit the *Intrepid,* the fightingest ship the world has ever seen. It hit her in the rudder and jammed that rudder so the ship could not be steered. It was going around in a circle. Can you imagine a 35,000-ton warship going around in a circle?

At Pearl Harbor, the Japanese sank or damaged the majority of our battleships, and now they were looking for our aircraft carriers.

They tried to figure out how to straighten out the *Intrepid* from going around in a circle. So some young navy chief got a bright idea. They had a lot of canvas sail aboard, so they put some sail up on the bow of the ship. That straightened the ship out until they could get a tow line on her and take her out of the battle area. The sail straightened that 35,000-ton aircraft carrier and acted like a rudder, and allowed the ship to get back to the dry dock area in San Francisco at Hunters Point. That's when I came aboard.

I saluted the quarterdeck, saluted the officer of the day, and got permission to come aboard. The ship had 3,000 mates on it, from the captain all the way down to a young fellow like me, seventeen years of age. They put us in line and said, "What did you do in civilian life?" I said I was still in school like the rest of these fellows. "What were you in training for?" I said I was training to be an electrician. "Would you like to be an electrician? We can make you an electrician on board here."

I said, "No, I want to get into the thick of things. I want to work with aircraft machine guns, bullets, bombs, and whatever destructive measures are used to defend this ship." So I became an armorer. I took care of the bombs, the rockets, the small missiles, and napalm.

Everyday life on the *Intrepid* was tiresome, because bombs were heavy. You had 250-pound bombs, you had 500-pound bombs, you had 1,000-

pound bombs, and you even had the blockbuster 2,000-pound bombs. And you had to practically move them by hand. We would be down in the storage areas, where there was no ventilation. The bombs were stacked like a pyramid and were lashed with cables. We put fuses in the bombs, in the nose and in the tail, and then loaded them on an aircraft. You had something like a giant fishing pole that hooked the bomb and brought it up into the airplane. It was hard, but everyone pitched in and did their job.

Every inch of that flight deck and every inch of that hangar deck had an airplane on it. We had 100 or 105 aircraft, and the wings were folded, so you could place them on the flight deck or hangar deck like sardines in a can. The planes were synchronized so that the fighters would take off first, and then the dive bombers would take off, and the torpedo planes would take off last. My job was to load the fighters. When that was done, we had to load the torpedo bombers, then we had to help with the dive bombers.

When we met the Japanese fleet, we had what is called "general quarters." When the bell sounds "general quarters," you hear that whistle, then "general quarters, general quarters, man your battle stations." You had three minutes to get from wherever you were to your battle station, or else they'd close the compartments on you. If you were stuck in a room and they closed that watertight door, you couldn't get out until the battle was over. You never wanted to open that door, in case your ship got hit and the water would rush in.

But there were very good times when, in order to stay in shape, we played jungle basketball. We had three elevators on this aircraft carrier, and we'd lower an elevator, and play basketball there. That was called jungle basketball. We even had boxing matches. We'd drop an elevator and put a boxing ring there on the number-one elevator. And we had good food, three square meals a day. There were clean beds to sleep in, stacked four or five high in our sleeping areas because spaces were at a premium.

What scared me when I was going to enlist was an army poster I saw that had a man with a rifle, and he had a bayonet on the end. I thought I could never face another man like that, that I'd much rather go to sea, and that's what made me join the navy.

On the most fatal day of the *Intrepid*'s life, you could feel that ship was alive. November 25, 1944, was the greatest naval battle in American history, off of the Philippines. The Japanese were going to attack our landing forces in the southern part of the Philippines, and MacArthur was making his landings up at the northern end. Admiral Halsey, who was the commander of the naval forces, was instructed to support the landings.

Well, the Japanese had another plan. They sent a dummy force of ships from the southern part of Japan to try to intercept this invasion. So Admiral Halsey went north to try to head off the dummy Japanese force. In the meantime, the main Japanese force was coming in on the southern end to meet our forces that were going to land there.

Well we, the aircraft carrier USS *Intrepid,* had a fighter pilot who was leading a flight of dive bombers, and they spotted the largest battleship in the world at that time, the Japanese battleship *Musashi,* which led the attack at Pearl Harbor.

It took twenty-one bomb hits and eighteen torpedoes for that giant ship to sink. I weighed about 140 pounds, a skinny kid from Pittsburgh, and I had loaded those bombs. "This is for Pearl Harbor!" I would yell, or "This is payback time!" Other guys wrote their names on the bombs, saying, "This is from St. Louis," or "This is from New York," or "Remember Pearl Harbor!"

We had our hard times, too. One was November 25, 1944, Thanksgiving Day, when two Japanese kamikaze pilots flew their dive bombers right through the flight deck of the *Intrepid.* The bombs exploded and killed sixty-five of my shipmates. We buried those men at sea the next day, after they were identified. The first plane hit amidships when I was just forward of it, maybe thirty yards, but I was behind a metal pillar that saved my life.

I grew up quickly, just like the rest of the servicemen at that time. We became men overnight, and we had to because we had to survive.

When the war ended, I came back to the United States, and my chief, Chief Ross, said to me, "Walter, you enlist for another six years and I'll see that you get another stripe." I only had one stripe, but I put my pants back on and went to work back in the steel mill. It didn't agree with me, so I joined the Pennsylvania Air National Guard at Greater Pitt Airport, which had an air force base at the time, and I became the chief armorer, or ordnance man, because of my naval experience. I started a Veterans of Foreign Wars post right here in West Mifflin, and ironically, the name of the VFW post is "Intrepid," which means gallant, brave, courageous, and fearless.

I loved the navy life. It gave me a living, taught me to respect other people and to do the best you can with what you have. I served my country with pride when she needed me! I'm now over seventy-five years of age, but I remember my seventeenth birthday, and I remember November 25, 1944.

AFTER THE WAR . . .

....

Walter Kuczma went back to Pittsburgh and worked in the steel mills for a few years. He then enlisted in the Pennsylvania National Guard and became a full-time "technician" guardsman for thirty-six years. Kuczma celebrated his own "D-Day" on June 6, 1951, when he married his wife, Martha. The Kuczmas have three daughters.

....

☆ Edward Kyler ☆

Camp Hill, Pennsylvania

· ·

Ed Kyler joined the army on his eighteenth birthday.
He was a paratrooper and a member of the army's 501st
Parachute Infantry Regiment, 101st Airborne Division.
He served in the European Theater.

· ·

I was working at my uncle's gas station when I volunteered for the service. My mother and father said I should go in the navy, but I started to see these army guys walking around, and I took a second look at them. They looked different; they had big brown boots that were shiny, they had a garrison hat instead of the regular army cap, and they had those wings up there over their hearts. Those silver wings. And I said, "I think I know what I want to be: a paratrooper." And that was the start of me going into the paratroopers.

They were tenacious, and they wanted to be a little different. There was just something there that took me. That's why I wanted to jump. I had no other choice.

I went into the draft board and signed all the papers, and they said, "Come on back when you are eighteen." And on my eighteenth birthday, I couldn't get there quick enough. I went up to the old courthouse and the judge swore us in. We had a physical down on Cameron Street in Harrisburg, and they fed us dinner. The buses were waiting outside the restaurant; we loaded up, and off I went to New Cumberland. I was in the army.

I passed fourteen weeks of army basic training with pretty big colors. You had to take a second physical for jump school. Well, I passed everything but my weight. The major said, "Ed you need to gain eight to ten pounds before I can sign your papers for jump school." I felt bad about that, but I made up my mind that I was going to gain the weight. I went to chow a couple of times every day, and in the evenings I went to the PX for egg sandwiches and milk shakes. I did everything I could. Two weeks before basic training was over, I was back up to the medical hospital and stepped on the scale, and there was my eight pounds!

Well now I was in it. I was going through with it. They collected all the men who volunteered for airborne and sent us to Fort Benning, Georgia, for jump school. We had a lot of physical training and mental work in jump school. We ran everywhere, and if you were caught walking, you would drop down and do twenty-five push-ups. We had to do five jumps: four in the daytime, and one at night. It wasn't easy; it took determination.

We actually didn't need officers, even in combat. The sergeants of the corps, even the privates, we could handle any situation we got into. That was the difference between the Germans and us. We were great for being individualists.

After jump school, we were shipped to the dock in New York and loaded on the USS *American*. That was our biggest ship. When we landed at the seaport in Bristol, England, I stayed for a week at a college, where we slept in double bunks in the gym. From there we went to the southern part of England, where I joined the 101st in the 501st Regiment. They were already getting ready for D-Day.

When D-Day came, my regiment took off from the Merryfield airfield in England. A couple of the jumpers in the plane got airsick. They would usually pass a helmet around for them, but the helmet didn't get to all of them. When we stood up to make the jump on D-Day, we were sliding all over the place, you know, we just had to get out of that airplane. All I could think of was to get out of there and on the ground!

When I left the airplane, it wasn't dark and it wasn't light, it was between a black and white fog to me, it was so quick and so sudden. There were bullets going through the air, you know, tracers. But I didn't have a problem landing. I landed safe.

We never really organized as a big unit, but being so well trained, we didn't need that. All we needed was a bunch of guys who could get the job done. And that's how we fought for the next three weeks. And we accomplished all our missions by handling it that way.

My company's job was to take two small bridges near St. Come du Mont in Carentan, France, and to take the causeways so the Germans couldn't flood the area and hold us up. We did our job and we moved on, getting in different firefights occasionally until we met up with some of our troops coming in from the beach. It wasn't long after that that we were airlifted and sent back to England.

Field Marshall [Bernard] Montgomery tried to end the war a year sooner by devising a plan to jump into Holland. There was a sixty-five-mile road running from south to north. He figured if we could take that road, he could take his tanks up there and turn right into Germany at Arnhem, and that it would end the war in a year.

Well, as you know, that operation failed, because his 6th Parachute Division didn't take the "bridge too far." They didn't get the last bridge. But the 82nd and the 101st, we did our job. We overdid it. Every time that road was attacked from the left or the right, we did our job.

I had a little incident there that I'm pretty proud of. We were relieving the British near a dike. Now you couldn't get too close to the dike there, because the Germans had the high ground; they could look right down on us. So the trucks got us up as close as they safely could and we unloaded.

I can remember my particular company started toward the dike. We got about halfway up, and they got word up front that things didn't look good for the area we were supposed to relieve, so we held up there till it got dark. As it got a little darker, we took off toward the corner of the dike. We had to cross over a barbed-wire fence, and just about the time our lead scout of the platoon got on the top of that fence, the Germans shot a flare up right over the apple orchard we were in. The scout's training saved everybody's life. He stopped right there. The flares only lasted ten seconds, and he didn't move a bit. So he did it right.

We started into this apple orchard, relieving the British. I got to my foxhole all right, and then all at once they start throwing 88 shells in on the whole orchard. They just peppered us. I distinctly remember that an 88 landed right in front of one of my best friends. It took his hand off and most of the fingers of his other. He came running past my foxhole toward his, and the blood was just . . . you knew the poor guy wasn't going to make it. He never got to his hole. He did live most of that night, but his moans just kept getting less and less, and we knew.

The next afternoon we were holding the ground when all at once a Tiger tank appeared at the entrance of a viaduct there and started leveling in on us. Well, the British had left an antitank gun there, and they said they were coming back for it the next day. Thank God they left it there, but none of us knew how to fire the thing! Two of my buddies were in the foxhole beside me, and one said, "We are not going to just stand here, because pretty soon there is not going to be anything left of this orchard."

Life of a Paratrooper

The paratrooper was a highly specialized infantryman, equipped to fight on the ground but fully trained to be dropped into live combat from aircraft. It required a physically fit, courageous, resourceful soldier.

In World War II, the scale and scope of paratrooper invasions was spectacular, with thousands of men jumping from planes at a time, but the actual number of such operations was relatively few. As a result, paratrooper companies or battalions often had long periods between drops.

But when an airborne invasion was planned, the paratrooper had to be prepared. He took off as part of a "stick" of as many as eighteen paratroopers aboard a C-47 transport plane (military version of the Douglas DC-3), which was flown by a crew of four. When the plane approached the drop zone, a green jump light went on. Heavily laden with equipment, the paratrooper stood up as best he could, taking his turn to jump out a single rear left-side door of the plane. The plane was flying at 150 miles per hour at an altitude of 600 to 1,500 feet. Very few men got cold feet, but for those who refused to jump, it was a sure ticket to reassignment.

After having been sealed in a noisy metal airplane, the paratrooper found the descent to be eerily quiet. A paratrooper hoped for a clean, slow-speed landing, on ground that was not too rocky so as to avoid risking breaking a leg or ankle. If his rigging got caught in a tree, he used a pocketknife to cut himself down.

So he said, "Are you ready, Kyler?" I said, "I'm ready for whatever you are." He said, "I'm going to run over behind that antitank gun and see if we can fire it at the tank. Kyler, you and your friend get rifle fire going, and keep the infantrymen behind the tank so they don't come out." And that's what we did.

He darted over to the antitank gun, and it had a shield in front of it, so they were pretty safe. They picked up a shell and put it in the tube and shut the chamber, and nothing happened. Just about that time, the turret of the tank was coming down and aiming right dead for all of them. My buddy

---

Once on the ground, the paratrooper jettisoned the chute, evaded any enemy small-arms fire, tried to determine if he was anywhere near the target, and looked around for his buddies with whom to form cohesive squads, platoons, companies, and battalions—all in unfamiliar and hostile territory, with sketchy and perhaps inaccurate maps. The next task was to prepare to advance on the objective, without the usual ground-forces protection of tanks and artillery fire. It took nerves of steel.

Among the equipment carried, a paratrooper might have 125 to 150 pounds of munitions and supplies strapped to his back, legs, and torso. The gear included jumpsuit; helmet; M-1 rifle; .45-caliber pistol; ammunition; bayonet; grenades; antitank mine; two or three days' worth of rations; canteen; cigarettes; compass; gas mask; shovel; first-aid kit; musette bag with extra underwear, socks, and ammunition; and main and reserve chutes. Optional equipment could include a radio, binoculars, and if demolition was part of the plan, sticks of TNT. If gas warfare was anticipated, the jumpsuit might be impregnated with foul-smelling antigas chemicals. If the flight was going over water, the soldier also donned a Mae West life vest.

If a paratrooper was on the ground for any number of days without meeting ground support or established friendly troops, he might need to be resupplied with drops of ammunition or food. Once the paratrooper reached the objective and safely secured the target, he might be detailed to hold the position for a while or to return to a rest-and-recovery area. If that rest period became an extended time, the paratrooper would undergo continuing refresher training to keep his combat and jump skills up-to-date. ★

told us later that it irked him that the antitank gun wasn't firing. So he opened the chamber again and just slammed it shut, and he saw a little lever there, and not knowing how to shoot it, he pushed the lever. Lo and behold, darned if it didn't fire! And the tank fired at the same time. I remember it just looked like they were meeting, you know, but the German tank shells went over everybody and into the orchard, and exploded against a tree. But his shell hit the tank dead center. Boy did it ever!

The Germans threw the turret open and—there were five of them in there—they all came out one at a time. Our machine gunner and our riflemen were picking them off. The last two came out, burning, screaming, and rolling down off of the side. Well, that was the end of the tank and the Germans.

The good thing about that was that the tank blocked that entrance so they couldn't send any more tanks through. But it wasn't over.

About an hour later, the Germans came over the dike and went around behind us, and now we were totally surrounded. Here we go again. We thought we had it. So we radioed in and asked if they could send another company up from the rear to relieve us, and said if you don't do it quick, there is not going to be much left here. But they did.

They came in from the rear, and we had a big firefight there, and the Germans pulled back over the dike. Our machine gunner was picking them off as quick as they tried to go over. It just seemed like they were piling up there at the end bottom of that dike. Well, we got out of that mess. That was one of the things I remember most in Holland.

One time we moved up to an area we called the Island. I was in my foxhole, it was in the evening, and one of my buddies came up and said, "Ed I have to go out on the outpost. You want to eat some of this Spam I have here?" And I said, "Sure, why not." He jumped in my hole and we split it up, and he said, "I'll see you, Kyler."

He took off over the dike, and he got his password right. He went over the other side to the outpost and relieved his buddy. After two hours he was coming back to get relieved, and don't you know, he forgot the password. Well, you had to have the password or you're shot. So we had to shoot him. He never made it. You know what passwords are. A password is like "sunshine." If I say "sun," you had to say "shine." And it changed every two hours. Then if you know it, you can come on through. See, the Germans wouldn't know it. That was another incident that sticks with me. But all in all, I didn't do bad in Holland.

We spent seventy-two days on that island, and that's not good business for airborne. Finally the British relieved us, and we were sent to Camp Mourmelon in Rheims, France, for rest and relaxation.

But lo and behold, here comes the Battle of the Bulge. When it happened, we were not equipped. A lot of our buddies were on leave in Paris, and our general, Maxwell Taylor, was in Washington getting ready for another airborne jump. Well, you know what happened then. The Germans made a sixty-five-mile push. The Pennsylvania 28th Division and a couple of the other ones held them back as long as they could, but the Germans just hit them too hard, and they just started backing up and retreating.

The 82nd and the 101st were the only two divisions in reserve. Ike [Eisenhower] said they had to get us up to the fighting. So they collected all of the trucks they could get and packed us in there like sardines. We didn't know where we were going. We had no equipment, we were not ready for anything, and boy, did we ever hit smack into it.

We unloaded on Longvilly Road outside of Bastogne, at a little village called Mageret, where our infantrymen were retreating. They had no rifles and were starry-eyed, you know. We asked, "What hit you guys?" They said, "Don't go up there; you are going to get surrounded." We went where we were supposed to be surrounded. That's what airborne does. So off we went. We walked right into it.

My regiment, the 501st, hit Bastogne first. Luckily one of our officers had taken a gentleman's vacation before the Battle of the Bulge, and he went to Bastogne. When the generals heard that, they told him and my regiment to lead it off, because he knew the area and where the crossroads were, because he had just been there. So they sent my company out in front of the 501st that got into Bastogne. We were the first ones there.

Right away we hit a German roadblock that had a machine gun. They were coming in from the east, and we were coming in from the south. We had passed that machine gun placement and didn't know it, and they turned around and started firing on us. That was the first firing of the encirclement of the bulge right there.

Gen. Anthony McAuliffe, who took over for General Taylor, started spreading us around Bastogne by companies and regiments. We dug in and got the town surrounded, and he put what little artillery we had in the middle. What he did was pretty slick, and what the Germans did was wrong. If the Germans would have advanced around Bastogne, they would have cut us off completely; everything would have been different. We would have

Battle of the Bulge

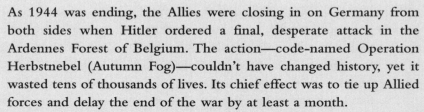

As 1944 was ending, the Allies were closing in on Germany from both sides when Hitler ordered a final, desperate attack in the Ardennes Forest of Belgium. The action—code-named Operation Herbstnebel (Autumn Fog)—couldn't have changed history, yet it wasted tens of thousands of lives. Its chief effect was to tie up Allied forces and delay the end of the war by at least a month.

On December 16, Hitler sent panzer tank divisions and a quarter million troops to retake the important port city of Antwerp, Belgium, as he had done in 1940. When the surprise attack struck along a seventy-mile-wide front at the Western Wall (Germany's defensive line), overcast weather helped mask the advance and prevented American aerial reconnaissance, giving the Germans an advantage. The attack, the last major German offensive of the war, smashed U.S. forces and

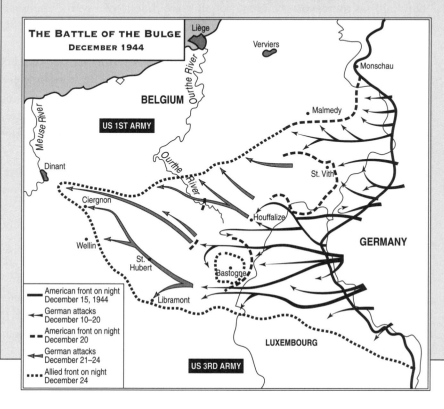

temporarily brought German occupation almost as far west as the Meuse River. The resulting protrusion—hence the name "bulge"—extended sixty-five miles into Allied territory.

One sideshow to this action was Operation Greif (Seize), in which about two dozen Waffen-SS troops who spoke perfect English infiltrated Allied lines in a Trojan horse–type deception. Dressed in U.S. uniforms and driving captured U.S. Army jeeps, they created confusion by changing signposts and spreading panic among U.S. troops. When some of them were captured, they falsely claimed that their mission was to reach Paris and assassinate Supreme Allied Commander Dwight D. Eisenhower. As a result, Eisenhower was confined to headquarters until the report was proven to be bogus. Those captured were ruled to be spies and executed the next day.

In the main fighting, American (and later, British) troops fought back in bitter cold and snow. When the weather cleared, they got help in the form of an assault by 5,000 Allied aircraft. On the second day of fighting, a chilling episode took place when eighty-four surrendered American POWs were herded into a field at the Baugnez crossroads near Malmedy, Belgium, and executed by machine gun. Called the Malmedy Massacre, the incident outraged American public opinion, stiffened the resolve of Allied troops, and reinforced the popular image of Nazis and Germans as subhuman.

Eisenhower dispatched a Who's Who of military leaders to push back the German army and relieve the siege of Bastogne. They were British field marshal Bernard Montgomery, U.S. lieutenant general Omar N. Bradley, and U.S. lieutenant general George S. Patton. Protracted fighting, through blizzards and fog and over difficult terrain, continued through the end of 1944 and into January 1945. With their supply lines shredded, the Germans fell back to their original position. Just two months later, the Allies crossed the Rhine en route to a final assault on Berlin.

American casualties were 19,000 dead and 15,000 captured, with total Allied casualties reaching about 80,000. But the Germans' toll was far worse: 20,000 dead, 120,000 total casualties, and the loss of as many as 800 tanks and 1,600 aircraft. The loss was both demoralizing and debilitating to Germany. ★

never held Bastogne. We would have been done. But what the Germans did was hit us periodically, then quit and move again. When they would do that, McAuliffe would move a regiment in front of them, and each time they moved, we moved with them.

Now you had nine Germans to one American there; those were the odds. You have to wonder how we got through it, but then again, we were airborne.

Then we got the surrender warning, when McAuliffe answered, "Nuts!" When word of that got back to the foxholes, we laughed. What nuts. We were going to be annihilated in the next two hours? Never going to happen. I'm in my hole, and the Germans are out of theirs. They had to come get us. It's just not going to happen. They tried for eight straight days of penetrating, and they never got in.

On that last day, I think I might have had two grenades left in my hole, and I had two clips of ammunition for my rifle. And once they were gone and my grenades were thrown, I figured that would be the end. But it never happened. Lo and behold, on Christmas Day the sun came out. You know the guy upstairs had something to do with that. We had fog and misery for eight straight days, and the air force couldn't leave their air bases in Belgium to drop us supplies. Then out comes the sun and off goes the air force bringing us supplies.

So after we were relieved, we got orders that General Eisenhower wanted to award the 101st Division the Presidential Citation for the stand at Bastogne. So we gathered in this open field, and he came by in a jeep and started marching down the front of the division. He stopped occasionally, talking to a few of us, and he said, "Soldier, why don't all of your troopers have your campaign ribbons on?" I heard my buddy say, "Well, they haven't issued them to us yet." The ceremony went on, and the very next day we were called out in the company street, and wouldn't you know it, we got our campaign ribbons. Now that's how much pull he had. So I got to see Ike there pretty close.

Then we were shipped to Germany for occupational duty at Berchtesgaden. We then visited Eagle's Nest, Hitler's mountain retreat. It was high in the mountains, and the hill that led to the place was so steep that the trucks had to use their lowest gear. When you got up to the top, you could see miles and miles of the Alps. It was beautiful. I got to see Hitler's wine cellar and his kitchen. I took a peek at his bedroom and that big bay window that was already blown out, where they held all their conferences. He had nothing but the best.

I made a mistake by not picking something up while I was there. We weren't supposed to take things, but if you did and could have gotten it back home, imagine what it would be worth. Some of the GIs did, but I never gave it a thought.

As the war was coming to an end, all of us wanted to go home. We were told that some of us were going to be in a victory parade in New York to represent the whole world. We got new boots, new class A uniforms, new rifles, and we started training for the parade. That day there were more than five million people watching. Both sides of Broadway from one end to the other were knee-deep with people. It took 2,000 policemen and army personnel to keep the crowd back. To this day I can see mothers and fathers finally seeing somebody they know. It was very touching. That parade is something I'll remember forever: to be selected to represent the world for that victory of World War II.

AFTER THE WAR . . .

Edward Kyler, who had always enjoyed bowling, took it up again, and through this interest, he met his future wife. Together they raised two sons. Kyler ran a service station for twenty-three years, working until the age of seventy-four.

☆ Frank Speer ☆

Emmaus, Pennsylvania

··

Frank Speer was a fighter pilot in the 4th Fighter Group
of the Army Air Forces, flying a P-51 Mustang. During
one of his missions, his plane went down, and Speer was
sent to the prison camp Stalag Luft 3 in Sagan, Germany.
He was forced to take the infamous "Death March"
to Nuremberg during the merciless winter weather.

··

At the time I joined the armed services, I was a cable helper with the Bell
Telephone Company. I had been out of high school a year or so and
had gotten married.

I enlisted. All my life I had wanted to be a pilot, particularly a fighter
pilot, but the qualifications were beyond my capabilities. For example, you
could not be married. You had to have all your own teeth. I guess you were
supposed to chew the enemy; I'm not sure. You also had to have a college
degree, which I did not have.

Gradually, as the need arose, they lowered some of those standards. You
could be married; the loss of two wisdom teeth was acceptable; and if you
could pass a two-year equivalency test, you were accepted. I breezed through

that with honors and was accepted into the enlisted Reserve Corps, where men were assigned while waiting for a training opening. At that time the buildup was such they couldn't immediately handle everybody they needed. About six months later I was called up and sent to the San Antonio Aviation Cadet Center, adjacent to Randolph Field in Texas. There you were classified as to whether you could be a pilot, navigator, gunner, or ground crewman.

I was classified pilot material and went into preflight training. There were many opportunities to "wash out" ahead of us. There were 1,900 hopefuls sworn in. Of those only 600 cadets made the first cut and were sent to preflight. Most of us wanted to be pilots, but our numbers continued to be decimated very rapidly, as one obstacle after another was insurmountable to some. Those who completed preflight went on to primary, then basic, and then advanced flight training. The attrition rate was such that only two of the six who started with me in primary were advanced to basic. After completing Advanced Training School, we had a short course in Aerial Gunnery School and then graduated as second lieutenants.

We went overseas in a barely tolerable way. New York was our port of embarkation, and one morning they marched us down to get on a boat. There sat the Queen Mary, but we walked right past it and got onto a little banana boat. It was a British ship that had seen better days. It was so small that going across the North Atlantic in the winter, there were times when the ship was up on a wave and you could see every ship in the convoy, 360 degrees around you. The next moment you would be down so low you could see nothing but water on all sides. It was like riding an elevator that went up and down eighty feet at a time, all the way across the Atlantic.

The ship was crowded. The hold was full of soldiers who were below the waterline, and they were sick all the time—vomiting. The stench was terrible. As officers we received slightly better treatment, but the food was awful. The only decent thing I experienced on that trip was that because it was a British ship, they had afternoon tea and crumpets. It was delicious! We had lousy food, but wonderful tea.

But we made it! We had a couple of submarine attacks, which were warded off by the destroyers, but we made it to England—Wales, actually. From there we went into advanced combat training and were assigned to various groups. When the United States entered the war, there was no separate branch of the service designated for an air force, but it was quickly formed as the Army Air Corps. I was assigned to the 4th Fighter Group, which consisted basically of American volunteers trained in the Royal

Canadian Air Force and assigned to the Royal Air Force. They were known as the Eagle Squadrons. Our assignment was to start escorting American bombers on their daytime raids over Germany. It was a very strict, very aggressive, and very gung-ho outfit.

When the group was established, they were still flying British Spitfires, maintained by British personnel. As time went on and America's production facilities increased, they were gradually switched to the P-47 Thunderbolt. Many of our pilots did not like them, because compared to the Spitfire, which was like a sports car, the P-47 was huge, like a truck, and it handled about the same. Through the aggressiveness of our group commander, we soon acquired P-51s—considered by most to have been the top propeller fighter plane ever developed. It sure was a great plane!

Pilots generally named their own planes, and I chose Turnip Termite, borrowed from the "Li'l Abner" comic strip. In the comics the turnip crop in the town of Dogpatch was decimated by Turnip Termites every year, and I thought I could devastate the enemy like that by myself in this plane.

Our group went on a lot of missions. On many of them nothing unusual happened, but some were very exciting. I recall flying as a wingman to one of my favorite pilots, named Kidd Hofer. He shot down a German ME 109. The pilot bailed out and Hofer almost hit him. Flying slightly behind Hofer, I came very close the German pilot dangling in his chute. To this day I remember his boots glistening in the sun. He was wearing a tunic, with his medals on his chest. He looked like he was about to lead a parade, and he was sitting in his chute waving to us. I was flying in a pair of grungy old overalls and GI shoes, thinking, "Boy, are we shooting down the top-level stuff here." It was almost humiliating that we should look so shabby in comparison, but it worked, and that's what counted.

I got into a real scrabble once when my wingman and I were attacking six German 109s. I didn't realize until the last minute that we were alone— just the two of us. I was thinking, "What do I do now?"

I said to my wingman, "I'll take the lead man, you take the second man, and hopefully the other four are trainees and they will just disappear and stay out of trouble." The Germans did that occasionally. And that's exactly what happened. I got close enough and hit the lead man on my first burst of 50s. He took violent evasive action, and I ended up in a vertical dive following him. Pieces of his plane were flying off and hitting my plane—I was that close behind him. We ended up approaching compressibility, which later was recognized as the sound barrier. His plane didn't pull out. I did.

It was very exhilarating, believe it or not! I pulled out just at treetop level, going about 700 miles an hour. I used my speed to climb back up and look for the rest of my group. There wasn't a plane in the sky. At the speeds we were flying, getting into such activity could get you separated from the group, and within three minutes you couldn't find a plane, they were all going so fast and in different directions. I couldn't even find my wingman, and so I had to come back alone.

As a fighter pilot, you have to have a sense of bravado and aggressiveness. It's not a matter of being fearless. You just don't think. Your ego overcomes your fear. Your regard for the enemy is such that you think, "You can't touch me, I'm better than you are." That's what makes a fighter pilot—that, good eyesight, and good coordination.

At that time a tour of duty was twenty-five missions, because it was so dangerous. We were losing too many planes and too many pilots. On my seventeenth mission, I was shot down.

In 1944, primarily for propaganda reasons, it was decided that with the long-range planes we had then, the group could fly from England to Russia in order to show the Germans they were vulnerable from all sides. A shuttle mission was planned to leave from England, bomb Germany, go on to Russia, and from there go down to Italy—not on the same day, of course. From Italy we could then go back to England. We more or less had Germany surrounded, and we wanted them to know it. My mission went from England to Poznan, Poland, which was halfway to our Russian destination. It was a pioneering run, so to speak—the longest mission that fighters had ever flown, and if successful, would prove we could make it to Russia for the shuttle run.

I was flying wing to Kidd Hofer, who was inclined to find trouble where he could, as was I. We left the group ostensibly because we saw something we thought should be investigated, and found an airfield. The two of us decided to strafe it. Now that's a very dangerous thing to do with just two planes. On our first run, my plane got hit. The engine was starting to cut out on me, and I knew I couldn't get back. So I turned and made another run, and each time, I hit German planes on the ground and left them burning. I got three that day and Hofer got four. I had only one choice to set down—a small clearing between the airfield and a village. It was the only open spot in the surrounding wood. I got it down in this tiny opening, dead-stick, wheels up. I don't know how I made it, but I did. Fortunately I didn't hit trees on either end of the clearing.

The P-51 Mustang: America's "Top Gun" Fighter

The P-51 Mustang fighter changed the complexion of the air war over Europe, gradually eroding and then destroying the Luftwaffe's onetime air superiority. Perhaps as much as any plane, it became the "Top Gun" American fighter of its generation.

Based in England, the U.S. 8th Air Force in 1942 began conducting a daylight bombing campaign over Germany (Britain's Royal Air Force conducted nighttime bombing), but it was dangerous and costly in both aircraft and men. Allied fighters such as the Lockheed P-38 Lightning and Republic P-47 Thunderbolt accompanied the B-17 and B-24 heavy bombers to protect them and fend off attacks by German fighters, but their range was curtailed by the limited amount of fuel they could carry. They could escort and protect the slow bombers only partway into Europe before they had to turn back over Belgium, the Netherlands, or northeastern France. That left the bombers vulnerable to Luftwaffe fighters, with only their onboard machine guns for self-defense, at a point when they still had hundreds of miles to fly to reach their targets—and then return to England.

A pair of disastrous missions in 1943 forced a reevaluation. In August, a 317-plane group of B-17s attacked a ball-bearing factory at Schweinfurt and an aircraft plant at Regensburg. Sixty B-17s were shot down. Two months later another attack was launched on Schweinfurt, with more than 60 bombers lost out of the 229 that had completed the flight to the target. Allied daylight bombing runs were briefly suspended, and U.S. officials ordered the development of a long-range fighter. They didn't care if it was a completely new design or an adaptation of an existing plane—losing 60 bombers in a single day was an unacceptable price.

The answer lay in a single-engine, single-seat fighter that the RAF had requested in 1940 and, along with the U.S. Army Air Force, had been acquiring since 1941. North American Aviation's P-51 (the P signified "pursuit" in the days before fighters were designated with

An armorer of the 15th U.S. Air Force checks ammunition belts of the .50-caliber machine guns in the wings of a P-51 Mustang fighter plane before it leaves an Italian base for a mission against German military targets, September 1944. NATIONAL ARCHIVES

the letter F) was powered by a 1,100-horsepower Model V-1710 Allison engine. Dubbed the Mustang, it could attain 409 miles an hour and was good for ground support and photo reconnaissance. But it lost power above 15,000 feet, so it was unsuitable as a bomber escort. However, Rolls-Royce's senior test pilot, invited to fly a P-51 in 1942, found that it was a fundamentally airworthy design, but underpowered. As an experiment, a Rolls-Royce 1,695-horsepower "Merlin" engine was installed in a P-51, and it proved that it could fly faster and higher (437 miles an hour, altitude to 41,000 feet) than the original version. Its range, up to 2,000 miles with disposable "drop tanks," also made it perfect for escort duty.

The modified Mustang quickly became the long-range bomber escort fighter of choice. Both the RAF and the Army Air Force began ordering the plane in mass quantities. Under license, Packard began building the Rolls-Royce engine in the States. More-powerful P-51s

(continued on page 56)

(continued from page 55)
began flying in combat operations in December 1943. It didn't take long for them to distinguish themselves. On January 11, 1944, American bombers—escorted over Europe for the first time by P-51s—flew a mission to hit aircraft factories at Halberstadt and Oschersleben, Germany. The sortie consisted of 220 bombers and 49 P-51s. While the bombers did take losses, the Mustangs shot down 15 enemy fighters and suffered no losses. On March 6 the U.S. felt confident enough to conduct its first P-51–assisted daylight bombing raid on the capital city of Berlin. Bomber crews quickly dubbed the fighters "little friends" (Boeing B-17s were "big friends"). By the end of the war, U.S. P-51s had shot down 4,950 enemy aircraft over Europe, more than any other fighter.

In all, North America built 15,386 P-51s, with 14,819 of those being delivered to the Army Air Force. Besides escorting bombers, they also were used for ground attack, dive-bombing, and training. They were deployed in nearly every theater of war. In the Pacific, they escorted B-29s from Iwo Jima to Japan; in the Korean War, they provided aerial support of ground forces. The original price of a P-51 was $54,000. Today, under private or museum ownership, about 160 P-51s are still operational. ★

I struggled out of the plane and suddenly became aware of a mob coming out of the village with pitchforks and clubs and other assorted unfriendly types of equipment. I sure didn't want any part of that, so I ran into the woods away from them. I shucked my parachute and my Mae West and ran. I hid in a clump of bushes the rest of the day, right at the edge of the village, while everybody was out there searching for me. By nightfall they returned, tired and disgusted. I waited until they went to bed, and then I took off.

I headed in the direction of Denmark on foot. Eight days and almost 400 miles later, with no food, no sleep, in constant fear, I was going on adrenaline alone. I finally became disoriented one night in the woods. I sat down to rest for a minute, and the next thing I knew it was daylight and I was being prodded in the head by a rifle muzzle, with another in the hands of a German soldier pointing at my head. It was a German patrol and I had no defense. I was on the outskirts of Kiel, and they had just picked me up by accident—they weren't even looking for me.

So began the road to Stalag Luft 3 prison camp. They took me to an air base, where they gave me some soup, the first food I'd had in over a week. I had no notion of the origin of the soup, but it was the best soup I ever ate in my life.

In solitary confinement, I crawled into my bunk and promptly fell asleep. I had no idea how long I slept, but eventually they shackled me to a guard, put us on a train, and we were taken through Berlin in the middle of the day. The Allies were bombing Berlin just about every other day, and I feared we would never reach our destination.

Finally I wound up in an interrogation center, Dulag Luft. The interrogator spoke even better English than I did and seemed to know more about me than I did. In order to develop camaraderie with me, so I would talk and tell him what he wanted to learn, the interrogator pulled out a dossier on me. He told me, "You went to Allen High School. You married Marjorie Poust, who was a classmate there. You worked for the telephone company. You were born in Pittsburgh, Pennsylvania." He tried to trick me. He asked about my flying career, "Who were you with, what group?" and the sorts of military things I could not disclose. So when he decided I wasn't going to tell him anything, he said, "Well, I'll tell you. You were with the 4th Group. Don Blakeslee was your commanding officer. You were flying today with a call sign of . . . (something he made up)." Since it was wrong, I agreed. He said, "Now don't fool with me, Lieutenant Speer. Your call sign was really 'cobweb,'" which is what it was. Finally, tiring of the game, he said, "You refuse to talk, you were picked up in civilian clothes, so you must be considered a spy. You will be put in solitary confinement for a week to think it over, and if you still refuse to talk, you will be shot as a spy." After an agonizing week I was returned to his office, where the questioning resumed, to no avail. Finally he said to his assistant, "Send him with the others to Stalag Luft 3."

Stalag Luft 3 was rather infamous, in that this is the camp from which approximately seventy-five British prisoners had escaped, in what came to be known as "The Great Escape." It is actually a true story. Fifty of them were shot when they were recaptured. Consequently it was not a very friendly camp to newcomers and security was very tight. Food was meager and of very poor quality. We would have starved to death on what the Germans gave us, were it not for the fact that their food was supplemented by

Red Cross parcels. I'm forever grateful to the Red Cross for providing us with food. A Red Cross parcel, as constituted as that time, was meant to contain the minimum amount of nutrients necessary to maintain a man for a week. The most we ever got was a quarter of a parcel for a week, except at Christmas, when we got a whole one—and when we were moved out on the infamous "Death March."

The German bread was black and soggy. When you ate it, so much gas was produced you could have fueled an airplane with it. It consisted of some regular ingredients, plus at least 30 percent wood fiber. This is a fact! We had two kinds of soup. One was "gray death" and the other was "green death." Gray death was like wallpaper paste and consisted of barley with no seasoning. The green death was generally made with some vegetable they had available, such as turnips, beets, peas, or cabbage.

Sleeping conditions were terrible. We had triple-deck bunks with fifteen men to a room. The rooms in the barracks were about twenty feet square. There was a tiny kitchenette-type area and a four-seat table with four stools but no heat. It was very crowded, with no privacy. The Red Cross parcel we received had a package of ascorbic acid pills in them. We presumed they were to fight scurvy or some such disease. The Krauts asked us what they were for, and we told them that the pills allowed us to see in the dark. Of course, they scoffed at us. So one night we set up a bridge hand on the table with four guys playing bridge. Others were on their bunks sewing or reading. It was pitch dark in there. When the goons came in to count us, using a flashlight, they looked around and saw all of us doing something that couldn't be done unless you were able to see in the dark. Their reaction was "crazy Americans." On occasion we pulled similar stunts and always retained our sense of humor in spite of the adversity.

About the time of the Battle of the Bulge, in the worst winter they'd had in Germany in decades, the Russians were headed toward our camp, and it appeared they would be liberating us. The Germans decided to move us south to prevent this. In the middle of the night, as a storm was approaching, they decided to move us. They gave each of us a Red Cross parcel, which was too heavy and bulky to carry, so we threw away everything that was not immediately usable and stuffed the rest into our makeshift packs. We then started out, and the snow began to fall fiercely. In addition to the snow, it was bitter cold, and the wind cut through our meager clothing. Those who did not have decent shoes suffered most. Looking at this motley group in the blinding snow, I was reminded of pictures of Washington's men at Valley Forge. As we went on, the snow got deeper and it grew colder. We were moving constantly. We got a five-minute break every hour, and continued twenty-four hours a day with no hot food and no water. We just kept going. After the first day, men were dropping by the wayside, too exhausted to continue. Some, I am sure, died from exposure and total exhaustion.

Typically we moved in a column of fours, with an armed German soldier and dog about every fifty feet on both sides of the column. The guards got to walk a tour and then ride in a wagon for an hour, so they got to rest; we didn't. After twelve hours, the dogs were gone, unable to continue with frozen feet. The group I was in traveled seventy-seven straight hours without any rest. At the end of that time, in that terrible cold, snow, and wind, we were just automatons, putting one foot in front of the other, no longer able to think, just suffering and moving along like robots. Many didn't make it.

At the end of seventy-seven hours, we had arrived at a little village with a river running through it. I happened to be standing on a bridge over the river. Men were collapsing where they stood. One fellow next to me said, "I've had it." He jumped over the bridge, headfirst through the ice into the river and didn't come up. None of us even knew who he was. Frankly, I'm not even sure any of us really cared. We had become completely numb, in mind as well as body.

A woman in the village saw these men collapsing and stuck her head out of a window and told one of the guards in German, "You can bring some of the worst ones up here." With that, I suddenly seemed to get a second wind. I grabbed the nearest guy who was on the ground, threw him over my shoulder, and carried him up the stairs. Then I came back and got another one. I don't know where I got the strength, but for the moment I seemed to be totally rejuvenated. I carried several up to the second floor and just set them down against a wall. Most of them were crying like babies; they had just totally had it. We were finally herded into a factory, where we crawled into the straw on the floor and went to sleep.

From there we were loaded onto a train. Most people have heard of the forty-and-eight boxcars, designed to carry either forty men or eight horses. They put sixty of us into each boxcar, locked the doors, and took off. We had to take turns sitting down and standing up. Being cooped up in a train without even a window, with some of the men sick and no latrines, was absolutely horrible. We were in there for several days before we got to our destination, Stalag 13 at Nuremberg.

That camp was the filthiest place you could imagine, with garbage, lice, and vermin of all kinds. I was fortunate in that, though I had fleas like everybody else, they didn't bother me. Every morning when I awoke, each little hair under my arms would have one little white egg on it. They were all lined up so beautifully it was a masterpiece; but with just one swipe I could wipe out a whole generation of fleas or lice, or whatever they were.

Months later, when Nuremberg was about to be liberated by Patton's army, the Germans decided to move us south to Munich to keep us from being repatriated. We were bargaining chips. So they marched us out toward Munich. As time went on, my buddy Nelson and I decided we would not be going back into a camp again, no matter what. We were marching along in our typical four-abreast style, and it was getting to be dusk. There was a village up ahead, and the column was coming up to an intersection and turning left, even though a road went straight up a hill and through the village. I asked Nelson if he was willing to take a chance, and he said, "Yes, what do you have in mind?"

I said, "When we get to that corner, you and I are not going to turn left. We are going to keep walking straight ahead. We are not going to change pace; we are not going to look back. We will just go along, talking as if we were in line doing what we are supposed to do, but we are going straight up that hill."

Well, we did it! We just walked out of that column, nodding to the people in the village as we went by. At that time, practically everyone in Europe was in uniform of one kind or another, so we attracted little attention. It was crazy, and I was wondering what it was going to feel like to have a bullet crashing into my back. But we walked right through the village, and no one stopped us or seemed to question it.

We were recaptured, but we escaped again by burrowing deeply in the hay in a barn where the Krauts kept us overnight. We had managed to get deep enough so the guards did not find us as they jammed bayonets into the hay to be sure no one was left behind when they rousted out the Kriegies. When all had gone, we left our retreat and found ourselves on a lonely country road in a dismal rain. We saw figures approaching and hid in the woods by the road to let them pass without seeing us. As they came near, they were talking, and it happened to be in French, which I understood slightly. I stepped out of the woods and spoke to them. They were forced laborers and told us to wait until dusk, and they would return and help us. They came back and took us to their compound where they were locked in at night. They hid us during their nightly bed check and left each day to work in the fields, returning with food that they had stolen during the day. They provided well for us.

One day, as we waited in the compound, a contingent of Luftwaffe personnel moved into a farm building adjacent to our compound. They obviously were retreating from the fighting front that was getting closer day by day, as evidenced by the louder noise of the artillery fire. Soon the goons left, leaving one man to guard their equipment in the barn. I recognized the man as one of our more friendly former guards in Stalag Luft 3. I approached him, and he made no move to bring his rifle to bear on me. I greeted him in the favorite manner the Germans greeted us under previous circumstances: "For you der var iss offer." He nodded and replied, "Ja, ja." I then told him I would like his pistol as a souvenir when the Americans came, and I would see that he got good treatment. Surprisingly, he unbuckled his belt and handed the pistol and his rifle to me. He said there were more inside if I wanted them. I told him to tell no one, and returned to our compound and armed Nelson. We were jubilant until there was a knock at the door. Peeking out, we saw an armed soldier. He was not belligerent. In fact, he wanted to surrender so he would also be treated well. We relieved him of his arms and swore him to secrecy. However, the word was out, and one by one soldiers appeared to surrender. By this time the Frenchmen were returning from the field, and we armed them and told them to put our prisoners in one of the barns and guard it well. We then sought the officer, who was in his office nearby, and he willingly surrendered.

Soon a jeep appeared, and we turned our prisoners over to Patton's forces. In return, they incarcerated Nelson and me and the other men in a one-room schoolhouse with a guard outside "to send us back through channels."

The first night we were awakened by an artillery barrage that was much too close for comfort. This was not our kind of war, so in the noise and confusion, we broke out a rear window and took off toward the rear of the fighting. We hitchhiked rides on trucks going back for supplies and eventually wound up in Nuremberg, where everything was being supplied by plane. We managed, by devious means, to hitch a ride on a plane back to France. This was the end of the line. At Camp Lucky Strike we were confined by the hospital group. They burned our clothes, deloused us, and assigned us to the hospital to recuperate. I had lost over sixty pounds as a prisoner and had many dietary deficiency problems. We were soon flown to England to board a hospital ship bound for the States. When we were sufficiently recovered, they let us go home. Thank God!

One thing I learned from it all—no one pushes me around. When I returned to civilian work, I had a supervisor, a huge man who enjoyed bullying and terrifying people who reported to him. One day it was my turn. He started ranting and raving, pounding on his desk about a job I had planned. I just stood there silently until he was finished. I asked calmly, "Are you finished?" He looked at me dumbfounded, and I said, "You don't impress me; I've been scared by experts." Strangely, after that I could do no wrong. He thought I was the greatest guy on earth! I've tried to live up to it.

AFTER THE WAR . . .

Frank Speer returned to Pennsylvania, bought a farm, and returned to his job with Bell Telephone. Under the GI Bill, he received an associates degree in industrial electronics. Speer later entered into a food-service business and real estate. He is the father of five children. Following the death of his first wife in 1995, Speer remarried. He currently writes books on military aviation and attends air shows, lecturing and selling his books. For more information on Speer's books, write to him at P.O. Box 283, Emmaus, PA 18049.

☆ John Agnew ☆
Huntingdon Valley, Pennsylvania

John Agnew was one of the original members of the
506th Parachute Infantry Regiment, 101st Airborne.
Later, as a pathfinder, he was one of a highly select
group of men who parachuted into Bastogne.

I learned to fly before I went into the service, so naturally I wanted to fly.
However, I did not have a college education, so I couldn't go to Naval Air
School. I took a test for the Army Air Force. They wanted me to be a bombardier navigator, and I wouldn't. I just didn't like the idea of dropping
bombs on anybody. So I got into the paratroops.

Our unit got a nasty reputation; we were the real "dirty dozen," and not
the movie version. We had fellows in the stockade because they got to feeling pretty good and shot out all the streetlights in town. The MPs got them
and they were going to be court-martialed, but our company commander
got them off, because that's the kind of men we needed.

We were shipped overseas to England. Most of us GIs referred to it as
Limey Land. The headquarters for the 101st was in Newbury; that's near
Reading. We did a lot of training over there. I volunteered for dispatch

service, so I was a regimental dispatch rider on a motorcycle, and I rode all over the place.

D-Day came along and we went to what they called a holding area. You are under guard and you can't get out, because if you spilled the beans, it could cause a lot of problems. A lot of people could get killed.

Colonel Wolverton wanted us to go with him on his objective, which was actually the farthest objective on D-Day, right outside Carentan. Our objective was to take the bridges over the Douve River and hold those bridges so the Germans couldn't advance and push the troops back into the channel.

People ask me what the night of D-Day was like. Well, if you ever go to a fireworks display, and at the end they have a lot left over and they throw it all up at one time and everything bangs—well, that's what it looked like when you went out the airplane door and your feet were in the air, and you had bullets going bang, bang, bang through your chute. You were lucky if you weren't hit; we lost a lot of men.

When I got on the ground, the first man I met was whimpering and crying, and I was really mad at him. I said, "If you don't stop that noise, I'll shoot you right now!" I think he was more afraid of me than the enemy, and I learned later that he went and surrendered.

The next one I met was one of our buddies, Mike Marques. Mike was a Mexican Indian. His brother Armando also was in our demolition team, which is rare, two brothers in the same platoon. Mike and I proceeded to our objective. We were told under no circumstances to get into a firefight. The main objective was to take and hold a bridge over the Douve River.

The first thing that we did on the way to the bridges was blow up the power lines and the telephone lines. We were running across Angoville-au-Plain to the bridges, and my buddy Clarence Ware got hit. He just bounced on the ground like a rat. We tried to get a medic to him, but we had to leave him because we had to take the bridges. We finally got down to the bridges and we held them.

You've heard about lost patrols? Well, they didn't know that we had taken our objective for four days, because we were cut off. We just held and waited until the glider troops and other troops caught up with us, then we assembled back at our headquarters and marched on the town of Carentan. We took Carentan and held that until we were relieved by the 4th Division. So that was more or less Normandy.

As a dispatch rider, I was given a motorcycle and laid a route out to Cherbourg. There were still German patrols all over the place, changing the road signs. I went all the way to Cherbourg and came all the way back. The next day I was leading our group to Cherbourg and got to a crossroad and said, "Something is not right here." One officer we didn't like too well said, "I'll take it from here." He did, but he took us the wrong way. He had collected a lot of mines and explosives to use for training when he went back, but that night the truck blew up and killed six men. After all that combat.

So then we went to Cherbourg and got on a landing craft and went back to Limey Land. From there we did a lot of training, because we lost better than half our men—killed, wounded, or missing in action.

On September 17, 1944, we jumped in the Netherlands. Our mission was to take the bridges on the Dommel River in Eindhoven. We jumped into a little town north of Eindhoven called Son. By the time we got to the Wilhelmina Canal, the Germans had blown up the bridges right under our nose. So we made improvised bridges, crossed the Wilhelmina, and got into Eindhoven, where we secured the bridges. We were supposed to meet the British coming up from the south. Well, they stopped and made tea, so they were two days late. And that's no joke, that's what they did.

So we had to hold that time. We jumped on the seventeenth, and on the nineteenth the German bombers came in and bombed us. They got a couple of my pretty good buddies. I picked my friend Jim Davison up, and my hand went right in his head; he was gone. And Sergeant Myers, we took him into a little air raid shelter there, and his leg was pretty well shot and he died. And a little Dutch boy was sitting there holding a baby, and he fell over; his arm was almost all gone. I took the baby over to the house. In later years I found the family and met with them.

From there we advanced up what was known as Hell's Highway, all the way to Nijmegen. That's where the bridge goes to an island and another bridge known as the "Bridge Too Far"—you have heard about that—well, that was the bridge from the island to Arnhem.

So we met with the British up there. We had about a twenty-six-mile stretch where we had to keep the bridges open so the whole British army could advance. They were cut off two or three times when the German tanks came across and took the road again, and we had to retake it. You had to watch the German armor over in Arnhem all the time to see if they were making an advance to come over and retake the ground.

We were seventy-two days on the line from the time we jumped until we got pulled out of the Netherlands. When we were pulled back, the 82nd Airborne came back first. They went on their passes and caused all kinds of problems, so when we wanted to go on passes, of course, we were blamed for everything.

Then they wanted pathfinders. Pathfinders are the fellows that jump in first and guide the other troops in so they assemble in one main area and are not scattered all over the place. They wanted demolition men to volunteer for the pathfinders, because if they were to pick a DZ, which is a drop zone, and an LZ, a landing zone for gliders, and if by chance the place they picked was mined, the demolition team could clear the area in a hurry with primer cord. We would just stretch out cord and blow it all up. We didn't have a lot of time, because the troops were in the air coming in. So six of us volunteered for the pathfinders, and we went back to England to do some further training.

That was when the Battle of the Bulge started. Hitler gathered up his army and started to push through the Ardennes. When it started, the only two units that were in reserve were the 82nd Airborne and the 101st Airborne Divisions. So they were rushed into the rear of Bastogne.

The German troops surrounded Bastogne on December 22, 1944, and we were alerted in England that we were going to jump in and try to resupply them. On the twenty-third we took off with two planes. At first we were going to use one plane, and then they thought, "Well, if one of us gets knocked out of the air, we'd better have another one." So I went with Jake McNiece, Mike Majewski, Bill Code, and John Dewey, and Lt. Schrable Williams—we called him little Willie—said, "If you guys are going, I'm going too." So our lieutenant went with us. He ended up as our stick commander.

We went in first and it was a pretty rough flight. We got a lot of flak. We were over the German lines and we had a gun pointing right at us, and Colonel Crouch, the pilot, drove our plane right at the gun placement. They thought we were going to crash them, so they all jumped out of the gun emplacement—it was lucky for us they did, or they would have shot us right out of the air—and then he pulled up and we landed at Bastogne.

We were supposed to signal the second plane with smoke, so Frenchie Blain, who was an original pathfinder, he threw the smoke out. I spotted a German tank, and I was undoing my tommy gun when I hit the ground and got a hole in my arm. I don't even know how it happened, but one of our officers came over and he patched me up. That's how I got my Purple Heart.

We ran into a place with a corrugated roof, but the Germans blew that off the top of our heads. Luckily nobody got hurt. The next place we got into was a chateau. When they bombed that, all the smoke broke loose and a lot of guys were trapped in the basement. I wasn't in there at the time. I went outside with John Dewey, because every time we wanted to go to the bathroom, a plane would come in and strafe us, and we would pull our pants up and run back inside. So he said, "I'll go out with you, John." After the chateau got bombed, I found a gas mask, and I went back in and got them because the smoke had filled the whole room and they couldn't get out.

Then we found a house that we more or less commandeered and made it a pathfinder headquarters. Then we found a brick pile where they had been building a row of houses, until the war came and they stopped. It was a great big brick pile on high ground, so we decided to put our radar sets up on there to guide the planes in. I happened to be the one on top of the brick pile that brought the first planes in, so I said, "How come you got me up there?" And they said because I was the dumbest one.

At Bastogne resupply we brought in a lot of planes. The troop carrier command really did a wonderful job with their planes shot to pieces. Almost every plane that came over there had twenty or thirty holes in it, and some were shot down. But they brought the resupply in, and that enabled the 101st Airborne to fight back and push the Germans out of the Bastogne area.

After Bastogne our commander, Col. Robert Sink, said he wanted his pathfinder teams back, so we advanced into Stuttgart and found a concentration camp, Landsberg.

The local people said they didn't know the concentration camps were there. Well, for miles before we got there, you could smell them. Something was radically wrong. If you ever lived in the country or lived near a slaughterhouse, you know what it is like. So we took Landsberg and made all the natives in the town come in and help move the bodies, and made them see what had taken place there.

You got to come home based on how many points you earned, and I had extra points for a Purple Heart, extra points for being a pathfinder, and extra missions.

One of the things that I'm proud of is that we accomplished every mission that we went on. And most of those missions saved a lot more lives than what we had to take. I think that's really something that kept me going for years. I'm pretty proud of the outfit I was in.

So that's about how I won the war.

AFTER THE WAR . . .

John Agnew worked for Western Electric Corporation as a telephone equipment installer, retiring from the company after thirty-six years. Agnew has been active in marksmanship and been instrumental in several police unit trainings. He has also been a Pennsylvania Game Commission hunter safety instructor and National Rifle Association instructor for more than thirty years.

☆ Anna Marie Cattuti ☆

Camp Hill, Pennsylvania

• •

Anna Marie Cattuti served as an army nurse in the
32nd Evacuation Hospital and was stationed in Europe
for most of her enlistment. She served for seven years.

• •

I was doing general duty at St. Joseph's Hospital in Memphis, Tennessee. I wasn't making very much money, and by the time you paid bus fare, bought uniforms, bought your food, there was nothing left over, so I joined the army because I could make more money. That was in '41, before Pearl Harbor. My father wasn't happy about me joining, but I just did it. I was about twenty-six years old.

I went to Fort Benning, Georgia, for training and worked as a nurse in the ward. At that time everything was very formal. You had to dress up in the evening. You had to have an evening gown or clothes that looked real nice, and you had to have little cards with your name on them to put in the colonel's wife's little dish. If you did, you would be invited to the colonel's house for a party or a tea.

At the hospital we took care of soldiers who had come back from over-seas, enlisted men and soldiers who were hurt or sick. They'd come in to stay for a little while, and if they were sick and got better, they would go back to the unit. If they were hurt, then we'd take care of them.

I was in the States about two and a half years before I found out I was going overseas. I was really excited but scared, too, because I didn't know what I was getting into.

I made two trips overseas. The first time, in 1943, I was with a ship platoon, and we sailed out and brought back soldiers who had been in the southeastern part of Europe. They were shell-shocked. My first trip was on the *Mariposa,* which was a luxury ship that traveled between California and Hawaii. The second trip was in our navy hospital—not a hospital ship, just a ship.

We saw a lot while we were over there waiting for the men to get well enough to bring them back. We used to see the dogfights up in the sky. It was amazing. You'd sit there with your mouth open, watching if they're going to come down or not. I don't think I ever saw a plane shot down, but we were watching.

We were billeted in Abergele, North Wales, up on the Irish Sea, and we were sent down to a little town named Cirencester, near Bristol, where we had a field school. There they tried to show us how to live out in the field—marching, digging foxholes, things like that.

On June 5, the eve of D-Day, one of the girls, whose husband was stationed at Swindon, wanted to get to a phone and call him. No one would walk with her, so I did. Everything was blocked up and we couldn't find a telephone, so we finally came back.

We were coming back at around 11:00 or 11:30 at night. Because it stays daylight for a long time in England during the summer, it was still pretty light out. The planes were out on the airfield, and these guys were getting in with packs and guns. They were coming out of the trees or the grass or shrubs all covered up, with their faces all blackened. They would go up the steps and get in the planes, which we later found out were gliders.

The MPs caught us. They thought we were German spies trying to infiltrate, so we were taken to headquarters and asked a lot of questions. They finally took us back to our post and told us, "Stay in, don't talk." And we were afraid to talk.

But that was the beginning of the invasion. As we went back to the camp, you could see the planes riding over the roof of the building. They were going out, one plane, two planes, and each one was pulling a glider.

When we got back, there was a phone call message for us saying, "Pack your things up. We're leaving." So we packed up.

Inverness
SCOTLAND
Atlantic Ocean
North Sea
Glasgow Edinburgh
Sunderland
Northern
Ireland
Belfast
York
Leeds
Irish Sea
Dublin ★
Liverpool
IRELAND
ENGLAND
Birmingham
Northampton
Gloucester
Cork
Wales
Newport
Oxford London
Bristol ★
Celtic Sea
Cardiff Bath
Southampton Canterbury
Exeter Dorchester Portsmouth
Plymouth Torbay Brighton
GREAT BRITAIN
Truro English Channel
FRANCE

At 6:00 the next morning we were ready to go. We waited half the day, and then we went down to Southampton to ship out. That was on June 7, but we didn't go into France until about July 12.

We landed at Omaha beach. We saw a lot of devastation. We went up the hill on trucks, and we ended up in an apple orchard. Late in the day we were putting our cots and blankets out, getting ready to go to bed, and we heard *ping!* A sharpshooter. So we started digging in.

After we left the apple orchard, we went to Saint-Mère-Église and stayed for a while. Then we got orders to move south down near Avranches, where we got cut off from the rest of the hospital. The Germans went right through our lines.

So we were on one side, and our hospital was back on the other side of the Germans. We didn't know what to do. We were in ambulances and were afraid to get out of them. But finally we did. One of us would get out and take a step, and the next guy that got out stepped in the same place. We were just scared.

Then, after that, the Americans broke through, and we moved on. But they never put us ahead of a column again.

We were always treating patients, but we moved every three days, so there'd be a gap where we wouldn't have patients. But you could always hear the guns going. And you could see the columns of trucks, jeeps, and ambulances going back and forth, all the time.

There must have been thirty of us altogether, divided between day and night shifts. You worked days and the other shift worked nights, and then you switched over and did the same thing.

We lived in tents, and the operating room was a U shape. They would bring the soldiers in, and we would check them out. A decision was made on whether there needed to be an operation, or if the guy could hold on for a little while, or if he could be sent back to his unit. When we were operating, we operated straight through until everyone was taken care of. If that was twenty-four hours, it was twenty-four hours. You didn't stop; you just kept going.

I did mostly anesthetics. If someone didn't need an anesthetic, I would circulate. I would take care of records, check on patients, or evaluate guys that were waiting for help. I saw people with legs shot off, a lot of back work, shoulders and lumbar region, abdomens split open, arms shot off— just about anything you could imagine. There wasn't time to think about it; you just worked. Ambulances kept coming in, and you put them on litters and just lined them up. As soon as one was taken care of, you'd move him back and bring another one in. Then we'd scrub up and go again.

In the wintertime it got so cold that we didn't scrub; we just cleaned up early in the morning and put gloves on. After that we'd just take off used gloves and put on clean ones. But they were always autoclaved, sanitized. We had an autoclave going with us all the time. Instruments, sheets, drapes, everything was autoclaved.

As I said, we traveled every three days. Sometimes we were in a field and sometimes on the edge of a little town. We might not move very far, maybe just a few miles, but we were always behind the troops.

When we were at Thionville, France, at the Battle of the Bulge, we took care of Germans who had been injured. We had very few Americans. Maybe some other hospital did, but our hospital was mostly German soldiers. You can't leave an injured man lying. You've got to pick them up, so they picked them up and brought them in. They were just like everyone else. You had to be nice to them, had to take care of them.

We crossed the Rhine River on pontoon boats and went over to Frankfurt, following the Autobahn. Then we got up near Essen, which is a big manufacturing place. It was also very beautiful.

But the Germans strafed at night. We got hit—got holes in our tents. We had one doctor who was a little silly. He got a flashlight and was looking at the holes in the tent, and of course, the planes saw it and he lost a leg.

Then the war ended and we headed south to Munich. That was beautiful. We thought we were going to be stationed there permanently, but orders came through that we were to move on to Salzburg. We did a lot of sightseeing around there, because there wasn't any fighting going on.

I came home because I had injured myself. I wouldn't say anything as long as we were working, because it was exciting and I didn't want to miss what was going on. I got hurt jumping out of a two-and-a-half-ton truck. I had to get out and go to the bathroom, and I got a popped cartilage. It was all right in the daytime, but at night when I'd relax, it was like somebody stuck a hot poker in there. So when I came back to the States, they put me in a hospital in Georgia. I figured that I had been in the army long enough. I got my discharge outside of Chicago, then I came back to New York and got married.

The most important thing I learned is to educate yourself to be ready to work. If I was twenty-six, I would do it all over again. If they needed me now, I'd go back, but they won't take me.

AFTER THE WAR . . .

Anna Marie Cattuti was employed by the U.S. Veterans in the FDR Veterans Hospital in Montrose, New York, until her retirement in 1981. She married Carl Cattuti, also a World War II veteran. Their son Michael was a marine who served in the Gulf War.

☆ Frank Lashinsky ☆

Cornwall, Pennsylvania

....

Frank Lashinsky was a tail gunner with the 455th Bomb Group.
He was taken prisoner by the Germans and was transported
in a boxcar that came in the path of Allied bombs.

....

I grew up and went to school in Mahanoy City, Pennsylvania. My father was a coal miner there, and in my junior year he was injured in a mine accident. He lost his right hand and his left eye. The family wanted me to finish high school in Mahanoy City, but before I graduated, I took a civil service test and went to work at the Middletown Air Depot at Olmstead Field. I finished school at the Farm Show building in Harrisburg. I became an aircraft electrician at a salary of $900 a year. A friend and I shared a room for $3 a week. I worked there for about a year before I went in the service.

When I was drafted, I went to Fort Dix, New Jersey, where I was put on a troop train that took us to Florida. During the war, the Air Corps had requisitioned hotels in Miami Beach, and that was where I took basic training. They had taken out all the hotel furniture and put in double-decker bunks. Instead of two people to a room, there were six of us.

From basic training in Miami Beach, I was sent to Tyndall Field in Panama City, Florida, where I underwent gunnery training and was made a tail gunner. I was assigned to a crew and we trained in Pueblo, Colorado, where we had to learn how to work together.

In August of 1944 I was shipped overseas. We picked up a brand new airplane in Topeka, Kansas, and flew from there to Grenier Field, New Hampshire, then to Gander, Newfoundland, then on to the Azores. That was a pretty tough test for a navigator, because the Azores were just a little pinpoint in the Atlantic, and there weren't many navigation aids. It was all done with dead reckoning.

We made it to the Azores and then flew to Marrakech in Africa, then to Tunis in Tunisia. As we touched down in Tunis, I looked out the window and saw the right landing gear. It was a very smooth landing, but when the landing gear touched down, the wheels started to wobble. It really became severe, and then all of a sudden the whole landing gear snapped off. The wing dipped down, tore out two propellers, and the wheel knocked the vertical stabilizer off the plane. We skidded to a crash landing. Fortunately no one was hurt, but we had to wait to pick up a new plane.

Eventually we continued on to Italy, where we were assigned to the 455th Bomb Group. We arrived in Italy the last day of August, 1944, and started flying missions on October 1. My twentieth birthday was eight days earlier.

On our sixth mission we were sent to bomb an oil refinery in southern Poland, near Auschwitz. The Army Air Force planners had decided that if they kept on hitting oil refineries, they could hinder all parts of the German Army—the tanks, the planes, everything. So that's what we were concentrating on.

We had a full load of bombs and ammunition, and 2,700 gallons of gasoline. We were flying "tail-end Charlie." They always put the new crew in the worst spot, and that was us. Typical squadron formations were ten planes. The leading three-plane V had another three-plane V stepped down on its left and its right. "Tail-end Charlie" was behind and below, and that was the most difficult place to fly, because it took more maneuvering to stay in position, and you also had to use more gasoline. So we had our engines running at pretty much full throttle most of the way and were using up a lot of gas. Inexperienced, we were learning on the job.

When you got near the target, there's a place called the IP, or initial point. At that point the whole bomb group turns and starts heading to the target, which would be maybe a five- to ten-minute leg. It's a straight run as much as possible, and the Germans knew that, so they would start putting up anti-aircraft fire into the predicted path of the plane. You couldn't deviate from it, because the pilot would switch on the automatic pilot, and the plane was controlled by the bombardier by keeping his crosshairs on the target. The formation would put on "full military power," as they call it, in order to cut down the time period of the bomb.

Well, when the rest of the bomb group went up to full military power, we started falling behind. After a while they disappeared and we were all by ourselves. Then two of our superchargers started to fail, and we began losing altitude. We had used up a lot of gasoline, so we started heading back by ourselves. That was very dangerous, because the German fighters looked for stragglers, but fortunately we weren't attacked by any of them. To maintain our altitude, we started throwing out our ammunition. Finally we stabilized it where we were flying okay. But when we got down into Yugoslavia, it became apparent we couldn't cross the Adriatic Sea and get back to Italy, so we looked for a place to jump out.

We bailed out over Bosnia. We never had any training for parachute jumps. All we were told was to make sure we cleared the plane, and if we were up high, to free fall until we were close to the ground, and then open up our chute. We never had any escape or evasion training either.

I bailed out and pulled my rip cord, and nothing happened. I was surprised at how clearly I could think. I figured maybe the pins that held the pilot chute were bent, so I grabbed the D ring with two hands and pulled it, and then all of a sudden the chute opened.

When I landed, I took off my helmet and I could hear voices all around. I was carrying a .45-caliber automatic, and I loosened it up in the holster. The first thing I saw was a group of women and children coming toward me. They stopped dead in their tracks when they saw me. Then behind me, there was a big group of men carrying rifles.

I positioned myself in a line between the women and the children, so it wouldn't be safe for them to take a shot at me, and I went up to the women. We carried a little folder that had an American flag and an official seal, and it had our picture in it. Text in about ten different languages said, "I'm an American airman." I showed them that and said, "Americanski." There was no change of their expression, so then I repeated, "Americanski." And then they started shaking my hand.

One of them could speak a little English, and he said the Germans must have seen me come down, so I had to get out of there real fast. They quickly gathered my parachute and clothing, and took me and some of my crew members to a barn, where I met another member of my crew. We were told to take off our flying clothes, and they made up a two-wheel ox cart with hay on the back. Our clothing was put underneath the hay, and we sat on the tailboard. For three days we traveled that way, passing quite a few burned-out German tanks and trucks on the way, until we got to the town of Sanski Most.

The town was a command point for Tito and his Partisans, and the British had sent a radioman in. We were billeted in a large house where there was a mother and her two grown girls, who provided us with food. They were Muslims, and they wore the veils on their faces.

When our entire crew was assembled, there were forty-five Allied airmen in town. The radioman sent out the information, and about a week later we went out to a meadow at night, and soon we heard engines overhead. There was a big contingent of Partisans who came along and lined a path in the meadow with torches, sort of like runway lights. As the plane landed, they extinguished the torches so it was totally black.

The plane was a C-47, which held twenty-one passengers. Obviously forty-five of us couldn't get on, so anyone who was hurt or wounded got first priority. We went back to town and waited for a couple more weeks for the right kind of weather conditions to take us out. During that time, they had the equivalent of USO dances for the Yugoslavs in the town square at night. The Partisans all wore German uniforms without the insignia, so evidently they must have killed Germans in order to clothe themselves. It was not unusual to see a woman with a bandolier of ammunition and a couple of hand grenades hanging off her belt, and you would dance with them dressed like that. Eventually another C-47 came in and we were flown back to Italy.

When we returned, I guess they figured we were seasoned fliers, because they selected us to become a lead crew, and from that point we flew as the lead of our squadron. On several raids, our squadron led the 15th Air Force. The 15th was flying 800- to 1,000-plane raids at the time, and as a tail gunner I could sit in the back, and as far as I could see were airplanes. It was quite an impressive sight.

That winter was one of the coldest winters of the century; in fact, the temperature at bombing altitudes was 50 to 70 degrees below zero. I'd always wear two pair of socks, a pair of long underwear, woolen pants, a woolen shirt, and then put on an electrically heated flying suit with electrically

The Mae West Life Vest

If their plane went down in the open sea, Airmen depended on survival techniques and an inflatable sleeveless rubber life preserver nicknamed the Mae West. During World War II, it saved many thousands of Allied lives. The vest got its name because when it was inflated, the wearer's chest expanded to resemble the well-endowed contours of the provocative star of vaudeville, stage, and film, Mae West (1892–1980).

An airman inflated his life vest by triggering the release of two cigar-shaped carbon dioxide cartridges. If cartridges failed or were lost, he could blow up the vest manually. Attached to the life vest was a plastic ditching whistle, which the user could blow to locate others in the water or to attract the attention of rescuers. Other gear might include flares, sea marker dye, shark repellent, flashlight, signal mirror, and bright yellow linen skull cap.

Exactly when the life vest got its nickname is unknown. Officially, it was cataloged as Pneumatic Life Vest Type B-3 (or B-4 or B-5). It reportedly was designed by James F. Boyle, who in 1935 founded a company that produced rescue gear.

The vest was manufactured in the United States, Great Britain, and Canada by defense contractors, in various colors—a tropical pattern for use in North Africa and the Far East, green or khaki for general use, and yellow for high visibility from airborne rescue planes. Some men who were marooned in the water with the yellow version took it off and hid it between their legs when they suspected that an enemy aircraft was near, and donned it again when they thought Allied rescuers were approaching. ★

heated boots. Then on top of that, I'd put a fleece-lined pair of pants and a fleece-lined jacket, and then a Mae West. Then I'd put on my parachute harness. And when we went over a target where there was antiaircraft fire, we put on flak jackets and steel helmets, which were supposed to protect us from antiaircraft fire. We also wore our goggles, which had little wires that defrosted them, and we wore oxygen masks, so you couldn't tell one person from the next. Everybody looked the same.

On February 22, 1945, we were sent up to bomb a railroad marshaling yard in Vienna, Austria. As we went over the target, a German antiaircraft artillery shell hit the plane a few feet in front of the wing. It tore a huge hole in the plane. It destroyed a big bundle of wires. It tore out an escape hatch behind the pilot, missing the pilot by just a foot or so, and hit the upper turret on the B-24, tearing the Plexiglas cover off. The shell stripped off the perforated cooling barrel of the machine gun and bent the barrel up into a ninety-degree angle, but fortunately it never exploded. I wouldn't have been here if it did. We brought that plane back and it was junked. That was the third plane our crew had lost.

Then on March 12, 1945, we went to bomb the Florisdorf oil refinery in Vienna, leading our bomb group. As we dropped our bombs, there was a loud screaming noise. Evidently one of the propellers ran away—in other words, it started speeding up. The pilot tried to control it, he tried to shut it down, but nothing would happen. By now it was vibrating the whole plane. We thought it was going to tear the whole thing apart, but it eventually froze up and caused a lot of drag.

We had been briefed before we left that in case we couldn't get back to our base, to go to an airfield that the Russians had taken over in Pecs, Hungary, which was right near the Yugoslav border. We dropped out of the formation and were losing altitude steadily, so we started to lighten up the load. We threw away all of our ammunition, we stripped our guns and threw every piece that we could throw overboard. The navigators set a course by dead reckoning, and we flew to where we thought Pecs was. The pilot told the navigator to descend, and when he got to about 4,000 feet, we started to break into the clear.

Suddenly we were attacked by three fighters and all sorts of antiaircraft fire. It turned out that we had stumbled upon a battle between the Russians and the Germans, and I guess both sides figured we were their enemy, so both sides were firing at us. We got a tremendous number of hits, and the pilot ordered a bailout. So I went to the escape hatch, and by the time I got there, everybody else in the tail section had jumped out except for one guy.

As he jumped out, the escape hatch came down and caught his flying boot between the hatch and the frame of the plane. I thought, "Oh boy, now what do I do?" If I opened the hatch, he would have fallen out, but he may have hit his head and been knocked out. Well, I decided, "I'm strong enough. I can hold him with one hand and lift the hatch with the other." I believe I could have done it, too, but before I could do anything, he fell right out of his boot, so I jumped out.

I looked up at the plane and saw somebody come out of the front section, and at that same time two large shells exploded, one under each wing. Then I tumbled and opened my chute. The next thing I heard was *fing! fing!* They were firing at us on the way down. I took my parachute shroud lines and started to spill air out of them so I would tend to swing and wouldn't make as easy a target. Also, you fall faster. When I hit the ground, I hit very hard and hurt my ankle and my leg.

The first thing I saw on the ground—I was in amongst barbed wire and trenches—was a guy sticking his head up from a trench he was in. Since he didn't take a shot at me, I ran and jumped in the trench with him. Well, there were about ten men in there, and they all had field gray uniforms that had the German eagle with the swastika underneath it. The guy who had stuck his head above the trenches put his hand out and said, "Pistol." I took out my .45 and gave it to him. They never searched me. I had about fifty rounds of ammunition on me.

They took me through the trenches towards the back, where I was put with a German officer in a dugout. He was seated on the floor, which was just a dirt floor, and he had a little metal desk and he was working away. I sat there for a few hours, until it started to get dark, and then they assigned a guard to take me back behind the lines. The guard could speak a little English, and he said to me, "If you manage to live for three months, you'll be a free man," because they knew that the war was just about over.

They took me to a river and into a flat-bottom boat, and they started poling us across the river. I was trying to think of how to get rid of the ammunition I had, because I didn't think they'd be too enthusiastic about me keeping it, so I decided that this was a good place to get rid of it. I reached into my pocket and dropped a handful overboard. When I did, it made a splash and everybody froze. I guess they thought there were some Russian frogmen in the area. They listened for a while and didn't hear anything, so they started poling again. It took me three handfuls before I finally got rid of all the ammunition.

We got to a town across the river, and they took me into the center of the town and up to the second floor of a building that the Germans were using as a command center. They had a guy who could speak English, and he was going to interrogate me. He told me to strip off all of my clothing, so I was standing there naked. There was a big potbellied stove in the middle of the room, and I could visualize all these tortures they would use as they tried to get information out of me.

We had been told just to give our name, rank, and serial number. So every question he asked me—where I came from, what unit I was with— I just replied with name, rank, and serial number. They said, "You're lying, because we know there was a captain onboard the plane." And our pilot was a captain. "We haven't picked any captains up and you're the last man we have, so you must be the captain." I just repeated my name, rank, and serial number.

They said, "What will you say when we say we're going to execute you?" I figured, well, it doesn't really make too much difference what I say, so I just replied with my name, rank, and serial number. Eventually they gave me my clothing and I got dressed. I figured, well, this is the end, because they took me downstairs where there was a brick wall, and they walked me over to it. I was relieved when we turned there and went down the street to another house. They had picked up five other men from our crew, and they were all in there.

It turned out that our pilot, copilot, and radioman were picked up by the Russians and got back okay. Three of our crew were killed: the two navigators and the radarman. They were probably shot on the way down.

We stayed in this house for a few days. There were shells going overhead and everything. Then I guess the Germans decided to retreat, because they put together a troop train complete with antiaircraft guns. We were put in a boxcar with three German guards, four Italian guards, and three German women. They used barbed wire to divide the car in half. In our half of the car, there were the six from our crew, another American crew of ten, and thirteen Bulgarian officers plus one Russian officer. The Germans had the other half of the car.

The first afternoon out we were strafed by some Allied plane. The antiaircraft guns opened fire, but fortunately they didn't hit anything, and we continued on toward Germany. The rail lines were bombed out in many places. We would go so far and stay for a while and back up, and we kept on doing this.

We finally got to Regensburg in Germany. We arrived early that morning in a big marshaling yard. Soon the air-raid sirens went off, and our guards opened up the car door and took us out of there. A little while later the sirens went off again. They assumed it was the "all clear," so they took us back into the car. The next thing you knew, you could hear engines overhead. The German guards just took off and left us in the boxcar.

There was a little barred window up in one corner of the boxcar, and it was screwed in. During our journey, we had been working on them, trying to loosen the window. We had no plan, but we had it partially loosened. Bombs started to come down all around us. There were fires and explosions nearby on all sides of our car. Some of the guys didn't want to leave the car, because they thought we'd get shot by the German guards because we were trying to escape, but I and a few others said, "I'd rather get killed that way than burn to death in one of these boxcars." So we pulled out the window. The bombardier from the other crew was small enough to fit through it. We lowered him down, and the door was just closed with a wire and a latch, so he undid it and everybody got out and ran.

Right next to us was a troop train full of Russian Cossacks, who had defected earlier and were fighting for the Germans. They told us that the war was just about over and said they'd like to surrender to the Americans. They said, "If you want, we'll kill your guards and you can come with us." But at that time the German SS were crawling all over the country, and anybody who looked like a deserter was shot on the spot. They didn't even bother to ask them any questions. So we thought it would be safer to stay with our guards, which we did.

We hardly ate at all during that whole period of time. There was a time we got four crackers a day; it was the only thing we got to eat. We never had a bath or a shower or a shave during all that time. The only place we drank was when they stopped the train near a stream, or if we were near a farmer's pump. We went to the bathroom wherever they stopped the train, but we didn't eat much, so we didn't have much need to go to the bathroom.

Eventually we got to Moosburg, Stalag 7A. We arrived there on a Wednesday, and that following Sunday some of our P-51s came overhead and started doing a kind of aerobatics and swooping around. They were trying to tell us that they were going to attack shortly and that we should take cover, but everybody started cheering.

All of a sudden they began strafing the perimeter of the camp, and we ran to our building and lay down on the floor. The firing went on for about half an hour and then it died down. I looked down to where the main gate was and saw American tanks breaking their way through the gates. The German guards were standing there with their hands held high in the air. It was the 14th Armored Division who liberated us. They were part of Patton's 3rd Army.

Later on, Patton came in with his cowboy outfit, and he got on his jeep and gave a little speech. Then he said, "I have to go chasing after the Germans," and he took off.

That's how we were liberated.

I was put on a hospital ship in England and was taken to Camp Miles Standish in Massachusetts. They processed us very briefly and gave us a set of clothing and some back pay and put us on a train. I was given a sixty-day furlough. I can't believe how good it was to get home.

AFTER THE WAR . . .

Frank Lashinsky earned a bachelor's degree in chemical engineering. He took a position with Pfizer and supervised production of newly discovered pharmaceuticals. Lashinsky and his wife, Dorothy, married in 1952. They adopted a son and two daughters from Italy.

☆ Raymond Miller ☆

Elizabethtown, Pennsylvania

• •

Raymond Miller was a radio operator in the Pacific
Theater, where he was infected with malaria, filariasis,
dengue fever, and food poisoning, among other illnesses.

• •

I was working for Sun Oil Company in Marcus Hook, Pennsylvania, and
a buddy and I had been talking for a long time about joining the Marine
Corps. We went to Philadelphia to see if we could enlist, but we had two
little problems. First, I was six foot tall and weighed about 120 pounds, and
the Marine Corps didn't want any 120-pound skins like that; they wanted
strapping men. The recruiting sergeant knew how bad I wanted to get in,
so he told me to go home, eat regular meals, a handful of bananas every day,
and drink a quart of milk with every meal. He told me to come back in
three weeks, and they would see what they could do.

After three weeks I went back. I was all bloated and could hardly keep
anything down because I was so full of milk and bananas. I got in by about
that much.

We had to bring letters from our family. My friend was fine—his mother
and father signed the paper. But my father would not sign mine. He said, "I

have six children and you are the oldest boy. You have a good job, a better job than I do, and we are just barely making it with your pay. If you leave to go into the Marine Corps, we may go under." I was upset, thinking I might not be able to go because my father wouldn't sign the papers. I went to my sister's house and told her about it. She said, "Don't worry about it, I will sign them." So she signed my father's name to the papers.

Boot camp was in San Diego. We had just about finished our training when we got a notice that the Japanese had wiped out about a quarter of the radio operators in the Marine Corps between Midway and Guam. They were in real need of radio operators. They sent three platoons over to radio school to take tests. I had been a Boy Scout leader for years, teaching boys Morse code, so I knew what it was. Out of the three platoons, I was the only one who passed the radio operator test.

You know a lot of boys and girls nowadays are sort of smart-mouthed, but you wouldn't do that then, because if you did, the next day you would come in with a black eye. We found out if we got real smart-mouthed, after dark the drill instructor would come in and take you out of your bunk and out of the barracks, and beat the devil out of you. After that you kept your mouth shut. You try that now and they will call the representative or senator or the governor or somebody, but then there was no one to protect you. Just the Lord himself, and he protected you most of the time.

There were a lot of kooky things that happened, and at that time we didn't laugh, but now I can laugh about. For example, all the cooks and bakers went to school in San Diego. So wherever you went in the world, any place, the Marine Corps had two kinds of pie: sweet potato and pumpkin. And since they all went to the same school, they all had the same flavor. One tasted just like kerosene, and the other one tasted just like the yellow octagon soap. Every place I went overseas, it was the same way every time.

When we got overseas, the mosquitoes were terrible. We unloaded the ships, and then we had to go put our tents up. A lot of the boxes said they were mosquito netting and mosquito bars, and we thought, "Boy, that's going to be great, we are going to be protected." So when we opened them up, the boxes were full of wool blankets. Someone had labeled them wrong, so that's why just about all the soldiers that were out there in the first part of the war got malaria.

Like I said, I was the radio operator, and when they needed information, they would take two radio operators and two observers, and drop us off on different islands to try to get information about the Japanese. You might go in on a submarine, then they would come to the surface and put you in a rubber boat and take you ashore at night. Or it might be a PT boat, but they would drop you off and say, "Now it's every man for himself. You guys have to protect each other and watch over each other, but if anything happens, if you can't bury your radio and hide it so no one can find it, then smash it so no one can use it. Now shake hands and separate." That's how it was. There was a certain day and time of the night they would come back, and they would flash a small light just one time. And if you didn't see it, you were missed. You may be there a day, you may be there a week, and you may be there a month. You may never come off of the island, who knows?

Down around the canal, we had a guy on perimeter all night long with a machine gun, and in the wee hours of the morning, the machine gun went quiet. We couldn't imagine what was wrong, but no one was crazy enough to go out there in the dark to try to find him. So we went out the next morning to find him. They had taken samurai swords and chopped him up just like liver all over the ground. Gives you nightmares.

How would you feel if you heard someone saying, "Help me, help me!" and you turn around and there is one of your buddies coming to you, and you say, "What's the matter?" And he says, "I don't feel good." And he has been hit with shrapnel, and he goes down and his guts all fall out on the ground.

During that time, a lot of us had problems. That's when I got messed up. My legs were full of shrapnel. I had malaria, fever, and food poisoning about ten times. Other than that, I was in good shape. I spent a lot of time in hospitals. In fact, I was in four different hospitals over nineteen months. I went from 180 pounds down to 118 in about two months.

About three years ago I had the last piece of shrapnel taken out of my legs. It was about the size of my fingernail, and my children and my grandchildren had fun. They would say, "Pop-pop, Mom-mom said you have some shrapnel in your legs." They didn't know shrapnel from the man in the moon. And I said, "Yes, why?" "Can we see it?" So I would pull my pant leg up and I would show them.

Different people ask if I went out to die for my country. I don't want to die for my country. I think most of your heroes in this country are the same way. They went out for the same thing. They went out to make the other guy die for his country. Not to die for ours. I heard a number of people out there say that.

AFTER THE WAR . . .

Raymond Miller returned to the Sun Oil Company in Marcus Hook, Pennsylvania, and worked there for more than forty-one years. He and his wife had a son and daughter and were married for fifty-one years before her death. Miller remarried in May 2003.

☆ Vincent Vicari ☆

Easton, Pennsylvania

....

**Vincent Vicari was aide to Gen. Anthony McAuliffe
in the 101st Airborne Division. He was assigned
to the 321st Glider Field Artillery Battalion.**

....

I was living in Union City, New Jersey, and worked right across the river in the apparel industry in New York City. It was still peacetime, but we all had to sign up for the draft, and we knew it was just a matter of time before we were drafted into the service. A number of my friends got called up, so I figured I might as well go with them. I figured we'd all stay together, but the only time I was with them was when we were down at Fort Dix for three days. After that I never saw them until after the war.

I was assigned to Fort Bragg, Georgia, a field artillery training camp. I went there for my basic training to learn how to shoot guns, and then I was assigned to the 30th Division at Fort Jackson, South Carolina.

Part of the artillery was sent to Fort Sill, Oklahoma, as school troops to shoot for the Officers Candidate School. These were enlisted men that had entered the program to become future officers. They would have to go out on the range and give us orders on where they wanted us to shoot, and control the fire. In other words, they'd have a target, and their objective was to hit the target and we would do the shooting for them.

One day the S3, who was the officer in charge of controlling all the batteries, came up to me and said, "Vicari, I'm sending you to OCS." I said, "Thank you very much, sir, I don't want to go." I didn't want to go because I had no education—I had quit high school after two years.

He answered me by saying, "Vicari, you have an option—you either go to OCS or I'm court-martialing you." I said, "I'm going to OCS, sir." And that's how I got into OCS.

It was very demanding. My class went in with 560 people, and when we graduated there were 345. And I did it in ninety days. I'm a ninety-day wonder. I wonder how I ever got through it. You had to take calculus, geometry, trigonometry, and you had to be able to repair trucks. I was able to take a transmission down and put it back together again. They put us through everything.

Truthfully, I cheated on the first test I took. I happened to look over at another fellow's paper, and he didn't have the same answers I had. So I changed my answers, and I got an F. I figured that if I was going to fail, I would do it on my own; I didn't need anybody else's help. But I ended up in the top 10 percent of my class at graduation.

Prior to getting our commissions, they posted up on a big bulletin board a list of units you could volunteer for. You had first, second, and third choice. Two of them were 101st AB, 82nd AB. We were trying to figure out what "AB" meant, so we asked our TAC [Tactical Air Command] officer, and he said, "It's a new way to fight the war. Before there's a big push, they put you on a plane and fly you three or four miles behind the enemy lines. The plane lands, you get out, you take the ground, and as soon as the ground troops come up to you, you fall back."

We went back to our huts and discussed it. We figured, what's the best way to fight the war? Two, three, four days at a time, and then you're out of it. Nothing was mentioned about flying in gliders or parachuting.

I volunteered for the 101st Airborne and was sent to Fort Bragg, where they were. I was assigned to the 321st Glider Field Artillery Battalion. I had never been up in the air in my life. Even today I'm afraid of heights—I will not get up on the roof of my house. But I love flying and I enjoyed parachuting. I loved being in a glider, but I will not get up on a ladder. People think I'm a nut, and I agree.

The third day I was there, we went down to the airfield, and the sergeant who was working with me said, "Lieutenant, that's your glider." At that time all the enlisted men would look at ninety-day wonders like me and see how I was going to react. So we walked over to my glider, and there was a jeep in it. I told him, "Take the jeep out." He said, "I can't. We need it to pull a gun." I asked, "What gun?" "The one that's in my glider."

We walked over to his glider, and there's a 75 sawed-off howitzer strapped down in his glider. Now the glider is nothing more than a light metal frame—like pipes with canvas wrapped around it—and the part the jeep was on and the part that the gun was on was nothing but a piece of plywood bolted down to the frame of the glider.

I decided to keep my big mouth shut, because everybody was looking at me to see how I was going to react. So I figured I would sit in the jeep so I wouldn't see where we're going. We were ready to take off, and the glider pilot said, "Lieutenant, you come up here and fly copilot." I had to go up front, because the three other men I had in the glider with me were looking at me to see what I was going to do. So I got into the copilot's seat.

When you taxi down the runway with a glider, the glider becomes airborne first, while the plane towing you is still on the ground. So we were up in the air, and I said to the pilot, "Take the glider down! The plane's on the ground!" He said, "I can't." I pulled out my .45 and said, "I'll blow your brains out! Take the glider down!" So he took the glider down and got directly behind the plane, and we got caught in the prop blast—that's the wind that comes back from the propellers—and our glider started to bounce like crazy, and I said, "Take it up!" That was the first time I was ever in the air.

The nice part of it is that after you are cut loose from the towing plane, it's like you're in suspended animation. You just float down.

The division was going down to Louisiana on maneuvers. Our unit actually had a live eagle in a big cage as a mascot. And I was told that I was in charge of the eagle. I had only ever seen pictures of eagles, but I didn't have any idea of how to take care of one. I went down to the mess sergeant and said, "Before you feed the men, feed the eagle." He said, "What do I feed the eagle?" I said, "Anything you want."

And it worked out until one day I was in my room, and the sergeant of the guard came running up and said, "Lieutenant, the eagle's dead." I ran out to the cage, and sure enough, there's the eagle lying on its back with its feet up in the air. I figured, "That's the end of my military career. I'm gonna get court-martialed." Since I didn't know what to do, I buried the eagle. We made a nice mound and put in a stake that said, "Young Abe Died 8 July 1943." I figured we would see what happened when the division came back from maneuvers. Then I went to my battery commander and told him.

About ten days later I was told to report to the battery headquarters, so I reported to the captain, who said, "General McAuliffe wants to see you." I figured that was the end of my military career. I went upstairs, cleaned up, changed uniforms, and reported to the exec officer. I was told to go in to General McAuliffe. We started talking, and he was a perfect gentleman. But I was thinking to myself, "If you're going to court-martial me, don't play games with me; tell me and let's get it over with." Finally, out of the clear blue sky, he said, "How would you like to be my aide?" I said, "Yes, sir." I didn't know what an aide did, but it was better than getting a court-martial.

We built up a relationship that was fabulous. He was a perfect gentleman. He's the only general I came across, and I met them all—Patton, Eisenhower, Montgomery, Bradley—and he was the only general that never used profane language. General Mac never used a cuss word the whole time I knew him.

When you were talking with him, he would say, "Nuts." That meant that was the end of the conversation. And if you continued, being that General Mac was Irish, he'd start to flush red from the neck up. But he would never raise his voice. Never yelled at anyone in front of anybody. Sometimes I think that's more effective, being polite and mannerly.

As an aide, I had to be available for anything he wanted to have done. Before anyone could see him, they had to come through me. All the reports would come in, and before they went to him to sign, I would go over them. I would go in to him with a stack of papers and put them on his desk and say, "General, will you please sign the papers?" And he would sign his name. He never knew what he was signing, but he would sign his name to it.

Brig. Gen. Anthony McAuliffe, artillery commander of the 101st Airborne Division, gives his various glider pilots last minute instructions before take-off. NATIONAL ARCHIVES

I also got the reputation of being a procurer. If he thought we ought to have something, he'd call me in and say, "Vicari, it would be nice if we had this," which meant, "I don't want to see you until you get it." When we were in England, he called me into his office and said, "Vicari, it would be nice if we had leather jackets like the fighter pilots have," which meant MOVE!

Now at that time, everybody wanted parachute boots, but unless you were airborne like we were, you couldn't wear the jump boots. So I got twenty pairs of jump boots from the supply sergeant, and I went out looking for a fighter squadron. When I found one, I got the supply officer and the supply sergeant, and we bartered. So everybody on the staff got a leather fighter pilot's jacket.

I brought them back to the general, and he said, "Vicari, good job, but they don't have the 101st emblem on them." So I had to go down to the supply sergeant, get the emblems, and then go into town and find somebody who was able to sew them on.

We were the first ones in airborne to have leather jackets. And then he did the same thing to me with the bombardier jackets. He called me in and said, "You know, it would be nice if we had one of those." So I went through the same process: getting jump boots, finding a bomber squadron, and everybody ending up with a jacket. I still have my leather jacket at home. It's about sixty-one years old now. It's the original jacket with the emblem on it.

General McAuliffe was originally a glider rider, and when I joined the 101st, I became a glider rider. One day as we were having lunch, General Mac looked across the table at me and said, "Vicari, we're jumping this afternoon." What do you say to a general?

We went down to the airfield, and the colonel from our parachute battalion was waiting for us. They had a mockup there about ten feet high. The colonel said, "When you stand in the door of the plane, you bend over and stand in a crouch. But the important thing is, when you land, you bend your knees and roll with the fall." He jumped off the mockup a couple of times to show us how we should do it. General Mac and I went up on the mockup and went through the same process. We jumped off the mockup twice. And that was the extent of our parachute training. Then they put the parachute on us, we got into the plane, the plane took off, and that was it. The next thing I knew, I was coming down in a parachute.

After D-Day, when we were in Normandy, I went up as a forward observer to direct the field artillery fire. When it got dark, I couldn't see anything, but I found a ditch where I saw three or four people laying with blankets around them. I figured at least if something happened, there were some people in the ditch with me, and we could get up and fight together. So I wrapped myself in a blanket and got down in the ditch with them. When it got light, I got up and saw that the people were still sleeping, or what I thought was sleeping. So as the sergeant walked by, I said, "Wake these men up and tell 'em to get moving. Last night when I got here, they were sleeping. I got up and they're still sleeping." The sergeant turned around to me and said, "Lieutenant, they're dead."

I was lying between them. They were watching over me—at least that's the attitude I take now. They were watching over me.

One night I got a phone call to tell General Mac to report to division headquarters right away. I woke the general up and told him he was wanted immediately. General Mac got dressed and I started to leave the building with him, and he said, "Vicari, you stay by the phone and don't leave it." So I went back and stayed in the room. About two hours later the phone rang, and I was told, "Vicari, notify all the battalions to pack everything up. They'll be moving out."

I said, "How could we move out? We don't have any trucks," because airborne doesn't have any vehicles except the jeeps that we use in our glider battalions. I was told, "There are vehicles coming." The vehicles came about five hours later. They had everything—cattle cars, trailers, two-and-a-half-ton trucks, every conceivable type of vehicle you can imagine. We hadn't had a chance to get new clothing, new jump boots, new shoes, new galoshes, and we hadn't had a chance to replenish our ammunition.

None of us knew where we were going. We drove with our lights on, then with our lights off, then with our lights on, with no rest stop to relieve ourselves. You did the best you could.

Finally the convoy stopped and Colonel Kennedy said, "There's a town up ahead. We're probably going into town." That town was Bastogne. We pulled into Bastogne, and the infantry got out of the trucks and started walking to make contact with the Germans so we could establish some semblance of a line, and when they made contact, that became the line. There were eight German divisions plus a full artillery corps against the 101st Airborne Division, and they just kept pushing us back and pushing us back, and they finally encircled us.

One of the men I went to OCS with was assigned as a forward observer with one of the infantry regiments. They needed time to establish some semblance of a line. Lieutenant Toth said, "I'll stay here as FO and direct artillery fire until you can establish some sort of a line." And that's what he did. After a while the colonel sent someone up and told him to fall back, and he went back.

I was talking to him after the war, and I asked him, "Did he put you in for a medal?" He said, "Yeah. When I got back, he tapped me on the shoulder and said 'Nice job.'" But earning a medal was the farthest thing from our minds. Nobody was looking for medals.

I think General McAuliffe was the turning point in the war. If he had surrendered, the Germans would have taken Bastogne—all they were after was gas. And if they would have gotten the gas, their equipment was so far superior, they would have overrun all our troops. I think General Mac saying, "Nuts!" was the turning point.

I tell you, during all of World War II, the 101st Airborne, with all we went through, had two Congressional Medals of Honor. One was Joe Mann in Holland, who had been wounded. He was dragged back into the foxhole and was lying there, and a German hand grenade went into the foxhole. And Joe, may he rest peace, threw his body on the hand grenade. There was also Colonel Cole in Normandy. He led an attack—the first man out—led his battalion. And, may he rest in peace, he was killed. That's the only two Congressional Medals of Honor.

But medals were the farthest things from my mind. I think about it now because I'd like to leave them to my grandchildren. But I've never worn them. They're in my drawer. I don't wear any medals. We did what we had to do, and that was it.

I'm one of the fortunate ones. I made it back. You honor the ones that didn't come back. They're the ones that made the supreme sacrifice. I complain about pain sometimes, but I'm here, and they're at peace, with the grace of God. That may not have been a nice way of going out, but in his infinite wisdom, he knows what he's doing.

AFTER THE WAR . . .

Vince Vicari was discharged from the service at age twenty-four and went to work in the women's apparel industry. He became a representative for the International Ladies Garment Workers Union for thirty-six years before he retired. Vicari was married to his wife, Emily, for forty-eight years and has two daughters.

☆ Lou Neishloss ☆

Bristol, Pennsylvania

••

Lou Neishloss was seventeen years old when he
went to boot camp in Bainbridge, Maryland. He served
on the USS *Brooklyn* in the European Theater.

••

I was going to Norristown High School and was on the track team. I ran
cross-country and I loved it. At the time, a lot of people were getting ideas
about going into the service. One day two or three of my buddies said, "Why
don't we join up instead of just talking about it?" So we all just went to the
recruiting station and joined the navy. We thought we were going to be
together, but it didn't work out that way. We all went in different directions.

I went to Bainbridge, Maryland, for my boot camp. Boot camp was
tough. We had to jump off a sixty-foot platform into ten feet of water. They
didn't ask if you could swim, and some guys couldn't. We had gas mask
drills with real mustard gas. You had to take the mask off to get an idea of
what that mustard gas did; it burned your eyes. You had to take the gas mask
off for five seconds, but that was enough. At 5:00 A.M. we would run three
miles with boots on. I didn't mind that, because I was on the cross-coun-

try team, but I didn't say a word. If they would have known, they would have made me go twice.

Then we went to Newport, Rhode Island, and learned to operate just about every gun made. We had .50-caliber machine guns, 40-millimeters, 5-inch guns, hand grenades, everything. We were under kind of secret orders there. There was a lot of espionage going on then. German U-boats came into Maine during the war, and they came up to North Carolina during the beginning part of the war. That's how close they got. It was kept quiet because they didn't want the public to freak out. But we knew about it because we weren't that far from Maine. The word came down to us about these German submarine guys who were caught by the Coast Guard. They tried to keep it from the press, since people would have freaked out knowing they were that close to the United States.

I had six weeks of boot camp, then I had a one-week furlough, then they assigned me to a ship, the USS *Ranger*—that's an aircraft carrier. That was my transportation to Casablanca. When I got on the ship, they gave me an envelope that said, "Destination unknown." They didn't want you writing letters home, because things were really bad then.

So we went to Casablanca and got off the aircraft carrier. Four other guys and I had to take these cattle car trains, and we went across the desert to Oran, north of Casablanca, where they gave us a day off. On my day off I was on this area where a bunch of marines were, and they had been out fighting Rommel. This one marine said, "Hey, what ship are you on?" I said, "I just got off the USS *Ranger*." He said, "Will you come with me?" And this is a U.S. Marine. I said, "Yeah, sure, I'll go with you."

He took me to this little village out there and said, "Now, there's something that happened here, so I hope you've got a lot of guts." In those areas at that time, you were told never to go out alone, never. Go with four or five guys. We went in this shack-type building, and there was a sailor nailed to a wall. Of course, he was dead. The marine said, "Do you know this guy?" I said, "No, but I can find out what ship he's from."

The marines knew who did it, and they took care of the whole thing themselves, if you know what I mean. They shot every one of them. And the marine said, "Tell your buddies, don't ever come out alone, because these guys will kill you just to steal your shoes." That was my indoctrination.

The next day, they put me on a PT boat that took me to the USS *McLanahan*, which was a destroyer. They're the ones that have the depth charges—they throw them off when they're attacked by submarines. And that's exactly what happened after I got aboard. We were attacked by a wolf-pack—German U-boats—the first night out. We shot these depth charges out, and you could see the water blowing up. And when you saw oil, you knew you had hit them, and the men would all start clapping. Bear in mind that I hadn't even gotten on my regular ship yet.

They took us to Palermo, Sicily, and that was where the USS *Brooklyn* was docked. I went aboard, and of course, you salute and say, "May I have permission to come aboard, sir?" And that was my ship for the rest of my time in the navy.

I don't think we were there more than a week before we went to Anzio beachhead, where a lot of soldiers went in. We had thirty marines on our ship, and we had two airplanes that went off on catapults. They were there for observation and would fly close to the shore off France or Italy, to see if anything was going on with the Germans. Then they would wire information back. Then, when necessary, we could open up our guns. We finished with the Anzio beachhead, where a lot of American soldiers died—but this was before the big invasion of France. We had all kinds of assignments like that, with the marines and the army, where we would back them up with our firepower.

Eventually we heard about plans for the invasion of France, and we knew it was going to be big. It started at about 5:30 A.M. on June 6, 1944. We woke up in the morning, and it was still dark, but we saw what looked like a thousand ships—battleships, light cruisers, destroyers, LSTs. Then the invasion started.

We were on general quarters—that's when you're on battle stations—so we slept for four hours and we manned our gun for four hours, around the clock for thirteen straight days. It was our job to fire our guns at the hillside to give the marines and army a chance to get up the hills and get dug in.

We actually ran out of food, so we ate turnips and raw potatoes. Since it was all we had, they started to taste pretty good. You couldn't reach out for another ship for food during the action, so we drank black coffee day and night, and ate potatoes and turnips. That's what we had—and lots of it.

My job was on the 40-millimeter guns, and I knew exactly what I had to do and when I had to do it. When we had general quarters, when the Germans were attacking us with planes and things like that, everybody knew exactly what their job was. Once in a while somebody choked up a little bit. That happened on my gun mount once. This guy from Brooklyn just froze. He was handing me the shells, and he just stopped, so I

The Anzio Beach Invasion

A surprise American invasion at Italy's Anzio beach on January 22, 1944, was supposed to smash the flank of a Nazi-held line stretching across the width of the Italian peninsula. Then, with British troops pushing up from the south, the Allies intended to force Axis troops to retreat northward, back into Germany. Known as Operation Shingle, the attack was advocated by British prime minister Winston Churchill, who saw a rapid liberation of Rome as a strategic and moral goal. American leaders were less convinced yet agreed to go along with it.

But it didn't work. What should have been an offensive thrust ended up with the Allies clinging to the beachhead at Anzio, thirty miles south of Rome, for four months before slowly breaking out, and then inching across Italy for another year.

The Nazis occupied Italy in 1943, soon after dictator Benito Mussolini was deposed. They dug in from sea to sea, establishing a defensive border called the Gustav Line. Its mission was to prevent the Allies from retaking Rome and attacking both occupied France and Germany, which was already fighting on two other fronts, Russia and Western Europe.

At Anzio beach the Allies mounted their invasion from 376 ships, supported by more than 2,500 Allied aircraft, some of which dropped paratroopers. On the first day the Allies landed more than 36,000 men and 3,200 vehicles, with losses of only 13 killed. Unopposed, they quickly moved seven miles inland, but an American commander erred by hesitating, thus failing to exploit an undefended route that led directly to Rome. More arrivals pushed the Allied troop strength to 100,000 men, but they stayed put.

Using the hesitation to their advantage, the Germans quickly reinforced their position and counterattacked, trying to drive the Allies back into the Tyrrhenian Sea. In all, the Germans lost 5,389 men killed, wounded, or missing during the five-day attack, while the Allies lost 3,496 killed, wounded, or missing. Neither side gave

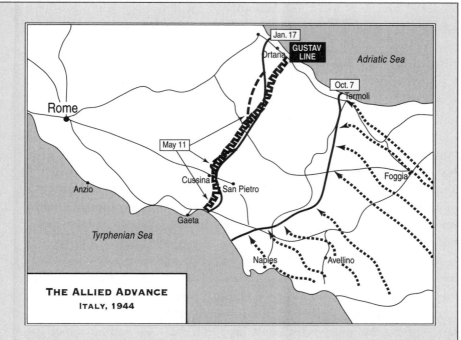

THE ALLIED ADVANCE
ITALY, 1944

ground for a few weeks. When the Germans counterattacked again on February 29, the Americans were prepared and stood firm. What followed was another holding action that lasted for three months.

In late May other Allied troops broke through the Gustav Line to join the Anzio troops. The Germans retreated to Rome. The four-month Anzio campaign had cost more than 29,200 Allied casualties (4,400 killed, 18,000 wounded, 6,800 missing or captured), as well as 37,000 noncombat casualties due to trenchfoot, exposure, or combat exhaustion.

The Anzio attack floundered because it was understaffed and undersupplied. In gearing up for the D-Day invasion of Normandy, the Allies diverted troops, equipment, and munitions to that venue. It was June 5—a day before the Normandy invasion—before Rome was liberated. But by landing behind enemy lines, Operation Shingle troops did tie up 135,000 troops that, strategically, Hitler couldn't move elsewhere, thus further sapping the already depleted German troop reserves, supplies, and initiative. ★

whacked him. It worked. I didn't want to hit him, but I really gave him a back-hander on the cheek, like they do in the movies. I said, "Come on. We're not going to win any war with you like that." Now, I was seventeen years old. I didn't know what was going on with this guy, but I really whacked him, and he started up again.

Every ship had a guy they called "the Swede." The Swede was usually a guy about six foot five and weighed about 225, and we had one. During some of our action, one of the 5-inch shells, the ones that weighed 135 pounds, instead of going out, it flew back onto the ship. It was a live shell. It could have blown the ship up! The Swede ran over, and when he picked it up, you could hear his flesh burning. This shell was hundreds and hundreds of degrees. He picked it up, ran to the side of the ship, and dropped it in the water, and then he went into convulsions. His skin was burned down to the bone. And he saved our lives.

We had planes on our ship, so they flew him ashore to a hospital somewhere in Italy. They didn't have the type of stuff that was necessary, so they took him back to the States. I'll never forget that, because I was only about thirty feet away, and I could smell this burning flesh. He didn't even think; he just did it. He knew what could happen if that shell had hit something sharp. There would have been fifty of us blown about fifty feet in the air. I never found out what happened to the Swede, but he was the best medicine we ever had. There are so many different things that happened that sometimes I forget some of them, but not that one. It's hard to talk about, because he sacrificed himself for everybody else, and that's a hell of a sacrifice.

After D-Day our assignment was to go down to Toulon, France—that's a little bit more south—because the Germans were digging in down there. They had a 16-inch gun that could blow a ship right out of the water. We sent our planes over and located the gun. What they did was put the gun on a railroad car, and the railroad tracks went back into a tunnel in the mountain. That's why you wouldn't know where they were. But a guy in our plane radioed back and gave the exact position, and that's where we fired. We fired where the mountain was, and the whole mountain caved in. But that gun—and we saw the gun with binoculars—that gun was longer than my house. It was huge. So we helped a lot of soldiers get a chance to get a foothold in that area.

During World War II there were two propagandists. In Japan there was Tokyo Rose, and in Europe there was Axis Sally. Axis Sally would get on our radio and say, "Well, boys, we know the USS *Brooklyn* is out there, and we know that everybody at home is having a nice Thanksgiving dinner," that kind of thing.

She came on our radio one time and said, "We know where the USS *Brooklyn* is, and any time of the day that we want to, we can blow you right out of the water." Now that's pretty scary! How did they do that? I don't know, but they did. The Germans had ways of doing that. They would talk about the people back home having a nice Thanksgiving dinner, or Christmas is coming up, trying to get into your head. This lady really got under your skin and made you boil inside. And she knew where our ship was, so their surveillance had to be unbelievable. I don't know how they did it.

After a while things got pretty settled as far as the navy was concerned. The army and the marines were doing their job, so we went back to our home port—if you want to call it that—in Palermo. That's where we docked, and we'd go ashore, and go shopping. You had to be careful when you went ashore, because a lot of the people were starving. Like I said, they would mug you or kill you. They had no money, they had no food, things were in bad shape at that time. In fact, I got my life saved by one guy.

At that time all military personnel were segregated, and the black guy who worked as a cook, his name was Trent, he was treated like dirt. I went ashore one time without thinking, and a gang of these Italian guys—mafia-type guys—were kind of coming this way, that way, and I knew something was up. But this guy Trent showed up, and he was a Muhammad Ali type of guy. He took care of all of them and saved my life.

May 9, 1945 was VE Day, Victory in Europe, when the Germans gave up. In August, our ship was back in Brooklyn, and we paraded down Broadway. Everybody was coming out, clapping, kissing us, shaking hands, we were all on cloud nine. We could have walked forever, because we knew the war was over in Europe. It was still going on in Japan, but that was the nicest feeling in the world, knowing that all that time you spent over there was worthwhile, that you accomplished what you went out to do, and that the war was over in Germany.

After VE Day we came back to Norfolk, Virginia, and went into dry dock—that's where you put the ship if anything needs to be repaired. They gave us a week's furlough, so I got the train to Philadelphia. My father and another fellow were partners in a garage business, so I walked down to his garage. I hadn't called him beforehand, and I just walked in. He saw me, and he grabbed me and started crying, and I held my dad tight, and he said, "We'll have a good dinner tonight." So we went home, and drove around a local park for a little bit. I wanted to see what it looked like. It was a whole different world after being on the ship and through war.

There is one thing I would want younger generations to know about the war. If you have a certain duty to do and you do it, and everybody else follows suit and does the same thing, things will work out in the long run.

There were times when I was on the ship, maybe I had my watch from midnight till 4:00 A.M., and I thought, "There's no end to this. I'm going to be on this ocean forever!" Sometimes I felt that way—I was just seventeen years old! But then I said, "Nah, this will end." We have too many good soldiers and marines and fighter pilots, and sometime this is going to end, and all of the stuff that I was involved in will have a happy ending.

AFTER THE WAR . . .

Lou Neishloss attended Lock Haven University and was employed by the Johnstown Rehab Center. He founded a wheelchair sports team called the Central Penn Wheelers, which won six consecutive women's state championships and two national titles. Neishloss married his wife in 1967, and together they raised a son and a daughter.

☆ Wendall Phillips ☆
Whitehall, Pennsylvania

∙∙∙

Wendall Phillips was a radio operator who served in both the European and China–Burma–India Theaters. He was taken as a prisoner of war by the Germans and then again by the Japanese.

∙∙∙

I was in my second year of college, and a lot of my buddies had already gone off to serve. I knew it was soon time for me to go. I couldn't afford to enter another semester of college knowing that I'd never be able to complete it and get credit for it. Some casualty lists started coming back, and some of my old friends from school who had been in for a year or two began to show up on that list. That's when I knew it was time to go—as a good citizen, this is what you did. When Uncle Sam needed us, we went. My dad had been in World War I in the navy, his brother had been in the army in World War I, so I knew I had an obligation.

I went for my physical in November of '42. I went through the process of physical exams, then mental exams, and then on into aptitude testing. If you were a plumber, you became a baker, and so on. It seemed that way, anyway. I was sent to Fort McClellan, Alabama, for infantry basic training, but they also had schools for telephone linemen and radio. I went through the radio school because, as I found out later, I had musical aptitude. So many guys in radio school could play instruments, and they wanted Morse code operators who had rhythm.

We were also required to complete the physical training as well. Every day we were in the field, and man, it is hot in the spring and summer in Alabama. There were guys who had been drafted in their late thirties and early forties and boy, they suffered. They were trying to keep up with us nineteen- and twenty-year-old guys. A lot of them dropped out; they just couldn't do it. We went through all kinds of obstacle courses. We also went through rifle calisthenics, and if you have ever seen that done, you know it is a chore. Those old army rifles that we used to train with were heavy as the dickens. It was tough, but it made hard guys out of us and was good for us—no doubt about that—but the older guys just couldn't do it.

As we graduated from radio school, we were assigned to various air force duties. Some went to the West Coast, some to the East Coast, some went to bomber outfits, and some went to fighter outfits. I ended up in Air Transport Command in Nashville, Tennessee. We used to call it ATC, the Army of Terrified Civilians, or American Trucking Company, or Allergic to Combat. There were several different names for it, but it was actually Air Transport Command, U.S. Army Air Force.

I was assigned to two pilots, who were just out of pilot training, and a brand shiny new Douglas C-47 transport plane. We took all of our stuff with us, and soon we got to Bangor, Maine, for refueling. That was the last I saw of the United States for a long time.

I was assigned to the ferry command of the Air Transport Command. We ferried airplanes from Goose Bay, Labrador, across the Greenland ice cap to Reykjavik, Iceland. We refueled there, and when we left Reykjavik, it was my obligation to radio either Belfast, Ireland, or Prestwick, Scotland, to see where they wanted the planes delivered. They were stockpiling airplanes in the British Isles, getting ready for the European invasion. We would land wherever they wanted the airplanes, and then we would all deadhead back to Labrador and start over again. I don't know how many trips I took across the North Atlantic. It was amazing flying. I had never flown before.

Ultimately I was stationed at Prestwick, Scotland, and after the invasion of France, we would go in with C-47s loaded with emergency supplies: mortar shells, blankets, medical supplies, food, ammunition and so on. C-47s were fabulous airplanes. The darn thing almost flew itself. It would glide forever, not like some of the airplanes. The minute you lost power, some of the airplanes just dropped like rocks, but not the C-47.

After they unloaded our supplies, first-aid stations would bring us the walking wounded and litter cases that had only been wounded for a few hours or so. We would take them over to England, and they would be in the hospitals only a few hours after they had been wounded. Most of them made it.

Ultimately we were sent over to the other side of Paris, where they had an air base called LeBourget. One day we went too far over the enemy lines, got shot down, and ended up in Belgium. The landing was rough. I had wedged myself between the radio compartment and the upright back of the copilot's seat. There was just room to squeeze in. I made it somehow, but the two pilots were killed when we hit. That was the second crash that I was in. We had to ditch a C-47 in France earlier, and I survived that one, too.

But the Germans were right there. The airplane split apart when we came down, and four German soldiers came and put me up on a truck. It was a two-hour drive to a prison hospital compound in Belgium. I was banged up pretty well. I had a dislocated shoulder and a few things that had to be looked after, and those German doctors were great. They did a nice job with the guys as they came in. There might have been sixty to eighty people in that compound from other planes that came down. Some were Canadian Air Force and, of course, American Air Force.

While we were there, they used to make us exercise. We would walk the compound, inside the fences. They would make us walk clockwise in the morning, and in the afternoon we would walk in the other direction. I liked it so well there that after thirty-three days I got out.

There was a guy in a bunk near me who pointed out that the compound was made of twelve-by-twelve wooden posts and fencing. And the fence was electrified. During our walks, he had been looking at a place where a fence had lapped—where they had run out of fencing and had to lap it and start again. And he kept looking at it until he found a place.

On the thirty-third night everything was in place. In those low lands of Holland and Belgium, in October they get a heavy wet snowfall where it gets so foggy you can't see your hand in front of your face. The guards would go by with the big German shepherd dogs, and of course the searchlight was going round and round, but it couldn't be seen in that fog. We waited until the dogs and the German guards went by, and we waited a couple of minutes longer, and three of us hit that fence to the left side of that big post, and darned if it didn't break! It pulled apart. We got burned a little bit, because it was an electric fence, but we were going through anyway.

All we had on was a jumpsuit with PW (prisoner of war) in big white letters and an old pair of worn-out German shoes. No socks, no underwear.

We decided to split up, because if they found three of us with PW on the back, we wouldn't have lasted long. I don't know if the other guys made it. I ran all night for three nights and hid during the day. All I had was a little snow for moisture. I knew that I needed to go northwest to get to American lines, so I just kept running. On the fourth morning I was in a barn up in the straw, and the farmer's dog got me, making all kinds of fuss. Before I knew it, I was face to face with a little boy around ten and a little girl a couple of years younger.

I couldn't speak Flemish and they couldn't speak English, so the little girl went to get the father. He couldn't speak English either, but through sign language, we determined that I was supposed to stay under cover until later. At night they came and took me into the cellar of the house. The mother came down with a broth of some kind. I don't know what it was, but it sure tasted good. That bowl of broth was a sacrifice for them, because the Germans stripped those people of everything when they went through there.

A day or two later a Roman Catholic priest came. He spoke English better than I probably ever will. It turned out that he had been educated at Notre Dame, in the United States. He told me how lucky I was. I had stumbled accidentally into the French Roman Catholic underground. And in less than a week they had me back to American lines in France. According to the Geneva rules, they can't send you back into the same theater of operations if you have been an escaped prisoner, so they sent me to London for debriefing.

They were supposed to send me home for thirty days, but I was a radio operator, and radio operators were scarce. They had lots of pilots, but you can't fly an airplane without a radio operator. The next thing I knew, I was on a British air base just north of Calcutta, India. I was assigned to a crew. Two pilots and another new airplane, and we flew the hump. The hump is the Himalayan Mountains—the worst flying conditions anywhere in the world. Mount Everest was 29,000 feet high, and our airplanes in those days couldn't gain the altitudes that they can today, so we couldn't fly over, but we could fly in between. We had to fly in the middle of the mountain ranges in order to get through. So we flew through the hump instead of over it.

We ended up in Kunming, China, in the Yunnan Providence, but they didn't want me there. The two pilots stayed there, the airplane stayed there, and I went on down to Chengkung, where they needed a radio operator. We flew out of there for the next twelve months. We had a lot of pilots, a lot of airplanes, C-47s and C-46s. I ended up making 116 trips over the hump. Again, we had lots of pilots, not enough radio people. Our radio guys were in the air all the time, it seemed.

The air war was pretty much finished as far as Japan was concerned by this time, so we didn't have too many problems with flying the cargo. The reason why we were in the China-Burma-India Theater to begin with was to keep China in the war. Japan had surrounded China completely, taken over all the seaports, taken over all the river transportation and all the railroad transportation. Japan had taken over most of China and was taking over Burma, Manchuria, and starting to get into India. The only supply route that they had was over the hump. We supplied China with everything imaginable, including American mules that were brought in from India. They came over on a ship to India, and we would fly them over the hump, three mules to an airplane.

I lived through five plane crashes altogether. We had to ditch a C-46 in central China above Shanghai. There were three planes that started out from Kunming one morning, going up to the Manchurian border for fresh fruit. The other two planes made it all right, but we didn't. The C-46 was a hydraulic airplane—almost everything was hydraulic assisted. Well, as we were flying, all of a sudden the two pilots and I were bathed in pink, hot hydraulic fluid. We lost all of it. It was all over everywhere, and you couldn't fly the darned airplane without it. So we had to ditch.

When we came down, one of the propellers on the C-46—it had a radius of seven feet—spun off, walked through the cabin, and made mincemeat out of the two pilots. I managed to survive that one. And the Japs picked me up and hauled me into Shanghai.

I don't remember what floor I was on, but it was up fairly high in the building. I didn't know there were other prisoners there, but I knew there were a lot of Japanese in the building. I was in a little cubbyhole. You would probably call it a clothes closet at home. I was naked and in the dark. There was a little straw mat on the floor that was my bed, and a tin can in the other corner for a bathroom. And that was it.

The first thing they did to me was put me in a steel chair, with my legs strapped to the chair legs and my arms tied together behind my back. When two guys take hold of your hands and bring them right up to the back of your neck, it doesn't feel too good. It's hard on the rotator cuff and the shoulder blades. They just wanted to let me know who's going to be the boss. While they had my hands back there, they pulled out my thumbnails. So anyway, I am sorry to say, I don't have much use for the animals that gave me that kind of treatment. I don't understand why one human being has to do that to another, but I can't call them human beings. I can't do it. I know it was previous generations involved and so on, and I understand that.

I was there twenty-six days. They would take you out in the hallway and beat you up just for fun. If there was an officer with those guys that were beating you up, he had a cattle prod type thing. If you didn't scream and holler and carry on, he would turn that voltage up to a point where you did, and of course, you know what he did with that!

I knew I was going to make it. I had faith. All my life I was brought up in a good Christian home and had a good, strong faith. Thank goodness for that.

So then days went by. They would bring me a little plate of rice once in a while, and a little putrid water once in a while, and that was it. I lost 80 pounds while I was there. I was a big, strapping farm kid, 185 pounds, husky, muscular. But I was skin and bones after that.

Then one day the door burst in, and there was an American MP and two British MPs. They had been going through the building, knocking in every door, and they found me stark naked and starving to death. The war was over.

They took good care of me. They got me clothes, shoes, a little money, and got me something to eat. Then they said, "Take off. Don't even report in anywhere. Just go. Get out of here." So that's what I did. I met a young married couple in Shanghai who were White Russian refugees teaching English in the school there. They took me under their wing and took me everywhere. I saw Shanghai from one end to the other. And I found a lot of good places to eat.

I think the main thing I would like people to know is that I love this country. I was in twenty-three countries of the world, and there is no place like it. I wouldn't trade it for any place anywhere. I'd serve again if I could. I would do what I could in a minute.

AFTER THE WAR . . .

Wendall Phillips returned home and graduated from college in 1948. He then married and began a career in marketing and management. In 1985 he retired from his position as senior statistician for Mack Trucks, but he continues to work part-time. Phillips and his wife are the parents of three children.

☆ John W. Berglund ☆

Elizabethtown, Pennsylvania

John W. Berglund was a marine in the Pacific Theater. He trained on Guadalcanal and served in New Zealand, Hawaii, and Iwo Jima, where he could see the flag raised on Mount Suribachi.

I was a senior at Rutgers University in New Brunswick, New Jersey, when Pearl Harbor was attacked. I remember the dorm stairwell filled with guys shouting and yelling up and down the stairs, "The Japs bombed Pearl Harbor!"

That night there were a lot of guys drinking beer at the Corner Tavern, which was a hangout for Rutgers students, and they made up parodies of songs; like, instead of "It's a long way to Tipperary," they sang, "It's a long way to Yokohama, where the yellow bastards grow," and other parodies like that. Many of those guys were either drafted or enlisted in the next six months. I asked my father if I could enlist. I was in the first semester of my senior year, and he pleaded with me to stay in college, at least for the end of my senior year. But at Christmastime, I tried to enlist in the navy as a hospital apprentice, second class. I was refused admission because of my eyes— my right eye was below the minimum.

So how did I get in the Marine Corps? I memorized eye charts. I memorized the eighth line from the top, which was d-e-f-p-o-t-e-c. I read it backward and forward with both eyes, and I couldn't even see it. I got down to Quantico in Officer Candidate School and thought I was home free, but I was there less than a week, and there was an announcement on the board: "Complete form Y tomorrow." That was a complete physical. Well, that night I couldn't sleep. I had visions of being put on the train under armed guard for fraudulent enlistment.

I was in a group of people going through the mill, and the eye, ear, nose, and throat room was the last place. I looked through a half-inch crack in the door while I waited my turn, and I memorized the top three lines on a chart of ten equal-sized lines. I gambled that the doctor would be too lazy to ask anything below the top three lines, and he didn't. So I was home free, and I didn't wear my glasses for two years. I kept them in my trunk. And I fired the M-1 rifle in OCS and made expert rifleman, which is a triumph of faith over reality, because at 500 yards, the bull's-eye was like a suggestion of a fly-speck on the front sight.

I stayed in Quantico for thirty-five weeks—ten weeks of OCS, ten weeks of reserve officers class, and then fifteen weeks of artillery school. From there I went to Camp Pendleton, California, where I reported to the 1st Battalion, 12th Marines.

In January or February I shipped out to New Zealand on a Liberty ship, at the dizzying speed of eight knots an hour, maybe ten when they pushed it. This was an experiment, putting troops on cargo ships. We had a deck-load of oil and gasoline, and we had 500 tons of high explosive in the hold next to where we slept. We had few troops, but we had a lot of seasickness, because we ate in the same place where we slept, which was a big mistake.

It took twenty-two days to get to New Zealand. I spent five months there and loved every bit of it. One of the features of the country was pastries stuffed with whipped cream, and I had a sweet tooth. Whenever I went on an errand, I'd stop at a bakery and get a dozen pastries stuffed with whipped cream. Most New Zealanders didn't have their own teeth, probably because of eating pastries like that.

After five months in New Zealand, we went up to Guadalcanal. At the time, Guadalcanal had been declared secured—the fighting was over. But nobody had told the Japanese Air Force. They used to bomb us every night. Not big air raids, just small, one-plane air raids. I used to lie in my hole wondering whether to put my helmet over my face or over my groin when the shrapnel fell from our own antiaircraft. It was very nasty. If it landed flat-side, it would bounce off a tent. If it landed on the sharp side, it would go through the tent and through you.

We trained on Guadalcanal. Because you can't see in the jungle, you couldn't see the rounds bursting in front of you, so we had to learn how to send howitzer fire commands by sound. We spent a day in the jungle digging into a stream bank, making splinter-proof shelters. Then we got in the shelters and we fired on ourselves. We were using 75-millimeter pack howitzers. The shell weighed fifteen pounds, and it had a bursting radius of about twenty yards. We were told to bring the rounds in, one round at a time, until we heard fragments crashing into our shelter. When that day was over, Col. Peewee Owens, who was in charge, called the roll over sound-powered telephones, and when he called each name, he went, "Whew!"

We went into combat at Bougainville, Empress Augusta Bay, and Cape Torokina. When I got onshore, everything was in confusion because the landing boats were "broaching to," which means coming in broadside to the waves, so the landing was in trouble.

We were being strafed by a Japanese plane. I was in a hole dug parallel to the beach, and at the time, I thought it should have been dug the other way so there was less exposure. So the Japanese plane came down, strafing us. It killed one man out in the water in a boat near me.

I was starting to dig my third or fourth hole of the day, when I saw five Japanese planes in flames all at once, above the fleet. The secret to us getting five at once was the proximity fuse. A proximity fuse was invented by Americans. It contained a small radar and a fuse a couple of inches long, and when it got fifteen yards from the target—any target, that's the bad point—it would go off. If you were firing over the heads of your own troops, unfortunately, they might go off, but against Japanese planes, they were deadly! So using the proximity fuse, we got five planes at the same time.

I spent ninety days in Bougainville, mostly in swamps, where I had to wring out my blanket at night in order to sleep. I learned that a wool blanket can be warm even if it's wet.

My closest escape from death was when a 500-pound bomb landed ten yards from where I was. We were in a swamp and had built an elevated foxhole using coconut logs and sandbags—it had to be raised because we were in a swamp. A Japanese plane flew over and dropped a stick of three 500-pounders on us. One landed across the road, one landed in back of our place, and the third landed next to our number-one gun—that's the one that was close to me. It dug a hole into the swamp twenty-six feet in diameter and ten feet deep. When it went off, I shook for half an hour. My mouth was filled with dirt. It was like standing in a subway, hearing a train come in and not stop—that was the sound of the bomb falling. I heard it click—the click of the fuse arming. I shook for a half an hour until I could light a cigarette under my blanket.

Another night, we were getting shelled by a Japanese 15-centimeter gun. And artillery men can't help it, it's second nature—they have to calculate what changes had to be made in the enemy shelling to place the next round right on where they were sitting. We had an old warrant officer named Bob Stutz, who was a Swiss national. He had to get permission from President Harding to enlist in the Marine Corps, because he was not a citizen, and he was due to retire and get a pension. While this shelling was going on, he said, "If that fellow goes up 100 and left 200, he'll save Henry Morgenthau a lot of money." Henry Morgenthau was secretary of the treasury in Roosevelt's regime. That's called gallows humor. It's a recognized psychological thing, that guys will joke in the face of death, because it lightens the atmosphere.

One morning we were told that somebody was firing at our place, and I was asked to climb a tree and look around. In artillery school I had learned how to climb trees using climber spikes, but I never practiced it before. I got seventy or eighty feet up the tree, and one of my men was up above me in the tree. Then some nut—one of our guys—started firing at us with an M-1 rifle, yelling, "Japs! Japs!" So the guy above me said, "I'm coming down, lieutenant, I'm coming down!" Well, I started down, and my spikes slipped out of the tree, and I slid sixty feet down the tree. It took all the skin off the inside of my arms and my legs. But I lived through that, and I lived through Bougainville.

I was back from Bougainville for maybe two weeks, and I was loaned to the 3rd New Zealand division. I was to supply them with naval gunfire to allow them to get their artillery ashore on Green Island. It was supposed to take two or three hours, but instead I stayed five days.

One of those days I spent two hours working with a navy lieutenant named Hearn, trying to dig a foxhole into the coral. We made it in about nine inches. Hearn was a very bitter man. He had enlisted in the navy so he could sleep between sheets and have hot showers on a ship. And here he was in the mud with the marines.

The New Zealanders were trying to find the Japanese forces on this beautiful atoll. It was like Hollywood's idea of the Pacific, with big trees and a coral reef with a pastel sheen. It was beautiful. By my last day with them, they still hadn't found the Japanese, but the day after I left, the company found the Japanese forces entrenched behind a cliff on the edge of the island. There were eighty of them, which was about the number of men we had. In the forty minutes of daylight that was left, the New Zealanders killed the entire Japanese force and lost four people.

When I left Green Island, I was ordered to go back to the States. I was chosen by lottery to go back to form another division. So I packed my bags and waited thirty days for transportation. During that time, I had no duties, so I perfected my skills in bridge, pinochle, and cribbage. Four times I had my gear out in the street to be picked up, and it wasn't picked up. The colonel said, "If Berglund has any more farewell parties, the battalion won't be worth a damn."

I finally got back to the States, but instead of forming a new division, I was sent to Fort Sill to take a course in sound and flash ranging. At the end of that, I went back to the Pacific, to the Corps Artillery of the 5th Amphibious Corps in Hawaii, the big island. Tough duty!

When I landed at Pearl Harbor, I was traveling with a friend named Rick Orstrom, who had been in class with me at Fort Sill. Rick was a child of wealth, and he was friends with a family named Walker, who were one of the five families who once owned all of the Hawaiian Islands. So he called Mrs. Walker and said, "I'm here in Pearl." And she said, "Oh, come out." So we went out to this beautiful home in the Nuuanu Valley, where we found these folks reduced to having only five servants because of the war—they were really suffering.

Rick and I had had several snorts in Pearl Harbor, and we had another drink at the Walkers', when all of a sudden—I can still hear it—there was a car in the driveway, and Mrs. Walker said, "That's our other guests." Well, into the room walked Admiral Nimitz and Admiral Lockwood, who was a submarine commander in the Pacific. You never saw two lieutenants get sober so fast in your life!

We had a very enjoyable dinner, and afterward we played nickel-and-dime poker upstairs. I was in the last few hands, and I won the last hand against Admiral Nimitz. Mrs. Walker told us, "Please don't tell anybody about this." And I thought, "Who's going to believe us?"

After Hawaii we went to Iwo Jima. I landed at Iwo on D-Day plus two. From a distance I saw the flag on Mount Suribachi.

I was in Corps Artillery, 5th Amphibious Corps. We had two battalions of our own, and we also coordinated all the fire of fourteen battalions of artillery. I was only a captain, and nobody listened to me, but I said they were doing it wrong. They were using World War I tactics. Every morning before the infantry advanced, they'd fire a great big barrage, and the Japs would just hunker down in their caves and shelters, and when the barrage was over, they'd come out and fight. There were a lot of people killed on Iwo. We had 20,000 casualties, including killed and wounded.

One night the ammunition dump next to us was set on fire. The Japanese were shelling us all the time, and I was in a sort of a splinter-proof shelter dug into the wall of the tent, with sandbags. It was covered on three sides but open into the tent. The tent got blown away by the explosions from the dump. I looked out in the sky, and I could see parachute flares and composition C—a plastic explosive—and dynamite. Everything was going off in the dump.

I had a flagpole outside the tent with a pair of black lace panties on it—this is what we were fighting for—and with all this stuff going off, bombs and artillery and flares, somebody said, "Through the rocket's red glare, our flag is still there." I never got a picture of that. I think the Catholic priest censored that picture. It was on the same roll as the pictures of his chapel.

When Iwo was finished, I was sent back to Guam. I was under orders to be in on the invasion of Japan, so I'm just as happy that the atomic bomb happened. I remember one day going to visit the old LST [Landing Ship, Tank] that I had ridden onto Pearl—it was in the harbor at Agana, Guam—and they told me about the atomic bomb being dropped. Well, I was raised on science fiction, so it was no surprise to me. I simply said, "That'll show the little yellow bastards we can outdo them at everything, including barbarity."

The most important thing I learned through World War II is, keep your sense of humor. The only guys I ever saw crack up—combat fatigue, psychoneurosis, you call it what you want—the only guys that happened to were guys that either lacked a sense of humor or lost their sense of humor.

AFTER THE WAR . . .

John Berglund married, and he and his wife, Rosalind, together raised four sons. Berglund worked as a microbiologist and in sales before entering the Lutheran Theological Seminary in 1969. He was ordained in 1972 and served the Grace Lutheran Church in Roxborough, Philadelphia. He retired in 1987.

☆ Harry McCracken ☆
Manor, Pennsylvania

....

Harry McCracken was a combat medic in the 99th
Infantry Division. His duty was to provide medical
supplies to aid stations and accompany battalions to
provide medical support in the event of injuries.

....

I tried to get into the Marine Corps before I was actually drafted, but they told me I had to wait until January of '43. However, the draft board contacted me in November 1942 and said that they couldn't wait, and I was drafted.

My first basic training was done in Camp Van Dorn, Mississippi, fifty miles north of Baton Rouge, Louisiana. It involved getting used to close-order drill, taking twenty-mile marches at least twice a week, and calisthenics. This camp was brand new, there were no sidewalks and no way of getting out of the barracks. Our sideline jobs were to haul sand to make pathways to get into our barracks. We did that as well as our medical training. We actually did the same training as an infantry soldier, except that we did not have to train with rifles or bayonets. All the rest of the training was the same as the combat infantry soldier. And we all qualified for the expert infantry badge.

When I went into the service, I had no idea about being a combat medic. I just assumed that when you went into the army, everybody got a rifle and went on the line and starting shooting. Once I got interviewed, we had to take IQ tests. During my interview, I was asked if I knew anything about first aid. I said, "Not much," and the interviewer said, "Good, then you will be a medic." Being a combat medic meant we had to learn all about the blood pressure points and how to use splints on arms and legs, how to treat a patient with a back injury, and also how to take blood pressure and temperatures.

I went overseas in September 1944. I'll never forget the trip. We were a large fleet of over 700 ships, including one aircraft carrier. Most of them were transport ships carrying supplies. Many of the guys were seasick, and they just hung on the rails of the ship for the whole trip. On the way over, we were alerted several times for submarine attacks. As soon as the emergency alarm came on, my job was to head for the rear gun of the ship, where I was to be the medic in case we were attacked and anybody was wounded. I didn't have a free ride over; I had to work.

Once we arrived in Europe, we headed right into Belgium. When I would write letters home, I said it was just like being home; the land, the hills, and the valleys just reminded me of western Pennsylvania, like the Somerset and Bedford area.

We would always try to set up our aid stations in houses with at least four walls. We tried to pick an area that was obvious, so that people who were wounded would see our flags in front of the building. A lot of civilians would come to us because they saw our Red Cross flags and knew we would have some kind of medical care that they needed.

As a medic, one of my assignments was to go with an engineer battalion to the Siegfried line. The battalion's duty was to blow pillboxes, which were made of a lot of concrete. Actually, you could have called them concrete houses. They had heavy walls, maybe three or four feet thick, with real small windows you could look out. The German soldiers would man these pillboxes and watch out for us walking around so they could shoot at us through the little windows. We would start out at 2:00 or 3:00 in the morning. They would put the charges in, and then they would blow the charges that would blow up the pillboxes. It was my job as medic to go along in case anybody was wounded.

We picked up a soldier one day who was hit in the forehead with a piece of shrapnel. The whole front of his forehead was removed, and you could actually see his brains inside his head. And he was talking to me just like I'm talking to you. He said to me, "Am I hit very bad?" And I said, "No I don't think so. I think you look pretty good." But I was pretty sure he wasn't going to make it. After we did the best we could for him, he was still conscious. I said to my doctor, who was the commanding officer, "Major, do you think this man will survive?" He said there was a good chance that he could survive. It didn't look like there was any damage to his brains or anything, but he said he was pretty sure he would be blind. I ran into a man five or six years ago at one of our reunions, and I was telling this story, and he said he knew the man personally. He said he never made it.

The incidents that bother me the most were not the injuries, because most wounds you got were in the arms, legs, or whatever could be repaired. What bothered me most was what we called combat fatigue. During the Battle of the Bulge, there was one soldier I knew personally, and I got called to go into a house where this soldier was. He was lying on the floor, digging into the floor with his hands. His hands were all raw, and he was trying to protect himself from artillery. So he was mentally gone, you know. I figured he was never going to come back.

There was another man in a corner of a building who was all curled up just like a scared rat. Your body's not built to go through combat twenty-four hours a day; bodies weren't built to withstand that. I think if I would have been in combat for another six or eight months, I might have been the same way. You're just under that constant pressure. I don't know how many of them ever got back to normal. There was really nothing that we as medics could do. We just sent them back to treatment, and it would be the end of their army career.

We were told that by the end of December 1944, we would be into Germany and the war would probably be over. On December 16, when the Battle of the Bulge started, we had an aide station in a farmhouse just on the edge of Rocherath, Belgium, the twin city of Krinkelt, Belgium.

It was about 5:30 A.M. when the shelling started, and I said to my commanding officer, "Now what's going on?" He said, "Look out into the field. Don't you see all of our artillery? That's firing going out, that's not shells coming in." I said, "Major, those are incoming shells. I was on line blowing pillboxes, and I know what an incoming shell sounds like!" And then, about two hours after that, everything stopped.

The next day it was the same thing: The shelling started again. Then all at once we started to pick up a lot of casualties, and our farmhouse had casualties everywhere. We had two ambulances available all the time, bringing casualties back for treatment.

The third day was the same. The shelling started getting heavier and heavier, and one of the shells happened to hit the farmhouse, so then the commanding officer realized that there was something big going on. But we still didn't know exactly what was happening. All we knew was, we were picking up casualty after casualty. By that night, we had the farmhouse full of wounded soldiers, and five or six dead soldiers that we placed outside of the farmhouse.

There was a lieutenant from the 2nd Infantry Division who said, "Why do you have these soldiers here? Why don't you evacuate and send them back for more care?" I told him that the ambulance crew said the roads were blocked, and that they couldn't get back to the collecting station. So the lieutenant said that he had a crew, and we could load everybody in the ambulance and they would try to get them through. To this day I don't know if they made it, or if they were captured or if they were killed.

All weekend we kept doing this. We would hear one of the soldiers ask if he could have more morphine; we were just giving them a shot of morphine to keep the pain down.

We treated casualties, but we also treated a lot of frozen feet, which we thawed out. The worst part was that we had been given orders that we were not allowed to evacuate anybody for any further medical care; that there were no replacements for them. As long as they could sit and hold a rifle, we had to send them back out on the line. That was the sad part. If we could have evacuated those men with frozen feet right away, maybe they wouldn't have lost their toes or even feet.

I remember one fellow in Elsenborn, Belgium. I gave him six pints of plasma, but he had very little reaction, so we just put him to the side and more or less covered him up. Soon we saw that the blanket was moving, so we knew this guy was still alive. So we gave him another IV and then loaded him in an ambulance. Whether he survived or not, I don't know. One thing about us medics—we treated the soldiers, but we never knew the end results. We just did our share, but we had no way of knowing whether the soldier survived.

My brother was in the air force, flying B-17s out of Italy. He had already been in combat areas before I got overseas. While I was in Camp Maxey, Texas, I got a call from my mother saying they got a telegram that he was missing in action. The following Sunday a telegram came saying that he was officially declared a prisoner of war. At the time, we were all trained and ready to go into combat; the only reason we were still in the United States was because there was no room in England for any more troops due to the D-Day invasion planning. Being a supply sergeant, I said, "Well, if I find him, he's going to need new clothes." So I ordered a complete set of clothes, shoes, socks, pants, shirt, jacket, and I loaded them up in a bundle and carried them with me all through combat.

While I was in combat, I got a letter from my sister saying where all the prison camps in Germany were, so I carried the letter with me. When we captured Nuremberg, my list showed that there was a prison camp there. So my buddy from Philadelphia and I went looking for this prison camp. We found it, but it was empty. Some civilians we found said that there were air force people in this camp, but the German Army had moved them out, down south. Well, we ended up heading south, toward the Danube River.

We crossed the Danube River and came to the town of Moosburg. We set up an aid station there, and I started to walk through the streets. There was a tank and two jeeps with guns mounted. I overheard one of the guys saying that there was a prison camp in the area, and that they wanted to find it. So I asked them if they wanted a medic to come along.

We all went back to my aid station and talked to my commanding officer. The officer told me it was okay for me to go, so we got in the jeep and followed the tank and two other jeeps. At one point there was barbed wire, and the tank plowed through it. We followed behind and ended up right in the camp. Of course, the guys mobbed us. The first thing I asked was where the American officer in charge of this camp was located.

Turns out the guy was a colonel from Pittsburgh. I asked him if there was any chance of a guy named McCracken in the camp. He told me that the name was familiar, but since we had come through the barbed wire in a tank, everything was in total confusion, and it would be difficult to find him. We talked a bit more about ways to locate him, and then I saluted and turned to walk out of the building. As I did, I saw my brother standing there. He said that he was watching the convoy come across, and he thought it looked like me in one of the jeeps, but he didn't even know I was overseas. So I had found him!

With the war still going on, they wanted to keep everybody in camp, but I told my major that I was taking my brother out. He told me that I knew what I had to do. He told me to take my combat jacket and steel helmet off and trade with my brother. When we left, they thought my brother was one of us.

The B-17: The Flying Fortress

One of the most strategic Allied weapons of the World War II air battle was the American B-17 bomber, known as the Flying Fortress, or often just "the Fort." The B-17 was designed by Boeing Aircraft Company in 1934, and the first prototype of the model flew the following year. The plane was used most widely from 1942 to 1945 in the European Theater.

While other military aircraft were built in greater numbers, the four-engine B-17 was a valuable "heavy" bomber, able to carry 6,000 tons of bombs on missions as long as 2,000 miles. The most advanced versions of the plane carried a crew of ten, which included the pilot, copilot, navigator, bombardier, and gunners.

The B-17 was intended to be a coastal defense plane, but the combination of its top speed (287 mph) and altitude (35,000 feet) made it a candidate for mass production as a bomber. When it was equipped with a precision Norden bombsight, it was capable of conducting highly accurate daylight drops on targets—not just hitting munitions factories, for example, but specific parts of factories.

The B-17's range made it suitable for the Army Air Force strategy of basing groups of bombers as close as possible to their intended targets in Germany, Italy, and occupied France, Belgium, and Holland. That meant flying them from England, North Africa, and—after the fall of its Fascist government—Italy. From those staging areas, crews could make flights that took them to the target and back in six hours.

Despite the "Fortress" name, early versions of the B-17 were underprotected and were vulnerable to attack by German Luftwaffe fighters. Later versions packed more defensive firepower in the form of additional machine guns (as many as thirteen, compared with five on early versions) and gunner positions. Even with the planes so armed, the German Luftwaffe airpower was formidable and losses were significant. As a result, bombing runs eventually needed the protection offered by escort fighter planes such as the P-47 Thunderbolt and the P-51 Mustang. Some sorties involved more than 1,000

A B-17 stands at rest at a Seattle, Washington, plant in 1942. FRANKLIN D. ROOSEVELT LIBRARY, HYDE PARK, NEW YORK

aircraft in a single strike. But even with defensive power and support fighters, the loss rate was horrific. In one week of October 1943, the 8th Air Force lost 148 B-17s, 60 of them in a single day, with more than 600 airmen killed or captured.

After the German surrender in April 1945, B-17s continued to fly in Europe, dropping food to alleviate hunger in formerly occupied countries. Within a year of the end of the war, most of the 12,500 plus B-17s built were out of service and already or soon to be scrapped. ★

Once we got back to the aid station, the guys were all excited to see my brother. They started running around, gathering us eggs, potatoes, and a ham to fix him a meal. The next morning he took off his old clothes and put on the new set I had for him. My brother wanted to go back to his crew, and the mess sergeant gave him a loaf of bread to take back to the camp. When I took him back to the prison camp, my brother Milton's buddies just kept staring at the white bread. They had not seen a loaf of bread like that in over a year. They hesitated about eating it.

The next day I returned to the prison camp to eat a meal they prepared for me made out of Red Cross parcels. I liked our GI chow better. After a short time the prisoners were flown out and eventually returned to the United States.

When the war ended in Europe, General Hodges was the 1st Army commander. He was reassigned to the Pacific Theater, and the infantry division he asked to go with him was the 99th Infantry Division. We were scheduled to leave and go through the Suez Canal to meet up with him to start combat. Fortunately two bombs were dropped on Japan, and they told us that we weren't going anywhere. That actually saved my life. I figured that I had survived the European Theater and only got hit once. I didn't figure I could survive the second war.

They deactivated the 99th Infantry Division. You had to have eighty-five points to go home, and most of us didn't have that many. I was reassigned to the 1st Infantry Division from July through December. In the middle of December I was on my way home. We landed on January 3, 1946, and I was sent to Fort Indiantown Gap, Pennsylvania, where I was discharged on January 9.

AFTER THE WAR . . .

Harry McCracken retired from Westinghouse Electric Corporation in 1982 after forty-two years of service. McCracken is a life volunteer fireman with the North Huntingdon Township Station 3 and a life member of Rescue 6 Ambulance Corp. He and his wife have been married for more than fifty-eight years, and together they raised two daughters and one son.

☆ Charles Steffy ☆

Ephrata, Pennsylvania

Charles Steffy enlisted in the army at age nineteen. He was
a staff sergeant in Company D, 318th Infantry Regiment,
80th Infantry Division, in charge of two 81-millimeter
mortar squads. He followed General Patton's 3rd Army
through France and Germany until he was hit by shrapnel.

I worked in a steel foundry for six months every day, even Saturdays and
Sundays. As a youngster of eighteen years of age, I didn't want to work
all the time, so I quit and joined the service. I wanted to be in the air force,
but I didn't have enough background in mathematics, so I joined the army.
Went to battle.

I went down into the desert in Arizona for training. I was an 81-millimeter
mortar forward observer. With mortars, you would fire a shell that would go
over the target, then another shell that fell below, then one fell beside the target, and after three shells you were on the target. Then you called for mass dropping of your shells. I was pretty good at it, and I advanced rapidly. I wasn't in
the army long before I was a staff sergeant.

We headed overseas in June of 1944 and landed on Utah Beach thirty-five days after D-Day. My first combat was with the Argentan Gap, where we were facing the Germans' 7th Army. We were told to march that first evening and get ready for a baptism of fire in the morning. When we stopped, it was dark. We bivouacked and dug our foxholes, and in the morning we found out that we were in a potato patch and we had destroyed this farmer's potato crop. As soon as it was daylight, we headed off for combat. I was up front observing mortar fire, and after a while one of our boys was directly hit with a shell. Sorry, but I have to say it, we picked up parts of him. A lot of the boys got so scared they turned and ran, and I jumped up and tried to stop them. A Colonel McVicker came along and helped me turn them around, and we never turned back after that. I got my Bronze Star through the effort of saving the men.

Later on that same day a colonel didn't listen to me. I was observing mortar fire, hiding in back of a rock and a tree stump, and he told me, "Sergeant you can't see your mortar fire hiding there. Get up and look!" I said, "Colonel, there is a sniper out front, be careful." And he didn't believe me. Moments later he was hit right in the chest, and that was the end of my colonel. I could tell you a lot of stories like that.

One time we were ready to go across a part of the Moselle River, and the water was high and running swiftly. Sergeant Phillips, my partner in the third and fourth section of the 81-millimeter mortar, and I watched the infantry that had been first to cross the river. Their boat capsized, and they were all dunked in the swift current and carried downstream. Whether they were rescued or not, I don't know. But this sergeant leaned over on me, and I held him in my arms, and he was crying. We prayed there together that we would be safe.

One time we were attacking this hill, and we were getting all kinds of fire—rifle fire, machine-gun fire, mortar fire, artillery fire. I wasn't the forward observer at that time; another sergeant was up. We always traded off. Sergeant Gray and I were there when the captain said that the forward observer had been hit and wounded, and we needed another front observer up there. He said, "Sergeant Gray, get up there," and he left. That's the last time I saw him alive, and he had been with us all the time.

That's the thing about combat—you never know when it's your turn or somebody else's turn. We would look in each other's eyes, and I would look back at myself and think, "Is it going to be me this time or is it going to be you?" That's a lot to think about.

One time we were in Germany and we were counterattacked by German tanks. I was in a building observing mortar fire and artillery fire, and a German tank came up so close to me at the window that I could see the carvings in the gun. He backed up after a bit, and I thought, "Now that's wonderful, he's leaving." Well, he backed up just far enough to fire a shell right into the side of the building, and it blew the whole thing in. I was lifted up, carried across the room, and knocked against the wall. I don't know how long I was unconscious, but when I came to, I picked up my rifle. My walkie-talkie telephone was all smashed. Then I picked up my helmet and I put it on, and my buddy said, "Sergeant Steffy, you'd better look at your helmet." So I took it off and looked at it, and there was a hole in my steel helmet as big as a golf ball. And it never hit my head. The Lord must have been with me!

One time we were advancing, and I was told to go ahead with another soldier and examine a house. We went into the house and found three elderly women with five little children less than seven years old. They were ready to eat their evening meal, and since I'm Pennsylvania Dutch, I could understand them and they understood me. They asked me if I wanted to stay for supper, and I said, "Well, what do you have?"

They were making sauerkraut soup. They put in an old piece of meat that they had used a couple of other times for the flavor, then they added a cereal bowl of peeled potatoes and a cereal bowl of sauerkraut, and they stirred it up until it was finished. Then they served me and the five little girls. We just had a little round bowl of soup. It wasn't bad, but it wasn't filling. Then the ladies said they had to put the children to bed. I asked why they had to go to bed so early, and they told me that when they fall asleep, they will forget their hunger.

So I opened up my pack and gave them my K rations and my candy bars. The girls had never tasted chocolate before that day. So I was the first boy that gave them the taste of chocolate. Isn't that something?

I was put in charge of a three-man patrol, and we were told to go out front a few miles to reconnoiter. So we went into this town called Pittsburg, or something like that, over there in Germany, to reconnoiter. If you ever were scared, that would be the time, because you are alone a mile or two into the enemy lines, looking around to see what was there. We made plans that we would meet on the left side of a church that was facing east. The reason I picked the church as a point to meet was because it was the tallest building in town.

Another soldier and I went into the town from one side, and the other two went in from the other side, and we investigated everything. It was a railroad station town, and we checked all the cars and trains and different houses for whatever they might have. We left our unit at 8:00 P.M., when it was dark, and we were supposed to meet at the side of the church at midnight. Well, we didn't get there until maybe 1:00 A.M. I got there first with my buddy before the other two, and I was thinking about what kind of people worshiped there. We were in France and Germany fighting and killing each other, and here we find a wonderful church.

One time we went twenty-five miles into German lines in jeeps and trucks. We had no problem getting there, but we had to fight our way all the way back. One time we had to get out of the trucks and jeeps because German tanks were coming. I was a bazooka man, so my buddy loaded the bazooka, and we were in the gutter right aside of the road that the tanks were coming up. I hit the first tank on the side and it stopped, and the trucks pulled it off the road and into the gutter, and there we had it. And that stopped everybody else on the road. I had knocked out a tank. Imagine that—I knocked out a German tank. So hallelujah, wasn't that something?

I brought home a German rifle and bayonet. I was up front observing mortar fire one time, and we moved on ahead a little bit, and there lay a German soldier, wounded pretty badly. He was acting like he was motioning to me, and saying, "Help me, help me!" in German. Well, I couldn't stop and help him, and I don't know if anybody else came along to help him, but he had a rifle in his right hand, and the bayonet was attached to the rifle. I said, "You don't need this anymore," in German, and took it. I carried it along all that time and brought it home, and I have it here—a rifle that says, "All for Germany."

I got the Purple Heart with two oak leaf clusters. I was hit in the chest on September 10, 1944. They took me to a hospital in England, and I stayed there for three months. That was the first time I got the Purple Heart. Later I got hit in the head, that was the second one, and then I got a bullet through my hip. That was the third one.

I left the hospital in England on Christmas Day in 1944 to go back to my unit. The doctor came and said, "Sergeant, you are going to go back to your unit." I asked why, since I still had a bandage on my chest. I was told that the chest bandage wouldn't hurt, and the medics could treat me for that. The doctor told me that they needed more cannon fodder at Bastogne, and he pointed at me. So I went back.

The most important thing I learned is to have respect, compassion, and love for one another. I learned a lot from those little girls and those three women in that German home. They were normal. The little girls didn't know anything about war, yet they had to go along with Hitler because they were in the country, the same as we have to go along with our leadership here in this country.

You know that German who was lying on the ground asking me to help him? I still have memories of that. Why didn't I help him? Well, I couldn't help him; I was fighting. But when the minister talks about the Good Samaritan, it always rings a bell. You must have compassion for one another, and if we understand other people's beliefs and reasons, maybe we could get along a little better.

AFTER THE WAR . . .

Charles Steffy was medically discharged from the service and enrolled in the Lancaster Business College. He graduated with a degree in bookkeeping and accounting. He eventually was named as the controller for Dutchmaid and was employed with the company for thirty years. Steffy married in 1947, and he and his wife, Dorothy, had two children: a daughter, who passed away, and a son.

☆ Chester Ogden ☆
Clearfield, Pennsylvania

∙∙∙

Chester Ogden was a flight engineer in the Army Air Forces.
His flight crew accomplished fifty missions over Europe. Despite
his crew's many missions, no one on his plane was ever injured.

∙∙∙

I was nineteen years old in January 1943, when I entered military service
and was inducted in Harrisburg, Pennsylvania. They assigned me to the
Army Air Force. I went to basic training in Florida, and after that, into various aircraft and engine schools. They sent me to the Ford Motor Company
plant at Ypsilanti, Michigan, where they were building B-24s. I got a firsthand view of how the aircraft was constructed.

They finally sent me to Topeka, Kansas, to pick up a new aircraft to take
to Europe. The pilot and I went to a meeting there, and they told us they
were assigning us a new B-24, with a value of $225,000. We took that aircraft through Florida; Natal, Brazil; Dakar, Africa; Cairo, Egypt; and into
Italy. From there we experienced the air war in Europe over the course of
fifty missions. I had a lot of experiences on those fifty missions.

During our time on base in Italy, we saw the faces of the people at the
chow hall every day. It didn't take very long to realize that the people you

saw yesterday wouldn't be there tomorrow. You could look around at the various crews sitting in certain places—the six enlisted men from each crew seemed to eat together—you'd look around at suppertime and see that the crew that was there that morning was not there. They were lost that day.

Day after day, you'd realize how fast crews that came into base would disappear and how accurate the German guns were. Because the crew exchange was so repetitive, you didn't get to know the men. You'd see their faces, see the aircraft that they flew on, the logo on the side of them, but when you came in from a mission, you might see various ones missing. This goes on for a while, and you realize the seriousness of front-line combat from the air war point of view.

I feel exceptionally fortunate to be here today to talk about what I saw. I brought back the memory of those fifty missions. To see the various aircraft blown from the sky in every imaginable way, and the ten men on the crew who went with it—to see this happen day after day—you realize the sacrifice that people made to have this country be what it is today. And to live with the memory of what my fellow man has done, there's no way my words can relate what my eyes saw. I'll never forget.

One event I can specifically relate happened on July 27, 1944. We had thirteen aircraft from the 743rd Bomb Squadron, flying at maximum effort. We went to Budapest and dropped, and we were on the way back to our base in Italy at about 1:00 P.M. It was a clear summer day, not a cloud in the sky. You could see forever.

We hadn't encountered any enemy aircraft or antiaircraft fire. That thought had just entered my mind, and in that instant we were in the heaviest antiaircraft fire I had ever seen. It was right on us, and it was everywhere.

As soon as the antiaircraft fire started, our tail gunner, Harold Schmiedeskamp, yelled, "There goes thirteen!" In no time at all, he said, "There goes number twelve!" From my position on the left waist gun, I could look back into the squadron, and I saw an aircraft going down. Schmiedeskamp said, "There goes ten; there goes nine." Then we lost number eight. In these few minutes, number-seven aircraft slid up alongside of us, tight in against our wing. I was looking right at it when they got a shot in the back of number-three engine, apparently right in the main fuel tanks, and it was on fire from the wings back.

Immediately the vertical rudder on the B-24 just melted like a piece of celluloid and disappeared. In the flash of the fire, I saw two men standing in the right waist window. Apparently one man had a chest pack on, and he had pulled a ripcord while he was still inside the aircraft, and the shroud lines were outside and caught up over the elevator. I don't know how in the world parachute shroud lines could get up over the elevator on a B-24, probably six feet above where he was standing. But in an instant the shroud lines and parachute were gone.

I saw where one of the men had bailed out and pulled his ripcord, but the chute just melted from the heat. I saw him going down with the trailing shroud lines. The chute was gone—melted. He went down like a plumb bob.

A third man that bailed out apparently didn't have his leg straps fastened. He must have been a gunner from the ball turret or the tail turret, because those guys normally didn't fasten their leg straps because of the bound-up condition they flew under. I saw his body go right through the chute, and the chute just puffed and disappeared.

Then the aircraft went into a steep dive. It wasn't rolling or out of control, so I could tell that the aircraft was still being piloted. I just watched it go down. That was a crew I had trained with in the states. Thomas M. Brown of Excelsior Springs, Missouri, the engineer from the crew, was on that aircraft, and I was watching him go down. In the course of watching them go down, there was still antiaircraft fire all around.

I had heard of German fighter pilots flying into their own antiaircraft fire to pick off American bomber crews. For the most part, when a bomber crew is subject to heavy antiaircraft fire, they're not so attentive to the fighters as they might normally be. As I watched this plane going down, I looked to my left, and there was an ME-109 German fighter coming in off the top of us. It crossed our flight path and was going down to our left at about a forty-five-degree angle, and he was really going.

At first I couldn't figure out what he was doing out there that far, because he was out of my gun range. But just in an instant, I realized what he was doing: There was a P-47 fighter of ours right on him. It was like watching three television sets at the same time: antiaircraft fire all over, my friends going down in flames, and here comes an ME-109 after us and a P-47 after him.

I went back to watching what happened to my buddy in the plane alongside of us. It kept going down, and finally I couldn't see any more flames. But I could see smoke, and they were still in a steep dive. I watched them going down for quite a while. The plane never rolled or dove or anything. It was just in like a controlled steep dive. Then I saw the plane level off, and there was no smoke. Then he disappeared under some clouds, so I don't know what happened to him after that.

After we had gotten out of antiaircraft range, way off to our left I saw a lone plane kind of sliding in. This plane kept sliding in and sliding in. He came right into our wingtip, right in tight. The canopy was back, and I saw a big gloved hand reach up and pull an oxygen mask down. I saw the pearly teeth and the smile of a black man. He gave me a big wave, and to this day, I can hear the engine in that P-47 as he wound the throttle up. He rolled over and went back to work. And I never saw him after that.

Another time we were attacked by fighter aircraft, an ME-109 was making a pass at us. We were on the back end, and I watched that plane coming in. When he came within my gun range, I started putting the .50-caliber ammunition out there. I closed in on that aircraft as he came closer. It was just seconds from the time he started his pass until he was right on us, so as he came in, I put the ammunition right in him. I thought he was coming right through us. The aircraft came in so close I ducked. He went across the top of us, but he didn't hit us. How that thing ever went across the top of us without hitting us, I don't know, but he passed over us and blew up on the other side. Our crew got credit for the aircraft.

But when I saw that aircraft coming in, I knew he was coming right at us. When he swung in close enough, I could see right at his guns, but he wasn't shooting. Maybe something happened from the time he got into range, because he had been shooting earlier. I know my ammunition was going right in there, but I don't have it on my conscience that I saw myself as taking the life of a person. But I did everything I was given a duty to do.

I went through fifty missions and never got a scratch. Not a person on our plane ever got an injury of any type. We had problems, engine troubles, but we had no injuries on the aircraft. We were never shot down.

The day that I was discharged from the service, my pledge to the American people wasn't terminated. It's just as valid today as it was then. I feel very fortunate that I can be here today, but the most important thing I'd like to do is recognize what my friends did for this country. And this country needs to be forever mindful of the sacrifice that people made for the pleasures that our society enjoys today.

AFTER THE WAR . . .

Chester Ogden was discharged from the service in 1945. He married in 1950 and entered the coal-mining business in 1953. Ogden has never abandoned his commitment to serve and defend the U.S. Constitution.

☆ Les Cruise ☆

Ambler, Pennsylvania

••

Les Cruise joined the army in 1943. He was a paratrooper
in the 505th Parachute Infantry Regiment of the 82nd
Airborne Division. His first jump was over Normandy.

••

I was a student at Stevens Trade School in Lancaster, Pennsylvania, when
Pearl Harbor happened. One guy after another started leaving to go off
to war. When the school year was finished, I went home. There wasn't anything I wanted to do, so on May 27, when I turned eighteen, I went down
to Philadelphia to sign up. I wanted to fly.

I tried to volunteer for the Army Air Forces, but they wouldn't take me,
because they said I was partially color-blind. So I went to the navy and tried
the same thing there. Nothing doing. I even went to the marines, and still
there was nothing. None of them would take me, so I went to the Draft
Board. They turned me down as well, all on the same day!

So I went back to school for the fall term to finish up. When I came
home for Christmas 1942, I went to the Draft Board again and told them I
wanted to go. On January 18, 1943, they signed me up in the army. I wanted
to be a paratrooper, since I couldn't fly an airplane. Eventually they sent me

to Fort Benning, Georgia, for training. I finished that in September and went over to where they put all the new recruits for airborne training.

You were required to pack your own chute and make five jumps. The last one was a night jump. After that we went through maneuvers at Camp McCall, near Fort Bragg, North Carolina, where they took the whole regiment and sent us out as replacements to the different airborne divisions, like the 82nd and the 101st, that were overseas.

They sent our whole group over to Northern Ireland. I left New York on February 11 with one of the biggest convoys they were shipping over. There were ships all over the place. I really loved going over. I thought that was great, because I didn't get seasick. We spent about five weeks in Northern Ireland, doing a lot of training and learning how to do jujitsu, until they decided what they wanted to do with us.

I was with about a dozen other guys who were sent over to England to the 82nd Airborne to fill in for some of the guys they had lost in Sicily and Italy. I joined the 505th Parachute Infantry Regiment in March 1943. We had a camp at Quorn, a little town between Leicester and Nottingham, England, and there I met all these guys who were already combat experienced. I think it was very helpful to me to be put in with them, because I was a young guy and I didn't really have any combat experience. I really thought that was great. They kidded you and said you probably wouldn't last the first day in combat. We were preparing with them and getting to know everybody. In our camp in Quorn there were eight men in a tent. You slept on a cot and had a couple of blankets and a potbelly stove, and that was our home away from home.

We were preparing for D-Day, and we made several training jumps in England. By the end of May we were pretty well trained and ready to go. They took us to Cottesmore Airport and gave us all the equipment that was necessary for combat. They gave us ammunition and a 9-inch round Hawkins land mine that we were supposed to put in our musette bags that we carried below our chutes. They were to be used at roadblocks for enemy tanks. They also gave us a composition C, which was an explosive made by the British. It was like clay. You put a sock around it and a detonator, and you carried it in your side pocket. You had to be careful you didn't set it off.

We left from Cottesmore Airport in England on June 5, 1944. We had so much stuff on us, it was very difficult to get on the plane. The plane's step is not even eighteen inches wide. There were three steps to get you up into the plane, and almost every one of us had to get shoved up the steps.

The "All-American" 82nd Airborne

Activated in 1942, the U.S. Army's first airborne division was the "All-American" 82nd, so named because its members were from all parts of the United States.

The 82nd Infantry Division had been demobilized following World War I; it was reactivated under Maj. Gen. Omar N. Bradley and redesignated as an airborne division on August 15, 1942. While the 82nd trained to go to North Africa, some members helped establish another airborne division, the 101st. By the end of 1942 the 82nd was training at Fort Bragg, North Carolina, under Maj. Gen. Matthew B. Ridgway.

In 1943 the division sailed for combat duty. At that point it consisted of the 504th and 505th Parachute Infantry Regiments (PIR) and the 325th Glider Infantry Regiment (GIR). After arriving at Casablanca and then relocating farther east, the division made parachute and glider invasions of the island of Sicily on July 9 (Operation Husky) and Salerno, Italy, on September 13.

With their first two combat assaults behind them, the 82nd was redeployed to England to prepare for Operation Neptune, the airborne component of Operation Overlord, the cross-channel amphibious invasion of Nazi-occupied Normandy. One PIR, the 504th, had been detached and assigned to fight on the ground in the U.S. invasion of Anzio beach, Italy, and therefore did not accompany the rest of the division. Two additional PIRs, the 507th and 508th, were organized and incorporated into the division in preparation for D-Day. Thus on June 5–6, the 82nd's three PIRs and one GIR joined the largest invasion in history, landing behind Utah Beach and engaging in fighting to secure the Normandy beachhead over the next several weeks. During that time, the division lost 5,245 paratroopers, either killed, wounded, or missing.

Once the Allies were established in Western Europe, the 82nd joined the 17th and 101st Airborne Divisions to create the newly designated XVIII Airborne Corps, which was commanded by General Ridgway. His assistant, Brig. Gen. James Gavin, was promoted,

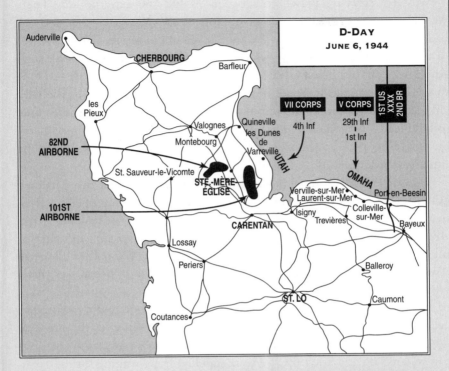

assuming command of the 82nd. The next action for the All-American was the failed Operation Market Garden assault on September 17, 1944. The strategy had been to land airborne troops behind enemy lines to seize bridges over the Rhine and other rivers. But Allied ground troops failed to move eastward to meet and reinforce the airborne soldiers. That, combined with a fierce German counterattack, brought an Allied retreat. The 82nd remained in combat in Holland until November 1944.

In December, the Germans unexpectedly pushed west into Belgium's Ardennes Forest in what became known as the Battle of the Bulge. The 82nd joined ground troops in fighting and did not again perform any combat jumps in World War II. After Germany fell, the 82nd was assigned to occupation duty in Berlin.

The 82nd returned to America in 1946 to be designated a regular standing army division. It was based at Fort Bragg, North Carolina, where it remains today. It subsequently saw combat action in Vietnam, Panama, and Iraq. ★

We were carrying anywhere between 80 and 100 extra pounds. There were about twenty guys on each plane. You sat opposite each other, and you had other equipment sitting in the aisle. It was about ten feet from one side of the plane to the other, so you were pretty close. Some guys took their equipment off, but I never did, because I figured it would take me too long to get it back on again. Some of us had a rifle pack. You had to take your rifle apart in three pieces and put it in the pack and put that under the chute to hold it in. Then when you got down on the ground, you had to reassemble it and be ready to shoot it. A lot of the guys didn't want to spend the time reassembling stuff, so they kept it in one piece.

We formed up in the air formation, and then flew over the Channel. When we flew over the Channel, we could see the silhouettes of all the ships that were waiting to land the troops on the beaches. If we had any doubt about this being the real thing, that's when we knew it wasn't more training. I was nervous, but I was more afraid that I wouldn't be able to perform. I wanted to do what I was supposed to do. My main concern was that I would not be the soldier I was trained to be.

We got over Normandy and the plane started to rock, and we started to get shot with all the flak. I don't know whether anything hit the plane or not, but it was swaying back and forth. As soon as we came to the coast, we had to stand up and hook up. We were standing there waiting for the green light, and when the green light went on, everybody was supposed to go. You could just feel the whole line of guys tightening up and waiting to go. I was trooper number nine. We were jammed in there, and as soon as the green light went on, everybody from the back would start to push, because they all wanted to get out and be as close to each other as possible.

When we landed, I missed a hedgerow and landed flat on my back. My helmet shot over my head and hit my nose. I couldn't tumble. When you go through jump school, you practice tumbling right, tumbling left, but when you get all that gear on, you can't move. You couldn't tumble left, you couldn't tumble right. You just plunked down.

I landed and there were guys all around me. We had close to 200 guys in the third battalion right in the one area, so we were able to move into the town of Sainte-Mère-Église and take control of the town. Our company, H, set up roadblocks, and the other companies went in to clean out the town. I was on a roadblock for the next couple of days, and the other companies cleaned out the town. We held the town until the beach forces came to link up with us.

Then the Germans in the area started to shell us. I could swear they had a high point somewhere, because every time somebody got up to move, they would throw artillery at us. Some of the roadblocks were attacked by German infantry, but they were beaten off.

Three of us were in a foxhole at one of the roadblocks. They wanted us to move, because several troopers got killed on the other side of the roadblock. As soon as we got up to move to the other side, we started to get artillery. I ran across the road and flopped down with the trooper who was with me. A shell landed right beside my buddy Vargas and just shattered his leg. So I dragged him behind the hedgerow and started to cut away his pant leg. I tried to give him morphine and a tourniquet on his thigh and sent another guy for a medic. The medic came back, and we had to move to the new position, so we left him with the medic.

That night I went back to the first-aid station, and I told the sergeant I wanted to see how Vargas was doing. They told me that he had died. I stopped for a moment, and went across the road and sat down and cried my heart out. Then I got up and went back to the roadblock. That was probably my most traumatic experience.

Once the beach forces reached us on Normandy, we were directed to isolate Cherbourg. We started to attack across the Cotentin Peninsula, one city and one village after another. On July 8 or 9, we were finally relieved by the 8th Division and were taken off the line. We went back to the beach area, and they had army trucks there equipped with pumps and water. We were able to get a shower and clean clothes. On the twelfth, we went back to the beach and boarded a transport back to England. So our days in Normandy were over.

When we got back to England, it was like going home. I took a fourteen-day furlough and went to visit areas around Birmingham, Walsall, Sutton, and Stratford-on-Avon, and places like that.

Once I got back from furlough, we got new recruits in and tried to assimilate them into the regiment. We had a couple of new guys in our tent. I guess we must have had sixteen or eighteen guys killed in Normandy from our company, and a larger number that were wounded. About half of them would not come back. So we needed replacements to fill those gaps.

We were spending our time in training and just enjoying life in England. Maybe once a week or two or three times a month, we would go to the airport with all our gear on, as if we were going to make a combat jump. Then they would either call it off or decide to just have a practice jump. So we were always on the tip of going somewhere. I think they did this to keep any spies in the area off-guard.

In September 1944, the British general [Bernard] Montgomery, who was in charge of the airborne forces under Eisenhower, decided to jump into Holland and take all the bridges up to the last bridge over the Rhine, leading to the plains of Germany. So we were all a part of that. We jumped into Holland on a beautiful Sunday in September at 2:00 in the afternoon. I landed in a plowed field. It was the best landing I ever had. Then our group took the town of Groesbeck, and the rest of our regiment went up to Nijmegen and tried to take that bridge. But it took almost a week before they got over the bridge. If you saw the movie *A Bridge Too Far*, it shows the 504th Regiment rowing boats across the river to get to the other side to take the bridge.

They finally did take the bridge, but there was no advancing from Holland. We were just in a holding pattern. We were to hold what we had taken, and the British Army was supposed to be doing the rest of the fighting to take the other bridge. But it didn't materialize, because they were a little too slow in getting there.

We had a lot of problems because there was only one road. Everything had to come up or back on that road, so it got to be a very congested place. In fact, some of the places below us were called Hell's Highway. It was where the 101st Airborne Division was serving, and sometimes they had the road and sometimes they didn't. Sometimes the Germans overran them or made it impossible to take anything up. We were in Holland until the third week of November, just holding the places that we had taken. We lost guys because people were sent out on patrol and never came back, and the artillery shelling was constant.

One occasion in early October, the Germans attacked our position and overran the front lines, but we knocked out one of their tanks, and a lot of their infantry were killed. I had strung out telephone lines to each of the platoons that were down in front of us, about a quarter of a mile, so we had constant communications. But the German tank ran over the wire, so I had to go out at night and put it back together. I had to take a roll of wire with me, hook it up, and then find the other end, wherever it was. That was a traumatic time for me, because I was silhouetted against the burning tank, running around looking for this piece of wire and trying to find the other end. But I did manage to find it and restore the communications.

We were finally relieved by the Canadian Army in November. They didn't have any trucks available for us, so we had to walk a couple of miles back to our positions to get transportation, because our own trucks could not get up there. There was still this problem with the highway. Then we came back, not to England, but we came to back to a French artillery camp at Suippes, near Rheims, France.

On December 16 the Germans broke through the lines up in the Ardennes. We didn't hear about it right away, but on the night of the seventeenth, the sergeant came down and started to wake everybody up, and said, "Come on, you are going to the front." Nobody would get up. It was about 1:30 in the morning, and everybody figured this guy was drunk and nobody moved. So the captain had to come down and read the riot act, and told us it was true—that the Germans had broken through, and that we were going up to the front to fill in the gap.

We spent the entire day of the eighteenth on the army transports, moving this whole division up to this area called the Bulge in the Ardennes, and we landed up there. I almost killed myself when we jumped off the back of the trucks. I fell over backward, and half my equipment was shaken loose. So I had to pick everything up, but it was dark and there was no light.

We got up to the front and had good positions on a brow of a hill called Petit-Halleux. There was a little village, Grand-Halleux, and the Salm River down below us. You could see for miles. We were defending those positions until Christmas. I didn't know it, but according to General Montgomery, our lines were sticking into the German lines with our own bulge, and we were very vulnerable, so he decided that we were going to move back. On Christmas Eve they ordered us to move back about five or six miles to a new position. At midnight the main company moved back.

We left a rear guard, and I was in the rear guard. After about four hours, they gave the first group a chance to go back to the new position. We left the line about 4:00 A.M., and of course there was snow all over the place. So we left our position and went to the new position at Basse-Bodeux.

On January 3, 1945, they decided to attack, and we were going over the same area that we had just given up in order to get back to where we were originally. We were coming into a wooded forest of evergreens, and the artillery laid in on us, and stuff was flying all over the place. A couple of guys got killed, and I got wounded, along with about a dozen other guys. So that ended my battle career.

I was taken back to the first-aid station, where we had to wait for an ambulance that took us to Verviers and Liège. I stayed in Liège overnight. And the guy that bandaged my hand was killed later that day with several of the other men. Nobody looked at me or did anything for me, and I was not

Operation Market-Garden: "A Bridge Too Far"

The idea was simple: Drop 20,000 paratroopers behind enemy lines with orders to seize strategic river bridges in far northeastern Holland. Send attacking armored ground troops to meet and reinforce them, thus seizing a foothold on Germany's doorstep for a final attack on Berlin that would end the war in Europe. But Operation Market-Garden collapsed in Allied defeat and retreat.

Operation Market was the airborne part of the attack; Operation Garden was the ground advance. Together they were intended to build on the Allied occupation of Western Europe after D-Day, June 6, 1944. By early September an Allied front stretched from the North Sea to the Mediterranean, directly facing the West Wall—Germany's western defensive line along its own border. British field marshal Bernard L. Montgomery got Supreme Allied Commander Dwight Eisenhower's consent to advance with a narrow thrust rather than the broad-front approach that Eisenhower favored.

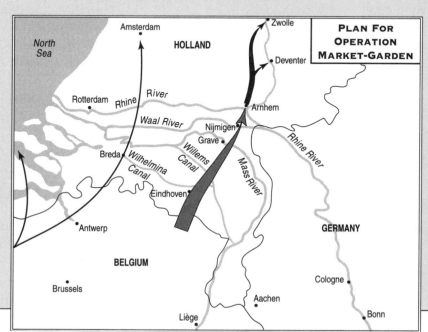

On September 17 some 1,500 transport planes and more than 400 gliders delivered Allied paratroopers as far as sixty miles behind enemy lines, with instructions to take a series of bridges that would become stepping stones for a headlong assault on Germany. Two of four target bridges were secured by the U.S. 101st and 82nd Airborne Divisions, at Eindhoven and Grave. The British 1st Airborne Division, with a Polish brigade of paratroopers, landed at a bridge over the Lek, a Rhine estuary, deepest in enemy territory—at Arnhem. By the end of the second day, the Allies had captured a fourth bridge, over the Waal, another Rhine estuary, at Nijmegen.

But the ground part of the war—Operation Garden—bogged down, both in combat resistance and in self-imposed delay. A decision by one British commander to stop advancing for the night gave the Germans time to regroup from the surprise attack.

The Germans fought furiously along Highway 69, nicknamed "Hell's Highway" by members of the 101st Airborne Division. That was the route the Allies intended to take to reach the airborne troops at the bridgeheads. It was the battle for control of this highway, plus the concentration of panzer tank forces at Arnhem, that caused Market-Garden to fail. The Germans prevented Operation Garden from joining up with the now-stranded airborne troops at the final bridge—the "bridge too far," as it was later called by author Cornelius Ryan—at Arnhem.

Those airborne troops were to hold the bridges for forty-eight hours, until the arrival of the armored corps, but as the wait stretched to a week, they ran out of food and ammunition. Bad weather prevented airlifts of either to the isolated British-Polish force, which was effectively abandoned. Finally, on the night of September 25–26, about 2,200 troops were evacuated out of some 10,000 men dropped on Arnhem. They left behind some 1,400 dead and more than 6,000 who were captured as POWs. For the Allies, heady with the success of Normandy and the liberation of Paris, it was a sober reminder that they still faced one of the most formidable foes in military history, and it was not giving in easily. The Allies did not cross the Rhine for another six months. ★

given morphine. The next morning they took us up to Brussels and sent us back to Paris. Yet there was still no morphine and nobody looking at my hand. The next day they shipped us out to a tent hospital in Le Mans. That's where I finally had somebody look at my hand to do what they could to put it back together. They sent me over to England, and that's where they operated on my hand. Then they sent me back to the United States on May 4.

When the war ended in Europe on May 8, I was in the middle of the ocean on a hospital ship. We were the first wounded to arrive back in the States at Camp Shanks after the end of the war in Europe. They sent me to a hospital in Martinsburg, West Virginia, where they did a final operation on my hand. They wouldn't take out the shrapnel; they just left it in there, because they said they couldn't assure me that I would have use of it if they operated on it. So they left it in there, and I have been living with it for over fifty-eight years.

It really wasn't bad. It was what we would call a million-dollar wound. It would get you off the line and out of the line of fire. It was pretty bad then, but it's fine now, because when I came back, I was able to play baseball. So it's all right. It's just missing a joint, and I'm carrying a couple pieces in my wrist that keep showing up on the X-rays. I was finally discharged from the hospital on September 27, 1945, and I came back to Philadelphia to study architecture at Penn under the GI Bill.

I didn't realize how important what we were doing was at the time we were doing it. I knew it had to be done, but in the terms of total history, I didn't equate it with what it equates with today. And you know, hearing everybody say that this was critical and a key point, it didn't seem to be that much then. I didn't really digest all that. We were just there to do the job and liberate Europe.

AFTER THE WAR . . .

Les Cruise received a bachelor's degree in architecture from the University of Pennsylvania in 1950 and went on to work for a number of Philadelphia-area firms. He also worked as a consultant to develop architectural fiberglass components for Disney's Epcot Center. Cruise married in 1946, and he and his wife, Shirley, raised two children together.

☆ Paul Daugherty ☆
Columbia, Pennsylvania

···

Paul Daugherty joined the service in 1942. After completing
gunnery training and navigation school, he was assigned to
the 450th Bomb Group. During one mission, his plane was
shot down, and Daugherty was taken prisoner by the Germans.

···

Just before the war I was on a survey crew for AT&T, working mostly in
the states below the Mason–Dixon line: Virginia, West Virginia, and North
Carolina.

The day Pearl Harbor was bombed I was home for a weekend, and that
morning I went to church. After church I walked downtown, where I ran
into a cousin of mine. He asked me if I heard Pearl Harbor was bombed. I
didn't know where Pearl Harbor was. We hurried home to listen to the news
on the radio.

In late summer 1942, I was in Richmond, Virginia, and noticed a sign
in the post office announcing examinations for aviation cadet in what was
then the Army Air Corps. Having nothing to lose, I reported for the exam,
took it, and passed. We were sent to Miami Beach for basic military training, then on to Butler University in Indianapolis for CTD, College Train-

The B-25 "Mitchell" Bomber

The B-25 "Mitchell" bomber was one of the best-known military aircraft of World War II, and the first to serve in every theater of the war. The model was named in honor of Brig. Gen. Billy Mitchell (1879–1936), who during World War I had coordinated 1,481 Allied aircraft to support ground troops during a battle in eastern France. A military visionary, he aggressively championed the idea of strong U.S. airpower and a separate air force.

Prior to the United States' entry into the war, the Army Air Corps saw a need for a medium bomber type and on March 11, 1939, issued a request for proposals. It took a very short time to design and build the B-25. The government awarded a contract to North American Aviation on September 10, 1939, and the prototype made its first test flight on August 19, 1940. By the end of the war, North American had built more than 9,800 of them.

The preeminent event for which the model is known was the daring Doolittle Raid of April 18, 1942. Less than five months after Pearl Harbor, sixteen B-25s under the command of Lt. Col. James H. "Jimmy" Doolittle took off from the carrier USS *Hornet* in the Pacific. The goal of the one-way mission was to surprise the Japanese and bomb the home islands, including the capital city of Tokyo.

Nobody had tried to fly fully loaded B-25s from an aircraft carrier deck before, but it was the kind of challenge that Doolittle, a former air racer and stunt pilot, relished. President Roosevelt had pressed for an attack on Tokyo to retaliate for Pearl Harbor, but the challenge was a stiff one. None of the Allied airfields were near enough, and any carrier venturing within 300 miles of Japan to launch planes would be sunk by Japanese warships, aircraft, or submarines. B-25s were ground-based bombers, but secret tests in Virginia proved that they could take off in as short a distance as 450 feet. They couldn't land on a short carrier deck, however, so the plan was to continue flying west to five designated landing fields in China, a U.S. ally.

A B-25 bomber receives its white star, 1942. FRANKLIN D. ROOSEVELT LIBRARY, HYDE PARK, NEW YORK

Doolittle's group flew 700 miles to Japan. Pilots split up and attacked from multiple directions to create maximum confusion, successfully bombing targets in Tokyo, Kobe, Nagoya, Osaka, Yokohama, and the Yokosuka Navy Yard from altitudes of 1,200 to 2,000 feet. Although attacked by antiaircraft fire and Japanese fighters, none of the B-25s were shot down. But because they had taken off early for security reasons and flown farther than initially planned, they ran out of fuel over China before reaching the airfields. Eleven crews bailed out and four more crash-landed. Surprisingly, most of the eighty crewmen survived. One B-25 made it to Vladivostok, Russia, where the plane and its crew were interned. Eight airmen were captured by the enemy in Japanese-occupied China. Of these, one, Robert Meder, died of illness in captivity, and three—2nd Lt. William G. Far-

(continued on page 146)

(continued from page 145)
row, 2nd Lt. Dean E. Hallmark, and Sgt. Harold A. Spatz—were executed by firing squad at Shanghai on October 15, 1942.

Although Doolittle thought the raid a failure and expected to be court-martialed, he was instead hailed as a hero, promoted to brigadier general, and awarded the Medal of Honor personally by Roosevelt. The raid inflicted minimal damage—50 fatalities, 250 people wounded, and 90 buildings destroyed, including military targets—but succeeded immensely in boosting troop and home-front morale at a time when American forces in the Pacific were suffering setback after setback. It also demonstrated to startled Japanese civilians that contrary to what military leaders had been telling them, they were not immune from attack. Even while World War II was still raging, the raid was memorialized in a 1944 Hollywood film, *Thirty Seconds over Tokyo,* with actor Spencer Tracy playing Doolittle, and actual B-25s being used in the filming.

Built from 1940 through 1945, the B-25 and its variants were configured not only for bombing, but also for submarine patrol (the B-25 was the first U.S. bomber to sink an Axis sub), strafing, crew training, and photographic reconnaissance. One B-25 was converted to serve as the personal transport plane for Gen. Dwight D. Eisenhower, supreme commander of the Allied forces in Europe, and two more were successively converted for the use of Gen. Henry H. "Hap" Arnold, commanding general of the Army Air Forces.

With a top speed of 300 miles per hour, the B-25 had a range of 1,200 miles and could fly at altitudes of 25,000 feet. Each plane carried a crew of five—pilot, copilot, bombardier, navigator and radio operator, and gunner—and a bomb load of 5,000 pounds. The cost for each B-25 was $96,000. In addition to the U.S. Army Air Force, the B-25 was flown by the air forces of Australia, China, Great Britain, Holland, and the Soviet Union. ★

ing Detachment. Here we took college courses in math, physics, meteorology, and such.

From CTD I went to Chickasha, Oklahoma, for primary flight training. After about 120 hours of dual and solo instruction, I graduated and was sent to Garden City, Kansas. About two-thirds of the way through, I took a check ride with a senior instructor, and I was told I was not pilot material. My classification scores were such that I was qualified for navigation training, so after attending gunnery school at Harlingen, Texas, I was off to navigation school at Selman Field in Monroe, Louisiana, from there to transition to B-24s at Chatham Field, Savannah, Georgia, with a full crew.

We did the Great Circle Route: Mitchell Field, Long Island, to Dow Field, Bangor, Maine, to Goose Bay, Labrador, across Greenland to Meeks Field, Iceland, to Valley, Wales, to Marrakech, French Morocco, to Tunis and up to Italy. The 450th Group was based in Manduria, just at the "arch" in the Italian "boot."

The only mission I flew with my regular crew was on Christmas Day 1944. The only mission I really remember much about was the last one. We flew roughly every three days, weather permitting. I had flown with another crew on the twenty-eighth, but we lost two engines near Venice so had to abort, so that didn't count as a mission. The next morning, the twenty-ninth, the CQ, charge of quarters, woke me up and said, "Lieutenant, you're flying today." I replied I had flown the day before. His reply was that it made no difference and I was flying again—today. In my haste, I took what I thought I needed but forgot my dog tags.

In the briefing, G2 (intelligence officer) told us the target was the Brenner Pass, "a milk run—no flak, no fighters." He was right on one count, in that we saw no fighters. However, the Germans had been bringing guns from the Eastern Front and massing them in the West.

We never made it to the IP, the initial point, at which the bombardier and the Norden bomb sight took over for the bomb run. Out of my box of seven planes, we lost three planes—not exactly a milk run. Our plane lost two men: the radio operator and the nose gunner. As far as I know, the nose gunner is still MIA. The radio operator had not fastened his chute harness, so when he pulled the ripcord, he fell out of the parachute!

Except for the pilot and copilot, I was the last one out. In order to clear the tail surfaces and to spend as little time floating as possible, I waited about ten seconds before I tripped the chute. When I landed, the snow came up to my waist, and I still had all my gear on. I was captured within about twenty minutes by a group of civilians, all with guns and four or five dogs. I had nothing but my .45, which was useless under those conditions. The party took me to a little town called San Felice near Bolzano. After a few days in the local jail, I, along with my pilot and a few others, was put on a train, eventually arriving at Frankfurt, the interrogation center.

I can't say I was prepared for that situation. Everyone knew there was the possibility of being captured, being wounded, or getting killed, but that was not the same thing as having it happen. I think I was in shock. One minute you're flying along with eight or nine other guys whom you know, or who

Luftwaffe: The German Air Force

The German Air Force flew under the name Luftwaffe, or "air weapon." Banned in 1919 after Germany's defeat in World War I, it was reconstituted in 1935 as part of Nazi dictator Adolf Hitler's rearmament plan. It became his favorite branch of service, and he personally oversaw every detail. He appointed Hermann Göring, a World War I flying ace, as its commander.

Hitler's philosophy of airpower was to use it as airborne artillery, in support of ground troops, a function that it fulfilled well during Germany's blitzkrieg invasion of Poland on September 1, 1939. On the eve of the war, the Luftwaffe consisted of some 4,000 aircraft, including Messerschmitt Bf 109 and 110 single-engine fighters, Heinkel 111 medium bombers, and Junkers Ju 87 dive-bombers. But German factories geared up quickly, producing a total of 5,700 Ju 87 dive-bombers, 16,000 Ju 88 bombers, almost 7,000 He 111 medium bombers, 5,900 Bf 110 fighters, and an incredible 35,000 Bf 109 fighters.

The Luftwaffe flew in a three-front war—on the Eastern (Russia) and Western (Britain) Fronts, and in the Mediterranean. Its staff increased fourfold over the course of the war, from 400,000 to 1.7 million. A total of 3.4 million people served, of whom the war claimed 165,000 dead, 155,000 missing, and 192,000 injured.

at least wear the same uniforms and speak the same language, and the next minute you are surrounded by men in different uniforms speaking another language.

Fortunately for those of us in the air force, the Luftwaffe treated us pretty much the same as we treated them. It sounds corny, but there is a sort of brotherhood there, and I assume this to be true not just of the air force, but of the submariners, ground forces, everyone. There was a bond between those who served in the same services.

Fortunately most of the question–and–answer sessions I had were with the Luftwaffe Oberleutnant, who spoke Oxford English, and we got along

Initially the Luftwaffe dominated the air war, but eventually it lost pace. From July to October 1940, it flew mass raids against Great Britain's military targets, bombing radar stations and aircraft factories in the Battle of Britain. Defending its homeland, the Royal Air Force lost 1,149 planes, while the Germans lost 1,782 planes. In retaliation for an RAF raid on Berlin, Hitler then changed tactics, bombing British civilian targets. Known as the Blitz, this campaign lasted through May 1941. Raids struck as far north as Glasgow, Scotland, and Belfast, Northern Ireland. In all, 2 million houses were destroyed (60 percent of them in London), 60,000 civilians were killed, and 87,000 were injured.

In 1944 Germany became the first air force to fly a jet fighter, the Messerschmitt Me 262. But Hitler had interfered, insisting that it be converted to a fighter-bomber, slowing development and delaying production. Thus it came along too late to reverse the tide of Allied victory. The arrival of the U.S. Army Air Force in Britain to bolster the RAF was a decisive factor in the Luftwaffe's decline. Also, Germany failed to develop a long-range four-engine heavy bomber, because Hitler and his aides believed that they would win the war quickly. Other factors were the attrition of aircraft in fighting on three fronts: the loss of experienced pilots; and Germany's insistence on keeping experienced pilots in combat rather than cycling them back to train new pilots. At the end, the Luftwaffe was so desperate that it resorted to airborne ramming of Allied bombers. ★

fine. There was no animosity. The only two times I felt threatened were once when I was questioned by the Gestapo and once by the SS, the Schutzstaffel. That was a little harrowing. Several times I was threatened with being shot as a spy, since I was not wearing my dog tags.

Before I was sent to Frankfurt, at the little jail in San Felice, the noncommissioned officer in charge was a Wehrmacht sergeant. He and I got to know each other rather well. We heard the troops complaining that he was giving us too much charcoal for our burners, too much food, etc. One day the sergeant and I were playing chess, and I asked him, "Sergeant, why are you treating us so well?" He said, "You know who's going to win the war and I know who's going to win the war, and I want to be treated the same as I am treating you." The SS simply didn't operate that way. They were the "Master Race." I didn't find that with the Luftwaffe or the Wehrmacht, or even with many civilians.

I was in Stalag Luft I less than six months, no big deal. There were about 9,000 of us in the camp. There were prison camps all over Germany, with anywhere from 4,000 to as many as 18,000 in them, but what we had to put up with was nothing compared to what the prisoners of the Japanese had to put up with. We didn't eat very well, but neither did the Germans. There were one or two guys in my room who really had a problem with being a POW, but for most of us it was part of the deal.

One day we got word that when we woke up the next morning, the guards would be gone; and when we got up, they were gone, along with the dogs, the guns on the towers, everything. We were free. There was already an Allied organization in place, so there was no pandemonium, no chaos, no guys running around. We cheered a little bit, then we packed up and sat there.

We sat for two days, five days, seven days, ten days, and nothing happened. Then the Russians moved in. I'm sorry to say this, but if there is one group to this day that I will not trust, it is the Russians. They were our allies, but I saw them in action. We discovered the reason we were there so long after the Germans left was because a Russian general who had been captured by the Germans offered his services to Germany to form a group to fight the Communists. Stalin said that until that general and all other Russians with him were turned over to Russia, there would be no one leaving Luft I. They smashed down barracks and other buildings with their tanks, and treated us as if we were their prisoners. We couldn't move unless we got permission from them to do so. There was a flak school near Luft I that was using some captured Russian women soldiers as instructors. They were treated worse than the Germans were. The situation was finally resolved because the C-47s and B-17s began to fly in.

Coming home was almost anticlimactic. Being released, knowing I didn't have to get up in the morning and stand inspection and roll call by the Germans, knowing I didn't have to see the guard towers with the guns, knowing I was free was the big thing. People who have never lost their freedom cannot understand that, and there is no way I or anyone else could tell them what it's like.

We would sometimes look up and see our B-17s or B-24s or others going over, and we'd say, "Those are our guys up there, and they're flying along just as we did." Then we'd drop our gaze down and see a guard tower, and they'd turn the dogs loose at night. Unless you've been there, you simply cannot understand it.

I'm not saying we suffered. I'm saying that the loss of freedom is worse. I know fellows who were in Japanese prisoner-of-war camps, and they'll tell you the same thing. It was not going down in the coal mines or whatever that bothered them—it was being free or not being free.

At that time, I thought we were doing something worthwhile. I thought the Germans were the bad guys and we were the guys in the white hats. I'm not too sure of that now. Knowing now what I know about the way we were maneuvered into World War II and almost every war since, well, what the American public should do is read and understand. Politicians get us into wars and—I was twenty-three at the time—the twenty-two- and twenty-three-year-olds get us out. It is a hell of a way to operate, but that's the way it is.

I don't think I'm being unpatriotic. Patriotism to me does not mean waving a flag and singing the "Star-Spangled Banner" and all that. Patriotism is being aware of what's happening in Washington and Harrisburg and acting properly. I would like to see citizens do something first and have the politicians react rather than the other way around.

AFTER THE WAR . . .

Paul Daugherty returned to his job with AT&T for the Altoona and Harrisburg areas. He retired from the company in 1985. Daugherty adopted two children; he lost his son in a 1999 car accident, and his daughter now lives in Australia. He is a member of the Conestoga Chapter of American Ex–Prisoners of War Service Foundation (AXPOW) and has traveled overseas to Ireland, Central America, and Australia.

☆ Harvey Possinger ☆
East Stroudsburg, Pennsylvania

Harvey Possinger was drafted while he was still in school.
He was a machine gunner and then became a medic in
the 25th Infantry Division. Possinger received twenty-eight
medals and believes he is the second-most-decorated
combat soldier of World War II, after Audie Murphy.

I was still going to school when I was drafted. I was in the eighth grade, living in Stroudsburg. I told them I wanted to go where the fighting was, and they sent me. In thirty days I was over there. I don't know if everybody felt the same way, but when they bombed Pearl Harbor, I just couldn't wait to get over there and pay them back for what they did. I wanted to chase them back where they belong.

The U.S. had just landed in Guadalcanal when I went into the service. The marines landed there, and we came in to relieve them and secure the island. It was three or four months until we got it cleaned up and chased the Japanese out. Most of the Japanese were taken out on barges at night, because the Japanese had air superiority and navy superiority, and they could bring their ships and planes in easier than we could. We had no airfields, and the U.S. wanted to build one to get some air support, because in the early part of the war there was very little.

Guadalcanal was my first fighting experience. I was scared to death. We all were, for that matter, but the longer you were there, the more you realized that you had your job to do. You might not have liked it, but you had to do it.

What the Japanese did to our soldiers is unbelievable. We felt that they were such an enemy that we had to kill them all, so we didn't take any prisoners while we were in Guadalcanal. Every prisoner that tried to run away was shot, because we didn't want to be bothered with any of them. And that's how Guadalcanal was until we got it secured.

At Guadalcanal I was a machine gunner at first, and then a rifleman until I got wounded. The first time I was wounded, I was shot in the foot, and then hit in the leg with a flamethrower.

Combat was hard. I was most afraid at night and early in the morning. That's when Japs would come and jump right in the foxhole with you, and you had to kill them. If you didn't, you'd get killed. They'd wait until dark, and try to come in and kill you when you were asleep, but we never slept. If we did, we took turns. That's the only way you could get any rest at all. In the daytime you got more rest than you did at night. And you were always scared to death. In fact, I can still hear Japanese singing to us, "Marines, you die, marines, you die."

We had no kitchens or anything like that. We ate C rations, and most of them were left over from World War I. It was mostly canned hash, baked beans, and biscuits. You didn't get a decent meal for months.

The malaria was awful. We fought the malaria more than we did the Japanese, but you got used to it, and the longer you were there, the harder you got. They made you a soldier, whether you wanted to be one or not.

We slept in foxholes. Many times you would dig a foxhole along the shore, and you'd think you were safe, but then you'd wake up in the morning and be in a puddle of water. The tide would come in and fill the hole up, and you'd be soaking wet.

Most of the toughest fighting was in the mountains. The Japs had good positions, and it was hard to move them, but we finally drove them off the island. It took months, but we did it. When the battle was finally over, we thought we'd all go home, but in no time they sent us to another island. We went from Guadalcanal up to New Georgia and Vella Lavella, Bougainville, and all the Solomon Islands. The ship I was on got hit going into Vella

Lavella. I remember helping take the wounded off the ship as it was still burning. The Jap planes would come over us and you could see the pilot— that's how low they flew. The only air protection we had was rifles and grenades and a few mortars. It was small stuff, but that's all we had.

Then the Japs dropped bombs on the aid station and wiped out practically all of our medics, so I volunteered to help. There were two medics assigned to each company, and they were responsible for all the wounded men. As a medic, you went right along with the rest of the men. You carried a gun just like they did. In the South Pacific, they armed you and you had to kill or be killed, the same as a soldier did. And when they got wounded, you tried to get them out. I saved many, many lives by bringing them out. Sometimes it was kind of tough. I learned how to give soldiers morphine and how to bandage them and to put sulfa powder on the wounds. We made splints, but most of the guys you carried out on your back. To me it was just a job, because I got so used to it. Whenever you heard the guns going and they said, "Go get them out," you knew what to expect.

I was in the Philippines for almost a year and a half. I was in combat 165 straight days without being relieved. We went up Highway Five—they called them highways, but they were nothing but dirt roads—and it took us 165 days to drive the Japs out of there. And the war didn't end then. They were still in the caves, and you had to go in with flamethrowers or go right in there after them. That's the only way you could get them out. A lot of times they'd have cannons in the caves, and they'd roll the cannons out and fire them, and then take them back in so you couldn't hit them. Our American planes went over and dropped fire bombs, trying to get them, but they were sealed in. They had about four years to build those caves, so they were well equipped to hold, and it took a long time to get them out of there. But we finally did.

I was awarded the Distinguished Service Cross, that's the second-highest award you can get for bravery, and I have two of them. I got one when I went in and brought six or seven wounded men out. I got wounded going in after them, but after I got wounded, I still helped carry them out. That was at Putlan Bridge in the Philippines.

I got five Purple Hearts for getting wounded five different times. Each time you were taken back to the field hospital, they would come through and say, "Oh, you've got to get a Purple Heart, you got wounded." It didn't bother us at all. We could care less about the medals. We just wanted to come back alive if we could. That was what we were after.

AFTER THE WAR . . .

Harvey Possinger returned to his work at Pocono Textile, a company that he had worked for prior to his service. Possinger and his wife had three children. He got involved with the VFW and was commander for twelve years. In addition, Possinger was one of the original coordinators of the Stroudsburg Little League.

☆ Paul Miller ☆

Elizabethtown, Pennsylvania

Paul Miller was a paratrooper in the 101st Airborne
Division. He received a Purple Heart when
he was wounded upon landing in Normandy.

I worked for the Harrisburg State Hospital as a night ward charge. I was a
young man then, and decided to go down and enlist in the paratroops.
Trouble was, they sent me to Carlisle, which at the time was a medical facility. They reviewed my reports and sent me to Walter Reed Hospital, where
they put me in training as a medic. But I kept trying to get into the paratroops. Every day I reported to the first sergeant, and he'd say, "Yeah, Paul,
we're looking into it."

After about two months I got a little bit discouraged, so I wrote a letter to
the commanding general of the paratroops at Fort Benning, Georgia. He
wrote back to my major and said if I could pass the physical, he would trans-
fer me to the paratroops immediately. The major felt that I was going over his
head. So he instructed me to have a physical at Walter Reed Hospital. They
really worked me over but couldn't find anything wrong. So the next day I
was on my way to Camp Toccoa, Georgia, where the 1st Regiment trained.

That's where we went through basic paratroop training. Every day we ran a mountain. It was three and a half miles up, three and a half miles back. That was besides the physical training—running the obstacle course, judo, the whole bit. Then they bused us over to Fort Benning, Georgia, for our jump training. They had us jumping out of mock airplanes, and then they took us to a 250-foot tower, where they raised us up and gave us the experience of coming down in a parachute. After your fifth jump, you got your parachute wings.

Camp Shanks in New York was our port of embarkation. We got onto a boat and went over to England for more training and more jumps, until the D-Day invasion. The night before the invasion we all got on the planes, ready to go, but they called it off because of the weather. So Ike—General Eisenhower—decided within the next twenty-four hours we would be ready. There was a break in the weather, so we got back onto the planes, and at 2:00 in the morning we jumped into Normandy, France.

It was a little dark, but not that dark. As we jumped, you could hear bullets going through the plane. It was *ping, ping, ping*. Then, when you jumped, you heard them going through your chute. They'd go *psst, psst, psst!* But for about two seconds it was one of the most beautiful sights I ever saw in my life. You could look up and see all those red and green tracers and bursts of ack-ack. It was probably the best fireworks display I have ever seen.

The landing was hard. The ground came up awful quick. We didn't know where the Germans were. The air force fouled up a little bit, to be honest with you. They say that some of the pilots were new, and they got confused and broke formation. So we were scattered over about thirty miles instead of being in one unit. Some of our men didn't get back to our regular unit for thirty days, we were scattered out that far. It wasn't a fun time.

Right before I got in the plane that morning, I had a wisdom tooth that was starting to pound. I knew if I said something, they'd take me out and send me to the dentist and have it pulled, and I would miss the jump. So I kept my mouth shut. Well, after I landed, there were times that my wisdom tooth was just pounding, and my eyes were watering so badly I could hardly see. We were going from fencerow to fencerow, and I fell down behind a log about halfway through the rows. I yelled back to some of our fellows, "If you can see Captain Fowler (a dentist), tell him I need him." I really had no hope of him coming, because we were scattered so far apart, but I'd say within fifteen minutes, here comes old Captain Fowler!

He jumped behind a log with me, and chips from gunfire were flying off of it every now and then, and he said, "What do you want, Miller?" And I

Gen. Dwight D. Eisenhower

Gen. Dwight D. Eisenhower was a career army officer who rose from undistinguished beginnings to become supreme allied commander in Europe, overseeing the greatest amphibious invasion in history, D-Day. That success, and his leadership in the final defeat of Nazi Germany in 1945, made him enormously popular among U.S. troops and the American public, who later twice elected him U.S. president.

Born in Texas in 1890 and raised in Kansas, Eisenhower graduated from the U.S. Military Academy at West Point in 1915. He rose steadily if slowly through the ranks of the army, and after the Japanese attack on Pearl Harbor in December 1941, he became an aide to Army Chief of Staff George C. Marshall. By June 1942, he was named U.S. commander in Europe, with headquarters in London.

In that role, he directed the November 1942 invasion of North Africa (Operation Torch), and later oversaw the Allied invasions of Sicily and Italy. At the end of 1943 he was named to lead the invasion of Normandy in Operation Overlord—the massive air and amphibious assault on German-held France by American, British, and Canadian forces.

After months of preparation for a June 5, 1944, deployment, stormy weather over the English Channel threatened to unravel the invasion. Eisenhower had to decide whether to proceed or to wait until the next favorable combination of tides and daylight, which would mean a two-week delay, eliminating the element of surprise. He opted for a twenty-four-hour delay, and the weather cleared just enough for the attack to proceed across the English Channel. It was a massive exercise in coordination, involving dropping airborne fighters (more than 20,000 paratroopers) behind enemy lines, landing troops from more than 5,000 ships along a fifty-mile-wide string of beaches, and providing air support with bombers. Despite confusion and bloody fighting on the beaches, the plan was successful, and by the end of the day, 156,000 troops and 30,000 vehicles had been landed. It was the turning point of the war. The liberation of Europe had begun.

Gen. Dwight D. Eisenhower gives the order of the day—"full victory, nothing else"—to paratroopers in England, just before they boarded airplanes to participate in the D-Day invasion, June 6, 1944. NATIONAL ARCHIVES

In that and follow-on campaigns (Operation Market-Garden in Holland, the Battle of the Bulge in the Ardennes Forest of Belgium, and the crossing of the Rhine River for a final attack on Germany), Eisenhower faced internal rivalries, arrogance, resistance, and demands for position and power. His skills as a coordinator, negotiator, and leader were severely tested by the dueling egos of those under his command—British field marshal Sir Bernard Law Montgomery, U.S. generals Omar Bradley and George Patton, and French general Charles de Gaulle. Eisenhower was enormously popular with the common foot soldier, visiting troops often, eating C rations with them, and even, on occasion, driving his own jeep.

After World War II, Eisenhower became chief of staff for the army, served a term as president of Columbia University, and became the military commander for the North Atlantic Treaty Organization (NATO). Finally, he ran for and won the presidency in 1952, becoming the thirty-fourth U.S. president, and was reelected in 1956. ★

told him. So he got out this probe and he touched it to my tooth, and I almost stood straight up. I said, "I can't take this." He said, "I'm going to pull it." I said, "We're in the middle of a battle right now and you're going to pull it?" His exact words: "I don't have time to fool with you, Miller. I'm going to pull that tooth, and that's an order." And he pulled it. Almost immediately the tears stopped coming, because the pressure was off, and he said, "I've got work to do. I'll see you later."

We had combat as soon as our feet hit the ground. In fact, you were in combat before you hit the ground. They were shooting at you. I got a Purple Heart because, when I hit the ground in Normandy, I got it in the knees. I reached down and could feel something wet there, and I thought, "Oh, don't tell me I've got trouble." So I pulled out these big bandages that we had carried, and I put them over each knee, right over my jumpsuit.

Suddenly it seemed like everybody was shooting at me, and I couldn't figure out why. I couldn't see them, but they apparently could see me. So I looked down, and there were these white bandages sticking out. "Well," I thought, "I can't keep this up." So I took the bandages off and dropped my pants, and put the bandages right on the skin. Then I pulled my pants up and kept on going. After a little while I got to thinking, "I wonder what people would have thought if they'd seen me with my pants down in the middle of a war?"

Later that morning we made contact with the troops coming in from the beach. We had a tremendous number of casualties. Eisenhower and his aides said that we would have approximately 82 percent casualties, and he didn't miss it by much.

A lot of cattle were killed there in the barrage, before the troops hit the ground. And by the third day, if you had a real good friend and you were hiding behind one of these dead cows that was swelled up, he might shoot a little bullet hole right in front of your nose, and all this gas would come out. Then you had a choice of lying there and smelling that stuff, or getting out and running. The choice was yours. Little things like that broke the monotony.

We were in France for thirty days, and then we got on a boat and went back to England and started to retrain, regroup, and resupply. Then we jumped into Eindhoven, Holland. That was the first town that was to be liberated whenever General Montgomery was to come through. All the airborne people—the United States Airborne, the English Airborne, there was some Polish Airborne people there—they were to form a corridor straight through to this bridge across the river.

We took our objectives and had everything lined up for General Montgomery to come through. But I think he must have been having tea or something, because he never made it. And it was because of his hesitation, or whatever you want to call it, that the operation didn't pan out. The English paratroopers lost an awful lot of men up there. It was a hot place to be.

Then we went into Bastogne and got completely surrounded. Bastogne is a small town where five different roads come in, and our orders were to hold it. No exceptions. We had to hold the ground. The Germans wanted to go through there because this was the main road to the coast, where they had to go to get gasoline. But we stopped them long enough that their tanks ran out of gas. But you could look out and see tanks in any direction, and guns pointing everywhere. The town wasn't worth very much after that siege. Many of our men have gone back, and they said it's a nice town now; they've fixed it up. They welcome us back every year.

I've often wondered how we held the Germans. We were behind the lines then, and all of a sudden we got this order, "Get to Bastogne. Right now!" We hadn't resupplied yet. We hadn't any winter gear. They opened up a warehouse and said, "Take what you want." But in the meantime, the officers were saying, "Get on the trucks, get on the trucks!" So basically, we had just our jumpsuits on. We had some ammunition, but not all we needed. We had no galoshes, no overcoats.

We were taken in there by trucks, and we had hardly gotten there when the Germans had us surrounded. We were fighting them with small-arms fire. We had a few bazookas and a few antitank guns, but we almost ran out of ammunition.

It was the coldest I've ever been in my life. I never want to be that cold again. A lot of men got hurt, a lot of men died, and a lot of men froze to death. A lot of people lost some toes and fingers, besides being shot at, but I think the weather saved a lot of lives, because the cold stopped the infections, and that was a godsend.

We slept on the ground. They didn't furnish cots out there. We didn't have any blankets; we just had our clothes. We tried to dig holes, but our shovels would hit the ground and bounce back. It was frozen solid to about a foot down. It was very, very cold. And we had no place to evacuate anybody. We were surrounded.

The Germans sent a three-man delegation right into the regimental headquarters of the 101st to ask for our surrender. General McAuliffe was there; he looked at the note asking for surrender, and he said, "Nuts!" Well, the Germans, on their way back, asked one of the sergeants on the front line, *"Was ist 'nuts'?"* I won't tell you what the sergeant said, but it amounted to, "Well, blow it." After that we just kept going.

We liberated a concentration camp at Landsberg. It was awful. Some of us wanted to open the gates and let those poor people out, but thank God there was a major there who said, "Keep the gates locked." If we had let them out, they would not have known where to go. They wouldn't have had any food or any medication. So they got a medical company to come in and service them. But it was probably like every concentration camp—a lot of death, a lot of bodies lying around.

The 101st Airborne: The Screaming Eagles

The 101st Airborne Division—the "Screaming Eagles"—was organized during World War I but never fully equipped. Thus its real history begins with its activation as an airborne infantry division in August 1942 at Camp Claiborne, Louisiana.

Soon the division was training in glider and parachute warfare in Georgia and North Carolina. One unit, the 506th Parachute Infantry Regiment, was assigned to Camp Toccoa, Georgia, where a daily run to the top of Currahee Mountain hardened the men for battle. Currahee, reputed to be the Cherokee word for "stands alone," became the cry of many parachutists as they exited the plane on their first jump, and it became a rallying cry in combat as well.

In September 1943 the division sailed for England, where Maj. Gen. Maxwell D. Taylor took command.

As part of the June 6, 1944, attack on Normandy, some 6,600 soldiers of the 101st boarded 1,432 C-47 aircraft for the predawn invasion of Utah Beach, the westernmost site of Operation Overlord. Confusion, bad weather, and enemy fire hampered the operation, and many paratroopers were scattered far from their intended drop zones. Some 1,500 were killed or captured. Still, the paratroopers and glider pilots succeeded in taking important targets, securing the exits from Utah Beach to allow troops landing off the English Channel to begin to penetrate inland.

We left there and moved on to Hitler's Berchtesgaden, Eagle's Nest, up on the mountain. We had bombed it the night before, and when we got there it was still smoldering. There were still German troops there, a few SS boys, most of them were the Wehrmacht. I sat there in Hitler's big living room, and there was a huge window there that looked out over the mountains, but of course, it was all blown out, and things were scattered around. We liberated Göring's art collection—what he had stolen from all the different countries he was in—and we liberated his alcohol. We thought that was a good thing to liberate.

Over the next week, the 101st seized the towns of St. Come du Mont and Carentan. The division remained in France for about a month before returning to England. Its next airborne combat drop came on September 17, 1944, during the failed Operation Market-Garden attempt to secure bridges over the Rhine in Holland. In a daylight drop, the 101st landed, liberated the town of Eindhoven, and fought to hold positions. The Germans prevented ground troops from linking up with the easternmost airborne troops, who were isolated at Arnhem and eventually had to be evacuated by the 101st. Although Market-Garden was a failure overall, the 101st did help to secure positions in Holland for later action.

In November the 101st was relocated to France to recuperate and start to train again for the next jump, which never happened. On December 16 the Germans launched a surprise offensive into the Ardennes Forest of Belgium—the Battle of the Bulge, where the 101st fought alongside ground troops.

After the fall of Germany in May 1945, the last assignment of the 101st during World War II was to occupy "Eagle's Nest," Hitler's vacation hideaway in Bavaria. The division returned to France to train for an airborne invasion of Japan, but the Japanese surrendered. The 101st was deactivated in France on November 30, 1945.

The division later was reactivated and saw action in Vietnam, Laos, Cambodia, Saudi Arabia, Iraq (twice), Somalia, Bosnia, and Afghanistan. Today the 101st is based at Fort Campbell, Kentucky. ★

About a month later, good old Harry Truman dropped the bomb in Japan, and the war was over.

Now I don't want to brag, but we were crack troops. We had men who had serious wounds in Normandy who were taken back to hospitals in England, and when they were going to be transferred to some other unit when they got better, they'd say, "Oh no, we want to go back to the 506." In fact, some of them went AWOL so they could report back to us. When they did, the colonel ended up with a lot of paperwork to do, but he said, "If you're smart, and you want to come back to this outfit, you're always welcome."

I still keep in contact with a lot of—well, not a lot, there's not that many anymore—friends in California, Pennsylvania, and New York. Anybody who wears the parachute wings is a brother.

They called us heroes, but the heroes are the ones who are still over there.

AFTER THE WAR . . .

Paul Miller took a well-deserved year off when he left the service. He worked for Pennsylvania Power and Light (PP&L), and then passed the civil service test for the Pennsylvania Game Commission and served as game protector for more than thirty-three years before retiring. Miller and his wife, Frances, have five children and have celebrated more than fifty-seven years of marriage.

☆ William Smith ☆

Columbia, Pennsylvania

••

William Smith was a pilot who flew fifty missions over Europe. The missions involved photo reconnaissance, escort, and strafing activities.

••

I was a seventeen-year-old senior in high school when I enlisted. I always wanted to fly, and two months later I was inducted into the Army Air Forces. At primary flight school in Americus, Georgia, I flew seventy hours in the Stearman Trainer. After that I went on to Greenwood, Mississippi, and flew BT-13s for seventy hours, and then to Dothan, Alabama, for my advanced training. I got my wings in February 1944.

We had a chance to go to a P-38 outfit or P-51 outfit. A P-38 has two engines, and none of us were trained in two engines. We were single-engine fellows and didn't want to take a chance. So we decided to take the single-engine P-51. We got assigned to the 308th Fighter Squadron in July, and on August 18 I flew my first combat mission.

I was prepared for flying, but not for combat. Even fellows that came into the outfit before me and experienced pilots said they weren't ready for combat. But when you go to a target, there are 500 antiaircraft guns that can shoot you and 300 fighter planes that try to destroy you. Guys that say they weren't scared were crazy.

We were going through Ploiesti, the oil fields that the Germans had in Romania. Our job was to escort B-24 bombers to the target, wait for them to come off the target, and then pick them up so the fighters didn't shoot them down. But most of the planes were shot down with flak. I realized then that bomber crews were the real heroes of the air war.

One time we lost a couple of guys—they just pulled out of formation, went down, and that was it. They surmised that it was a loss of oxygen or something else. Once at around 32,000 feet, I felt a tingling in my feet and I saw spots in front of my eyes. I happened to look down, and the oxygen hose on the mask had pulled out of its plug. I was on the verge of blacking out, so I pushed the hose in, turned the oxygen on full, and everything came back to normal. But if you were without oxygen a couple of minutes at 35,000 feet, you would black out and may get into a spin and never recover. We lost guys and they never knew what happened.

You always flew the same plane. Some days were rained out, some days you had a rotation. But if you were going to fly, you flew that plane. Mine was Weary Willie. I had an aunt that was close by, and she called me "Weary Willie" when I was a kid. Since I didn't know what to name the plane—I wasn't married, I didn't have a girlfriend—I chose Weary Willie. That stuck.

When you went to bed at night, you never knew what was coming up: an escort mission, a strafing mission. At about 5:00 or 6:00 A.M. we'd go to a briefing, where they prepared us. The bombers always took off before we did, because they were slower. Then we would take off and beat them to the designated time and place, where we picked them up in fighter territory. It took about five and a half hours.

For a strafing mission, you shoot up anything that moves. One day I destroyed three enemy oil barges with machine guns. Get a couple of shots in there and phew, up they go. If you saw trucks, if you saw high-tension wires, shoot them up. Things with military value like trains and trucks and oil barges were called targets of opportunity. Everything was game except civilians.

One day we were on a strafing mission and we got separated somehow. I saw this one fellow in our squadron and told him I didn't have any ammunition. I figured I'd let him fly off my wing, since he had ammunition; if anything jumped, he could help me. We flew back and landed, and started talking a little bit. I said, "Boy I'm glad you came along," He said, "Why?"

I told him I was out of ammunition, and he said, "So was I." Here we were, two guys tooling around Germany with no ammunition!

Another time we were strafing, and I saw a train and went after it. I was going fast and I didn't know what was on the train. It could have been important people or full of munitions—anything. I got the engine, but then all hell broke loose. Here it was a flak train. I never saw so many red ping-pong balls coming in all my life. I was amazed I wasn't hit. I got the train, but they didn't get me.

Strafing missions were pretty hairy. I lost a wingman during one raid. I didn't know whether he burned or crashed, but after the war I found that he was killed on that mission. Anything dangerous could happen, even flying itself. You would take off and not know what was going to happen—engine trouble, oxygen trouble, flak, fighters. We used to fly over the Alps and look down at their menacing snow. There was no place to land there, and you would swear that the engine was running rough because of the way it sounded.

You had two wing tanks of 102 gallons each, and you had a fuselage tank in the back. So you had a little over six hours' flying time. The only time I ran out of fuel was when I almost missed Italy. After that mission, they called me the best navigator in the 31st Fighter Group. They always kidded me about that.

We were over Blechhammer, Germany. It was bad weather and we got separated. I was by myself, and it's an awful feeling to be a couple hundred miles inside of Germany all alone. I wasn't sure what was going to happen, but I figured I would make a heading and get back to my base. So I kept flying and flying, and thought I should hit Italy soon. And out of the corner of my eye, I looked over and saw this island, but I didn't know of any islands in the Adriatic. I flew over, and here it was the heel of Italy—I almost missed it completely. If I would have missed that heel, nobody would have ever known where I was. I would have been a goner. And when I got back to the field, I just had enough gas to pull off the runway, and then I was empty.

The most traumatic thing was an accident with that P-51 that I brought in. There was a mechanical failure, and it came into the field and caught on fire. There were flames on both sides of the engine. How I landed that thing I'll never know, and it was a miracle I got out of it. I had a concussion and hurt my back, and was sitting there like nothing happened. Two enlisted men from another squadron pulled me out, and they both got the Soldier's Medal for it. I still have problems today with my back, but it's one of those things you get over.

You had to depend on people. When you flew, you depended on your wingman. And when you were a young pilot starting out, your flight leader depended on you, because you had to have your neck on a swivel looking out and back. When we said to a fellow, "I'm going to do this," we did it. No ifs, ands, or buts. Your word was your bond. Everybody that doesn't know what to do should go in the service, because it opens your eyes up.

I was once in a dogfight with a German FW-190. I didn't get him and he didn't get me—a Mexican standoff. There were eight of us that jumped twenty-four of those guys, and that was my only chance to shoot down a German plane.

We had a photo reconnaissance outfit at our field, and we escorted reconnaissance planes that flew over the territory to pick up film. Usually they were stripped-down P-38s, no armament, no guns, nothing. We escorted them and we escorted the mosquito, an English plane. They were South Africans, but they had an English officer that was in charge of them, and I got to know them. We used to go down to their club and they used to come up to our club.

We were at two bases in Italy. One was at San Severo in the southern part, where we had barracks the Italians evacuated when they gave up. It was just a big, long stone building. My roommate, Bill Markley, and I had a room that had been a urinal. Some other fellows had to sleep in tents outside because there wasn't enough room, and it got pretty cold. It snowed one January, and that was the first time they had snow in that area for years. Then we moved up to a place called Mondolfo, where we flew the rest of our missions. Italians would come and sell us eggs at 50 cents apiece. A pack of cigarettes was worth a dollar. A can of beer was worth a dollar. I didn't smoke, so I gave them a pack of cigarettes and got two fresh eggs.

We weren't always dealing with combat. We went to Rome on what they call a rest camp, a week away from flying. I went to St. Peter's and saw the Colosseum and the Forum and all these places I never knew anything about. A fellow and I took a horse and buggy all around Rome. After some other missions, we had another rest camp. We went to Cannes on the Riviera and stayed in the Martinez, where we had a beautiful view of the Mediterranean. I think we paid 50 cents or a dollar a day to stay. I sat next to film actor Robert Preston, who played in *The Music Man*. Then one day I was walking, and this little short woman comes up and says hello to me. It was Lily Pons, the opera singer, and she was over there with her husband entertaining the troops.

We weren't allowed to tell our families anything about what was going on. The way they probably knew where I was is that I took a picture and the fellow on the base would develop it, and I would send the negatives home. Once I took a picture of the San Severo railroad station, and in the picture was a sign that read, "San Severo," although it was very tough to see. That's how my family knew where I was located. Otherwise I never told my family anything about the war. I tried to forget it all.

On December 9 this HE III—which was a German bomber—landed on our field. I don't know how he got through all our fighter planes without being shot down. But here they were landing to get away from the Russians. It was two Hungarian officers, a man, a wife, and a child. The reason I remember it so clearly was that the five of them ate at our mess hall. They had their lunch there that day. Of course, our guys seized the plane and gave the five of them to the British to put in an internment camp some place.

I had fifty missions. Thirty-three of them were escorting bombers, six were strafing raids, and six were photo reconnaissance missions. The others were miscellaneous, like one when I escorted planes that threw pamphlets over northern Italy, asking the troops to give up instead of fighting. The most rewarding mission was one where we picked up prisoners of war from Bucharest, Romania. Instead of killing somebody, I was helping to save somebody's life.

There were three of us that finished our fifty missions before the war was over. I had a pretty good commanding officer, who knew that a few of us needed five missions to get fifty (and knew the war was soon going to be over), so he gave us two missions in one day to get our fifty missions in. They were milk runs; an easy target. You weren't getting a chance to get shot down. The other guys who didn't finish their missions had to stay with the outfit until they came back to the States, and then some of them were mustered out.

After the fiftieth mission, I went to Naples, Italy, and got a boat for home. I was out in the Mediterranean when they declared VE Day and the war was over. We went through the Straits of Gibraltar, and the next day the captain said, "You will be glad to know that there were five German submarines that gave up the day before we went through the Straits of Gibraltar," which made everybody happy. We didn't know if there were still any die-hard Germans that wanted to sink an American ship. Then I went to Santa Ana, California, to be mustered out and by train to Fort Dix, New Jersey, to get discharged.

I still converse with this one fellow, Parke Shee, from south of Chicago. And we kid each other—he will tell me things I don't remember, and I'll tell him things he doesn't remember. He hopes we are the last two guys left in the squadron so that we'll be able to lie and tell all these combat stories, and there won't be anybody to refute them. I saw him last at a reunion in Dayton, Ohio.

I belong to the VFW and the 31st Fighter Group Officers Association. And I belong to the P–51 Mustang Pilots Associations.

I'll sum up my fifty combat missions like the boys in the RAF and this flight commander of South Africans. They were a good bunch of fellows. They always said when they would come back from a mission and everything is happy—you don't get shot at, you know—that it was "a bloody good show." That was their favorite expression and how I cap my fifty missions: "a bloody good show."

AFTER THE WAR . . .

William Smith attended Franklin and Marshall College for one year, and then went into the family-run beer-distributing business for thirty-two years before retiring. He and his wife, Grace, are the parents of five children. Smith is still interested in aviation and attends air shows and expositions.

☆ Felix Lockman ☆

Norwood, Pennsylvania

• •

Felix Lockman was a crew chief in the 1st Air
Commandos of the Army Air Forces. He was involved
in the China-Burma-India Campaign, flying supplies
through the Himalayas to British troops.

• •

I was an automobile mechanic in Hazleton, and one day I took off from
work, went downtown, and found a recruiting officer there. We got to
talking, and he asked, "What would you like to do?" I said, "I'd like to go
to aircraft mechanic school." He said, "Okay, they're starting one very
shortly, and if you sign up, we can send you to the school. Why don't you
go up to this doctor and get your physical?" So I went up to the doctor's
office and they said, "Do you want to get in?" I said, "Yes." He said, "Okay,
you're 1-A." And that was it. A couple of days later I got on a train at 4:00
A.M. and went to Philadelphia, where I was sworn in and got my uniform.

I started aircraft mechanics school at Chanute Field, Illinois, on January
1, 1942. We went to classes five or six days a week, and I finished the course
in June. Toward the end of the course, they asked each of us what we wanted
to do after we graduated. I said I wanted to go to gunnery school in Colorado, but they told me I couldn't, because I had been selected to be an

instructor, teaching aircraft mechanics. They had spoiled my plans. All these guys were going overseas, and here I was stuck in school.

They sent me to Goldsboro, North Carolina—I was a private then—but the school wasn't quite completed yet, so I sat around and did nothing. The first thing I knew, I was a corporal, with stripes and more in pay—$21 a month. When school started, I made sergeant, and after a couple months I made staff sergeant.

I was teaching school and getting bored. I wanted to get out of there. So one day somebody came around with a letter that said they were looking for volunteers for a one-way trip. Everybody's reaction was, "A one-way trip? It's a suicide." And that's what it was.

A few of us signed up—we had to find out what was going on—so they told us to report to the other end of the field. We walked in and they started interviewing us. They asked if anybody was married, and one or two guys were, so they asked what the wives thought. They said that whatever they decided was okay with them.

Then I said, "Major, they told us it was a one-way trip." The major turned to the captain next to him and said, "You know, some SOB is giving us a bad name." Then he said to me, "Sergeant, it's this way: It's war. You're going over to India, and you'll be there six months. If you're lucky and if everything goes right, you'll be back." Well, that sounded better than a one-way trip. So I looked at my buddies and said, "I'm going to miss you guys." You know, at a time like that, there's a lot of black humor.

The organization I volunteered for was the 1st Air Commando Group. The commanding officer was Phillip Cochran, who turned up as a main character in the comic strip "Terry and the Pirates." In the comics they called him Flip Corkin.

We got orders to go to Florida. We stayed in a hotel in Miami for two or three days, and then they told us, "You're going up to the eighth floor." The eighth floor was like a prison. They had guards on the elevator, on the stairs, everywhere. When you went to the eighth floor, it meant that within twenty-four hours you were going to leave the country.

So we got all packed up, and early in the morning we went to Miami Airport, got on an airplane, and went to British Guiana. We stayed overnight before flying on to Natal, Brazil. Our next flight was halfway across the ocean to Ascension Island, where we had a pit stop, had breakfast, gassed up, and took off for the Gold Coast—Ghana. There we got into another airplane and hopscotched across Africa to India. That's where we grouped up and started to put airplanes together.

They had a big dirigible hangar there, and our planes—airplanes, gliders, and helicopters—would be shipped to us in a crate, and the natives would take the crate and make an apartment out of it. It was big enough, about eight feet by eight feet and about thirty feet long, made of two-inch plank. You could build a house out of it, and they did.

Often the planes would be covered with what they call Cosmoline. It's real gunky grease, a preservative. We'd have to wash all that off, put the wings on the airplane, and install equipment that had been taken out for shipment. After that the planes' mechanics—the ones assigned to the fighter groups—would take care of them.

We were assembling C-64s, and each mechanic was assigned to a pilot. I ended up with Captain Wagner. He asked me if I knew how to fly. I said, "No." He said, "You're going to learn, 'cause if I get my can shot off, you're going to have to bring me back." So I learned how to fly. After a while, it got to where I could land and take off with no problem, but I never got any credit for it, because I was just a crew chief as far as the military was concerned.

Until the invasion of Burma, most of our flights were what we called administrative. We'd fly down to Calcutta or some other base—it wasn't into combat—and we'd do business or haul supplies or something. When we'd come back, the pilot would go and rest, and I had to fuel up the airplane. If there were any discrepancies, I had to take care of them, and sometimes I'd work till 9:00 at night by flashlight just to make sure the airplane was ready for the flight the next morning. The pilot would be dozing off at the time or in the club drinking, but the crew chief had a full-time job. Flying was just part of it.

The night of the invasion of Burma is one I'll never forget. Captain Wagner and I were on a flight somewhere, and when we returned to our base in Asansol, we found out we were going to Burma. Our flight consisted of about eight airplanes of the light cargo type. We were "tail-end Charlie," which meant we would be the last in the group. It was our job to keep all the others in a very loose formation. Instructions were radio silence and no lights.

It was about midnight when we took off, heading for Broadway, which is the name they gave to the landing site for the invasion. I think only the lead ship actually knew the destination. Everything was okay as we approached Burma. The only way we knew where the other ships were was by the exhaust of their engines. Everyone stayed in formation, but after a few hours we began to have strays. My pilot tried to herd them back into formation, but after a while we lost sight of all the exhaust flames.

We did our best to find Broadway, but in the dark we couldn't see any landmarks. We had a moonlit sky, but we were in an area we had never been in. We couldn't find our position on the map, and we could see nothing but jungle underneath us. Our fuel was getting low, so Wagner decided we'd better head for home. We both felt terrible that we didn't get to our destination.

We were headed back toward India when our fuel started getting dangerously low. We decided that when the engine started to sputter from lack of fuel, we would turn all the power switches on with the hope that when the aircraft crashed, it would catch fire, and then as we parachuted down we could find it. We agreed to find our way to the burning aircraft if we could, stay in the area for about two days, then head back to India on foot.

As we were making these plans, I spotted two rows of lights on the ground. I showed the pilot and he asked, "Whose are they?" But we had no choice. We only had about fifteen minutes of fuel left. As we dropped down for a landing, since we didn't know whose field it was, we had to prepare ourselves again. We agreed that if the field didn't look friendly, Wagner would hit the throttle. We knew we couldn't go too far, but at least we would have a chance to escape.

There was no shooting at us as we made the approach, so we thought it fairly safe. A jeep pulled up and signaled us to follow. As Wagner parked the plane, I told him to try to stay clear, and if the natives weren't friendly to start running, and I would spray them with the tommy gun I had trained on them. After a while Wagner signaled me to join him. I got out of the plane still holding the tommy gun, and I heard an English soldier call, "Put that bloody thing down." It turned out to be a British field, and they were expecting one of their aircraft that night.

We sat around a fire and drank tea until daybreak. They gave us enough fuel to take us back to our base in India, but the rest of our flight had been scattered over Burma. Some of the crews had to bail out and find their way back. I hope we made up for it when we got to Broadway a couple of days later with needed supplies.

Another memorable trip was the time we were supplying the Chinese with food. We carried huge bags of rice that must have weighed 200 pounds. It was a free-fall drop. We located the drop zone and made a pass, and I pushed the rice out of the plane. After what was to be our fourth and last drop, I watched the bag head for the drop zone and noticed someone running after it. All I could figure is that one of the Chinese tried to catch the falling bag, and I believe he did. It looked like they both reached the spot at the same time.

There were a couple of occasions where we thought we were going to have to step out of the airplane because we ran into a problem.

One time we went down to Asansol and turned our parachutes in for repacking. We didn't have anybody to repack chutes up-country, but when we got to Asansol, they had a parachute rigger and a room for it. I turned mine in, and the CO called me back and said, "We want you to sign a statement of charges: $85." I said, "For what?" "For a parachute." I said, "Like hell. I turned mine in." He said, "Go up and take a look at it." I did. The parachute was made of silk, but if you picked it up, it would disintegrate in your hands. It got wet so many times it had rotted. I just about got sick.

Not too long before that, we had been flying along and there was a big thunderhead ahead of us, so the pilot stuck the nose down, and as he was going down, there was a big explosion—dust and everything else. So when the pilot leveled out, he killed the engine and everything was okay, but I looked around, and the top of the airplane was gone. It was made of rag, all fabric, and when you went into a dive, it just ballooned, and that was the weakest part. It took our antennas and everything off.

As soon as it exploded, I had my hand on the jettison handle so I could kick the door out and step out, but it turned out the engine was okay. I went all the way in the back, and the pilot kicked the controls to see how the tail services were, and they seemed to be all right. So I said, "Well, if anything starts acting up, we can always step out and we'd get rescued somehow."

The base was three-quarters of an hour away. We made it to the base and circled around to get ready for a landing, and we got a red biscuit gun, which was a signal light. Green meant it was okay to land, red meant don't land. After about three tries the pilot said, "Well the hell with them." And he came in and landed. As soon as we landed, the engineering officer came up in a jeep and said, "You got the red light. How come you landed?" The pilot said, "Take a look." He looked around the plane and said, "How come you didn't bail out?"

That was a time that we just about bailed out. And that's what came to mind when I picked up the parachute and it was rotten. I could just picture myself bailing out, looking up at my chute—and that would be it. Zoom, right down.

One other incident stands out. Mandalay had been hit pretty hard by the British and the Americans because it was a Japanese stronghold. We had a base that was ten or fifteen minutes from there, and after it fell you could go in and walk around. So I had one of my buddies fly me in there. I was supposed to meet them back at the airstrip at 4:00 P.M., so I walked around for a while, and when I was heading for the airstrip to be picked up, I had to go over a big pagoda hill that was 500 or 600 feet high, and there were steps on four sides.

As I started up, I met a Gurkha officer. Gurkhas are from Nepal, and they were part of the British Army. We chatted and he said, "Where are you going?" I said, "Up this side and down the other side." He said, "Do you have a strong stomach? Because there's a lot of bodies."

The China-Burma-India Theater: The "Forgotten War"

Many men who fought in the China-Burma-India (CBI) Theater of World War II considered it to be the "Forgotten War," because it got the least amount of supplies, support, troops, and publicity, compared with the massive European and Pacific Theaters. CBI operations were important for keeping military and food supply lines open to China, then led by Gen. Chiang Kai-shek, and for serving as a buffer to keep the Japanese from invading India. The United States supported China against both Japanese aggression and internal division by Communists, and also viewed China as a potential staging area from which to eventually invade Japan.

Starting in late 1941, Japan invaded much of Southeast Asia. Burma (today known as Myanmar), a British territory, fell on March 8 when the Japanese entered Rangoon, its capital. They closed the Burma Road, the last overland route to China, whose ports had been sealed off by Japanese naval forces. It was important to keep the Chinese military viable; that kept 750,000 Japanese troops engaged who otherwise would be fighting the Allies elsewhere.

In the invasion, U.S. lieutenant general Joseph W. "Vinegar Joe" Stilwell, who had been newly named Chiang Kai-shek's chief of staff to oversee CBI operations, was forced to retreat to India. He planned to retake Burma, but in the meantime, the Allies employed a two-pronged strategy: create an airborne supply route over the Himalayas from India, while hacking a new jungle road from India to the northern part of the old Burma Road. Extending 470 miles, the new Ledo Road took more than two years to complete.

The airlift began in July 1942. This was some of the most hazardous flying in the world, as heavily laden transport planes had to climb steeply in poor weather to clear 10,000- to 22,000-foot mountain peaks, the ridge of which was known as the Himalaya Hump. During the two-year-plus airlift, the Allies flew more than 167,000 trips and moved about 700,000 tons of gasoline, arms, men, and food, losing some 460 aircraft and 792 men to crashes and Japanese fighter attacks. On the ground, a group of 3,000 Americans fighting under Brig. Gen. Frank D. Merrill ("Merrill's Marauders") fought guerrilla-style behind Japanese lines, while also enduring tropical diseases and monsoons.

Allied troops, mainly British, slowly won back portions of Burma throughout 1944. By January 1945, the Ledo Road was completed. On May 3, 1945, the Allies retook Rangoon. China lost importance to the Allies, because Chiang Kai-shek became preoccupied with internal conflicts with the country's eighty million Communists rather than helping the Americans and British in Burma. When the Allies discarded China as an invasion platform for Japan's home islands, they abandoned the CBI Theater. ★

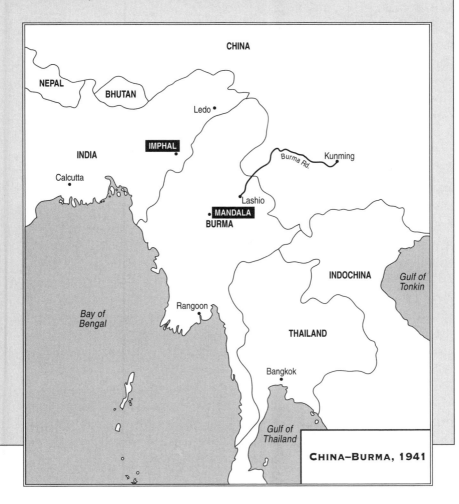

CHINA–BURMA, 1941

The bodies were Japanese. There were a lot of caves in this pagoda hill, and the only way they could get the Japanese out of the caves was with a flamethrower. They would throw a flame in there and burn them out, and they'd come out screaming and burning. Then maybe they'd shoot them, or maybe they just dropped dead themselves. On one side of the hill, the British had covered the bodies with lime, but going down the other side, they didn't cover them with lime, and there's nothing smells as bad as a rotting human body.

When I got to the airstrip, there was an airplane there and a couple of brass. I had a camera, so I went over and started taking pictures. It turned out to be Lord Louis Mountbatten. He came over to me and I took a picture of him. He said, "How long have you been in the area?" I said, "Since the beginning of the operation." He said, "I thought all you blokes went home." I said, "Well, they forgot a lot of us."

After a while my pilot arrived and I went back to the base. I was going past the commanding officer's tent—Buck Beasley was captain at the time—and I told him I had a conversation with Mountbatten and he figured that all of us had gone home. He said, "Well, you are. I just got a radio to send you home." I said, "See that? When you pull the right strings . . ." But I'm sure it was just a coincidence that they told me I was going home right then.

I stayed there a week before I left. I didn't do anything, just lolled around in the jungle, then I flew back to our base and stayed there two weeks. I didn't want to go home, because I was going from a known to an unknown, and I didn't know what was going to be at the end, so I was kind of hesitant. But then they said, "You have to go." I had been there sixteen months instead of the six months they told us it would be, and you get kind of acclimated to whatever you are doing. It becomes a life. Now I was going into an unknown. And it was a scary thing.

I learned one thing in the service: Never make fast friends, friends that are part of your life. Be friendly, but not to a point where it's an obsession. This friend of mine and I were kind of buddies, we'd date together and go out together, and we got to be pretty chummy. He went out one day and never came back. He was in an airplane hauling gasoline—we used to haul gasoline up into Burma for the airplanes—and they flew into a mountain. They found him hanging on a tree. The airplane had exploded and caught fire.

That hit me hard, so I made up my mind then that I'd have no friends that would upset me if they went. And I just live that. I have a lot of acquaintances, I have a lot of friends, but I don't have any deep friends, because after a while, you can't take that. And I'm getting too old.

Felix Lockman (L) and Capt. Sam Wagner (R) with a UC-64 Norseman in Burma.

My proudest accomplishment is that I made it back. That was my goal. A lot of my friends didn't, but I did. I would give a million dollars for the experience I had, but I wouldn't take $20 million to do it again. It was an experience you should never go through twice. But the main thing is, I made it. And I think I contributed to society.

AFTER THE WAR . . .

• •

Felix Lockman worked for thirty years as a mechanic, and later as an industrial engineer, building helicopters for Piasecki Aircraft and the Boeing Company. He was active in many community organizations, including the Boy Scouts, the VFW, and the Norwood Fourth of July Committee. He and his wife were married fifty-seven years and raised four sons. He died in April 2004.

• •

☆ John Wiest ☆

Williamstown, Pennsylvania

- -

John Wiest joined the navy while he was still in high school.
He was assigned to the USS *Vincennes* and was a ship's cook.
He was wounded during a battle with the Japanese.

- -

My dad had three farms, a lot of milk cows, steers, pigs, turkeys, chickens, and a lot of work. There were seven children in our family. I had good grades in Hubley School—in fact, I was the best in arithmetic for a long time. I played soccer and basketball, I was on the track team, and played baseball. My dad would always tell me, "You have to come home right after school—we have a lot of farm work to do." But I wanted to play sports. So when he insisted I come home after school, I decided to join the navy. I was in eleventh grade, and he didn't want to let me go, so I got my mother to sign the papers. That was in January 28, 1941. I enlisted in the navy before Pearl Harbor.

I completed my boot camp down in Norfolk, Virginia, and got transferred to the USS *Vincennes* CA44, a heavy cruiser with about 1,100 men on board. We made a couple of trips to Alaska and Iceland, where we experienced the worst storm I've ever been in. Everybody had to get off the ship's top deck and go down below, and close the door caps down so no water would get into the apartments.

After Pearl Harbor we were shipped back to the Pacific coast, and from there I was in four different kinds of battles: I was in the Coral Sea Battle, I was in the Midway Battle, I was over in Guadalcanal, and I was in the Battle of Savo Island. That was the last one, where the ship was sunk.

We were along some of the aircraft carriers, and one was the *Yorktown,* that was hit when we were alongside it. We were shooting airplanes down, and these suicide Japanese planes would come down at us. If they dropped the bomb and they didn't hit your ship, they would come straight at you with the plane. We were lucky—we didn't get hit with a suicide plane—but it was very nerve-racking. You didn't know what to expect. But we got through all those other battles until the time we took Savo Island from Japan.

We sent marines and soldiers and supplies in, and we were supposed to protect the harbor. We knew there was a Japanese fleet out there, but we did not think the Japanese ships were as fast as they were. They caught us at 2:00 in the morning, and they sank three of our heavy cruisers at one time. We were hit with three torpedoes; that's what sank the ship. We had fifty or sixty bombs and shells that hit us.

I was a ship's cook, and during battle, my job was to be in a passageway with ten men, and when they sent the shells up to that deck, we were supposed to pick the shells up and send them up to the guns. During the battle, the Japs sent a couple of shells into the side of the ship, and they exploded. Of the ten men in there, only two men came out of there alive—me and another fellow. We were taught, when we got in battle, if we were wounded or in need of help, to go to the mess hall. The tables were all tied up at the ceiling, clearing the floor.

Well, I was wounded, shot in the back, had shrapnel in my neck, and was shot in the legs. So I went to the mess hall, and while I was waiting for somebody to come, I saw a lot of dead sailors all over the floor—you had to crawl over them. While I was in there, they dropped some bombs on us, and one of these mess tables fell down and hit me on the leg. It tore the muscle right off the leg. They cut the leg open and tied it to the bone.

And then they announced, "Abandon ship!" One big marine helped me up through the manhole door and said, "Now you have to help yourself." I had to crawl over the dead sailors until I got up to the deck. I found one of my ship's cooks that worked with me in the galley. He was stunned—had shell shock or something. I asked him, "Would you give me a navy life jacket?" He reached over and got a jacket for me, and I put it on as best I could.

When the ship started to turn over, I slid down the side, and a sailor who was there grabbed onto me. When we hit the water, we went down—the suction of the ship sinks you down under the water—and he lost his grip on me. Well, I had a life jacket on and he didn't. I didn't see him after that.

When I came up, I held my breath as long as I could. I had some water and oil in my stomach. I spit that out and I started swimming away from the ship. I spent ten hours floating around in the ocean. It was around 2:00 or 2:30 A.M. when the ship went down. There were a lot of men floating in the dark ocean. A lot of sharks were in the water. Some people were grabbed by sharks and wounded that way—killed, maybe—but they didn't get hold of me. They say 337 were killed, 119 were wounded. Some might have drowned who were not wounded, but they didn't have a chance to get off the ship. I was just one of the lucky ones.

When daylight came, there were small lifeboats going around trying to pick sailors out of the water. When they came across me, they said, "We have room for one more sailor." They picked me out of the water and put me on the boat, and I said, "I don't believe I'll make it. I've been shot through the neck, in the legs, in the back." And they said, "Yes, Dutchman, you'll make it."

They took me to a destroyer, where they put me on a chair, tied my hands back, and slit my throat open, because I was shot through the neck and couldn't breathe, and I couldn't swallow. If that piece of shrapnel would have cut my windpipe, it would have killed me, but it just closed it halfway shut. So they slit my throat and got the piece of shrapnel out. Then they sewed my throat shut, and I could swallow and breathe again.

I was taken to a hospital in New Zealand for a couple of months, and after that they shipped me to San Diego, where I spent four months in the hospital. Then I went for rehabilitation leave, to heal and to go home. They might give you two weeks off once you were able to help yourself. At home there was a girl, Carolyn Kembel—she was a twin—and I had gone with her before I went in the navy. We decided to get married. We had a big wedding, all last-minute. So when I had to go back, I took her along out to California.

I was in pretty good shape, but I thought since I had been wounded so bad, they would give me shore duty. But I was assigned to the USS *Cree* 84, which was an oceangoing tugboat, and my wife had to go home alone. I spent a year and a half aboard the USS *Cree* 84. Never got off the ship anywhere.

We used to travel with the fleet to go bombard Japan, or wherever the fleet went. If a ship was hit or had to be towed in, a tugboat would tug them. So I didn't get any time off. We had seventy-five men on an oceangoing tugboat, and I did all the ordering of supplies. I had to figure out what we needed to have to eat for a month or so, and most of it was dehydrated food. When you got a turkey or a chicken, they were not cleaned the way they are now. The insides were left inside, and it was frozen that way. Then we cooks would thaw the chicken, take the inside out, finish cleaning it, and then cook it, too. That was my job.

When my time was up, they wanted me to stay. They said, "We'll make you ensign, we'll give you whatever you want to be if you will stay in the navy." Well, I had gotten married and wanted to get home! But the captain said, "I can't spare you." So I did something some people don't have the nerve to do, and maybe I shouldn't have: I went over the captain's head and wrote to Washington, D.C. My regular navy time was up, I was not in the reserves, and I wanted out. I got out real quick when I wrote to Washington.

AFTER THE WAR . . .

John Wiest headed up a number of businesses, including a farm, a grocery store, and a soft ice cream shop. He also had a restaurant and motel business for forty-five years. Wiest and his wife together raised a son and a daughter. He lost his wife of fifty-four years in 1999.

☆ Michael Mauritz ☆

Turtle Creek, Pennsylvania

••

Michael Mauritz was a fighter pilot in the Army Air Forces.
He wrote *The Secret of Anzio Bay,* an autobiography that describes
the resurfacing of his plane fifty-four years after it crashed.

••

A couple of years ago I got a letter from an amateur historian in Italy. He said that some people were fishing in Italy, just south of Anzio, and they were getting their nets caught on something. They complained about it to the authorities. Scuba divers were sent down, and they found my plane, the Skipper. They found my name inside the plane and looked through the American white pages and on the Internet, and found that there were only five Michael Mauritzes in the United States, so he sent a letter to the five. I wrote back and said I was the man that he is looking for. That's how the plane got to be removed from the ocean.

It's a P-40L, a Curtis Wright. It was a single-engine fighter craft with the Maryland engine, which is a British engine. Most of the P-40s had the Allison engine, and this is the only one of its kind. It's in a museum now. It's not operational.

I hadn't told my family much about the war. As a matter of fact, when I wrote my book, they read it and it was a surprise to them.

I was adopted when I was nine months old, and I was separated from my birth family. I learned German from my foster family, so when the Germans captured me, I could speak to them. Some people think that that saved my life, because the three Germans who captured me were younger than I was at the time. I was twenty-two then.

I joined the service when I was twenty-one. I enlisted in the air force, hoping that I could become a pilot. Eventually I went through the training, through aviation cadet school, and graduated as a pilot in Victoria, Texas. Then I went through replacement training in Sarasota, Florida, with P-40s.

I went overseas to Casablanca in the early part of 1943, and in the later part of '43 I wound up on the Italian front, flying combat in the 79th Fighter Group, with the 86th Squadron. Our outfit landed at Anzio around January 22. We established a beachhead, and then moved to Naples, Capodichino, from where I took off on January 31, 1944.

That morning my buddy and I went out to the airport on the motorcycle I had at the time. We went to the briefing, but we weren't supposed to fly that morning. So I went to repair some parts on the motorcycle. As I was doing that, the order was changed, and we were told that our group would have to fly the mission. It was a reconnaissance mission, in a sense that twelve of us would fly up to Anzio from Naples, which was about 100 miles, at about 10,000 feet, and protect men on the ground. I was in the group just about two weeks, so I didn't have a plane of my own—I eventually would have if I hadn't been missing in action—so I was assigned to Skipper.

Now a P-40 usually runs at about 130 degrees Celsius. It heats up really quickly on the ground as you are taxiing, and if you taxi around too long, your engine will get too hot and you will detonate on takeoff. But as soon as you get up in the air, it cools off. So mine was all right, and I took off with the group. But my plane kept getting hotter and hotter as soon as I got up in the air. I called Colonel Nielsen—he was the leader of the flight—and told him my plane was overheating. It got way over 150 degrees Celsius, and the temperature needle was hitting the peg. We were using 100-octane gasoline at the time, and it's very flammable. The colonel told me there was a landing strip at Anzio, so we were headed there, but the plane started acting up, so I had to make a 180-degree turn and land the plane in the water just below Anzio.

It turned out the plane had been sabotaged. Somebody had stuffed pieces of a parachute in the cooling system. That was done quite often with planes.

Somebody who didn't like us on the Italian side sabotaged the planes. That's what happens in war. So I made a very nice landing in the water, and got out on the wing and watched the plane sink.

That's when I was captured. They took me to their CO, and he took my leather flying jacket. He wanted it as a souvenir, I guess. They just gave me a blanket. Now this was January, and I had just come out of the Mediterranean Sea, and it was still cold.

They put me on a motorcycle with two Germans and took me back to Cisterna, to a building where they were keeping about 600 soldiers from the 1st and 3rd Ranger Battalions who were captured. I was interviewed by a German officer, who gave me a pack of cigarettes. He could speak perfect English. Then they took me upstairs, where they introduced me to Captain Schuster, the ranking officer of the Allies.

Right after that they took us to a railroad station and took us to Rome. They dropped us off at the Colosseum, and we marched through Rome as a propaganda show. From there we were taken to a prison camp just north of Rome.

Well, from the first day I was captured, it was my idea to get away somehow. One morning I told Captain Schuster, "These Germans are completely confused here. Things are not set up right yet and kind of disorganized, so I'm going to try to get out of here." He said he wanted both of us to go.

We were being kept in one barracks, and there were three empty barracks between us and the barbed-wire fence. I told the captain that maybe we could work our way through the empty cabins and get to the fences. When the guards weren't watching, we snuck into the next barracks and the next one, and finally got to the last barracks.

There was a guard at the main gate fifty or sixty feet away, just outside of voice range, and at the end of the barracks there was another guard who had some Allied prisoners cleaning up the area. There were two fences five or six feet apart, and there were two Italians working between them with some kind of electrical wires. They were young fellows and they were singing. Captain Schuster knew a little Italian, so he asked them if they were friendly with us or the Germans. They said they didn't particularly care for the Germans.

Now the guard at the right, behind the barracks, would walk back and forth, so while he was behind the barracks and out of sight, the captain went out and pried up the wire of the first fence and went over, and pried up the next one and went under, and made it into a ditch which was several feet on the other side.

Then it was my turn. I got under the first fence, and as I was getting up from the first fence, the guard at the main gate looked back toward me. So I just pretended that I was working with the two Italians. Then, when he turned around and went back behind the barracks, I went under the next wire. The Italians could have very easily given us away, but they helped us. In a way they saved our lives.

The first night we had to walk. My legs were sore because I was a pilot and I never walked much. The captain was infantry and his legs were fine. After that day walking up this mountain, my legs were pretty sore. We stopped at a house, it was dark already, and asked them if we could sleep someplace. They wouldn't let us in the house, but they said we could sleep in their little shed. We went in there, and the floor was covered with walnuts, so we had to sleep on walnuts that night. From there it was anybody's guess what we would do next. We didn't know how far we were from the front, but we knew we were north of Rome.

Instead of heading toward Switzerland, where it was cold, or to the Mediterranean, where the Germans were headed, we decided to go across the Apennine Mountains to Ancona. It was quite a distance. We traveled about 300 miles total during the five months it took us to get to friendly territory. We had a lot of help along the way. We had to watch in several places, but there were very few Fascists compared to the ones that helped us. We escaped on February 9, and it took us until May to get to the east coast, which was the Adriatic Sea. That's where we were hoping to get a submarine to pick us up.

As we got closer to the front, people were more afraid to keep us, so we had to split up into individual houses, because they couldn't trust their neighbors, or maybe a Fascist would see us and they would turn us in. We had trouble with some priests one time coming to the house. We didn't know whether they would be friendly or not. We were protected by the family, but they were scared of us getting caught in the house. They would have all been killed.

One morning I went to see where Schuster was, and I found out that he had gone and had been picked up by the submarines. And he didn't tell them that I was there. I never heard from him after that. He was a loner. And he was trained to be a killer. That was his business and he enjoyed it. I can't blame him for that, because I was trained to fly an airplane. I could kill people like babies by dropping bombs, but I didn't have to face them. But we had to have people who could face people and fight with them and kill

POW Camps

Conditions in World War II prisoner-of-war camps ranged from spartan to hellish, varying by combat theater, branch of service of an individual POW, and the personalities of the guards or officers in command of an estimated total of 60 million to 68 million combatants, 16.1 million were Americans, and of these, some 130,200 were taken prisoner between 1941 and 1945. Nazi Germany held about 94,000 American POWs, and Japan held an estimated 27,000 to 36,000.

The Holocaust exposed the evil of Nazi brutality, leaving 6 million civilian Jews dead, but the Germans were no less cruel to Russian POWs, killing—by starvation, exposure, or both—at least 3.5 million of 5.5 million men captured. Likewise, the Soviet Union took revenge on its 3.1 million German POWs, killing 1 million through execution, starvation, overwork, or exposure. Germany treated American and British POWs better. Of the 94,000 U.S. POWs held by Germany, only 1,100 died in captivity, or about 1 percent.

Japanese camps, by contrast, were universally condemned as the most inhumane, and least survivable, of all. Prisoners suffered lack of food and water, clothing, ventilation, and sanitation. Approximately 200 camps existed in Japan proper, with more in occupied lands. Contrary to Geneva Convention rules, to which Japan did not subscribe anyway, camps were often located near military targets and not identified as POW facilities, so Allied bombers sometimes killed their own countrymen. Of the 27,000 to 36,000 American POWs held by Japan, an estimated 11,100 to 13,850 died, producing a fatality rate of about 40 percent. In short, only 3 out of 5 survived.

Both Germans and Japanese used POWs as slave labor. In Germany, POWs were put to work on farms, cultivating and planting fields, and on railroad track, repairing damage inflicted by Allied bombing. In Japan, workers were put to work in both government-owned and privately held enterprises, including steel mills, mines, and factories. Japan's military tradition held that surrender or being captured alive was dishonorable, so Allied POWs were treated as being lower than criminals.

The Japanese government moved many thousands of American and other POWs to work sites throughout China, Japan, Korea, the Philippines, and Thailand, aboard twenty-three unmarked prison vessels known as "hell ships." Men were jammed, standing, in the holds for days with little food or water. At least five such vessels were sunk by U.S. subs, ships, or planes, resulting the death of an estimated 5,000 American POWs.

In addition, Japan was known for its Unit 731, a notorious secret research lab that carried out biological and chemical warfare tests and dissected many live prisoners. Doctors performed such gruesome and always fatal experiments as learning how a man reacted to being subjected to freezing temperatures or low atmospheric pressure, having a bullet fired into his stomach, being injected with seawater, having various organs cut from his body, or being exposed to diseases such as anthrax or typhoid.

Escape from Japanese prison was almost impossible. Because most American POWs were white Caucasians, they couldn't blend into an Asian population without detection, as they could in Europe. Moreover, civilians in Japan or occupied China were reluctant to help, fearing horrible retribution—such as extermination of an entire family or a whole town—if they aided an escapee. A related but different attitude applied in Germany during the final year of the war. Hitler encouraged civilians to take justice into their own hands if they found a downed flier. Some German soldiers actually saved Allied men from vigilantes by taking them to the relative protection of a POW camp.

Both Japan and Germany used physical and mental methods to extract information, including beatings, food deprivation, torture, and solitary confinement. But the Nazis more often used subtle psychological methods that didn't require physical force. The Geneva Convention held that a POW need give only name, rank, and serial number, although later in the war, the U.S. military loosened that for airmen caught by the Japanese to allow them to spare their lives.

More than 100 POW camps existed in Germany, which also ran camps in occupied Austria, Byelorussia, Czechoslovakia, France, Lithuania, Greece, Poland, Russia, Serbia-Croatia, Slovenia, and

(continued on page 190)

(continued from page 189)

Ukraine. The Luftwaffe (German Air Force) ran camps for airmen, while the Wehrmacht (German Army) ran camps for ground soldiers. Stalags held enlisted men and noncommissioned officers (sergeants); oflags held officer POWs; stalag lufts held air force POWs; marlags held navy POWs; and milags held merchant marine POWs. The roofs of many POW camps in Germany were marked as such so that they could be seen from the air. A typical camp was bounded by two parallel rows of twelve-foot-high fences, separated by barbed wire and a trench, and punctuated every 100 meters by elevated guard towers.

Germany's feeding of POWs, while not on the starvation level of the Japanese, was still inadequate. The International Red Cross shipped food, clothing, and medicine to all Allied POW camps in Germany except for those holding Russians (Soviet dictator Josef Stalin had rejected the aid), allowing the men to escape the depths of malnutrition. The YMCA sent books, sports gear, musical instruments, and religious supplies.

Escape from a German POW compound was rare, but not unheard of. On March 24, 1944, seventy-six officers broke out of Stalag Luft 3, an event that was portrayed in a 1949 book and 1963 film of the same name, *The Great Escape.* Although many recaptured escapees were simply shot on the spot, the more determined and repeat escapees were interned in a special high-security prison, converted from Colditz Castle in Saxony. ★

them, because you can't win the war just in the air. You have to contact people on the ground.

One thing I would suggest is that soldiers don't become too much of a buddy with anybody. That way you don't get hurt, because a war is a war.

When I got back, I had orders that I had to be out of the combat area within seven days. They felt that there might be somebody spying on our side who might do me in or try to get some information out of me. So I had to get out of the war area.

Through all of this, my folks back home didn't know any of what I was doing. Nothing. Not until I came back home.

After all of this, I feel that there is something in our lives that moves us into certain directions that we have no control over. I feel that destiny plays a big part. For instance, finding the two Italian men working in between the fences in the prison camp. Why were they in that spot working on abandoned wires? It's a big world, and to have two men working there at just that moment, is that a coincidence? I don't think so.

AFTER THE WAR . . .

Michael Mauritz retired at the age of sixty-four from his position at the U.S. Steel Company in the Edgar Thompson Works in Braddock, Pennsylvania. He had been with the company for thirty-three years. Mauritz and his wife, Louise, are the parents of a son and daughter. For more information on his book, *The Secret of Anzio Bay,* published by Word Association Publishers, call 1-800-827-7903.

☆ Robert Book ☆

Quarryville, Pennsylvania

• •

Robert Book joined the service when he turned eighteen,
and trained as a radio operator in the Army Air Forces.
He was part of the 345th Bomb Group.
His crew flew missions against Japan in a B-25.

• •

I was out traveling with some friends in an automobile, and it came over
the radio that Japan had attacked Pearl Harbor. I wasn't quite eighteen
years old, still going to high school. It seemed like all my friends were going
into the service, so when school ended, I decided I wanted to get into pilot
training and I signed up.

I went down to Miami Beach for cadet training. Well, I'll tell you, the
army was never like this, because they had taken over all the hotels there in
Miami Beach, and we were living in the hotels on inner-spring mattresses;
I mean, we were really living it up. We took our physical training out on the
golf course, and then we would go down to the beach for a swim. So like I
said, the army was never like that.

It was the Army Air Forces then, it wasn't the U.S. Air Force like it is today.
Our basic training included shooting, learning about the M-1 rifle and the

.45 pistols that the army used. I don't know why they taught us those, because I think you could have thrown the pistol at the target and hit it quicker than you would shooting at it. It had so much recoil that every time you would pull the trigger, the gun would fly up and you would have to re-aim it again. We also got acquainted with the submachine gun, and when we got into gunnery training in Yuma, Arizona, we trained with the .50-calibers, because that was our gun when we were flying on the B-25. I passed basic training and got into cadet training, and we took what they called a psychomotor exam, which was a three-day test, and by the grace of God I passed.

They sent us to Toledo University to take a lot of college courses, and we were getting three years of college in one year. We would get up at 6:00 A.M. and get breakfast; we were in class at 7:00 and we were done at 3:00 P.M. Then it was physical training and then chow, and after that it was studies until 10:00 P.M. when it was lights out. And the next day it was the same thing all over again, until we got to the weekend.

The government decided they had too many guys training to be pilots, so they said unless you have an A average, you are out. Well, I was running B+, but B+ wasn't quite good enough. One day our commanding officer called me in and said, "We've decided you show aptitude for radio school, so you are going to be going for radio training." So I shipped out to radio school in Sioux Falls, South Dakota. When I got there, it was 35 degrees below zero, and it stayed that way. We lived in tarpaper barracks, with about twenty of us in a barracks, with just potbellied stoves to heat the place. Things were pretty chilly, but you kind of got acclimated to it. I passed radio school, and after we had gotten accustomed to the cold in Sioux Falls, they shipped us down to Yuma, Arizona, to gunnery school.

We got off the train, and it was 110 degrees with no shade and we about died. It took us about two weeks to get acclimated to the heat, and we started in our gunnery training on B-17s. Now that's a heavy bomber—four engines, one big tail. We would go up to about 30,000 feet and shoot at tow targets—a plane that was towing a target. Some of the guys were pretty reckless gunners, and they would even shoot the tail assembly on the plane of the guy who was towing the tow targets. Those guys took their life in their hands towing targets for the guys who were getting acclimated to firing a .50-caliber machine gun.

In order to pass the course, we had to be able to fieldstrip that .50-caliber machine gun blindfolded. They would put a piece in there that was defective, and we had to take out the defective piece and call for the piece we needed, and put the gun back together. There was a good reason they made you do it blindfolded. When you were flying at a high altitude, and it was dark and you were being attacked, you didn't want to turn on a light to let the enemy know where the plane was.

After we passed gunnery school, we were transferred to Greenville, South Carolina. Our crew was made up of fellows mostly from Pennsylvania. Our pilot came from Hanover and his name was Charles Fred Shultz, and we called him Dutch Shultz, after the gangster up in New York City. Our tail gunner was from Pittsburgh, and the bombagator was from Allentown. We all had two jobs on the B-25. First, we were gunners. My second job was radio operating. Then the engineer took care of the engine. The tail gunner also took care of fusing the bombs once we loaded them in the bomb bay. The pilot and copilot were gunners at the same time they flew the plane. But we all worked together as a team, and we had a bunch of good guys.

We were assigned a brand spanking new plane in Savannah, Georgia. We flew down to West Palm Beach, Florida, and the next day we flew down to Puerto Rico, then down to South America. We took off from Natal, Brazil, and flew over to Ascension Island, which is a great big rock out in the middle of the South Atlantic. We ended up in Dakar, French West Africa, when orders came for us to halt right there. We hung around there probably a month, until orders came that we were to return to the States.

When we got back to Savannah, they took our plane away from us, put us on a train, and sent us to San Francisco. They shipped our planes out to us by rail. I don't know why they didn't let us fly out to San Francisco, but that was the way it was.

Then they had us go over to Hawaii, where we took off and headed for Manila in the Philippines at what they called a replacement depot. That's when we were assigned to the 345th Bomb Group. They were over on Ie Shima, which was the island where Ernie Pyle was killed. In 1945 we arrived and replaced a crew there, and they were able to come home. The 345th was a fairly old outfit, and we were flying out of Ie Shima, making raids on Japanese shipping and other targets.

Our plane had four .50-caliber machine guns in the nose, and then on each side of the plane they had what they called package guns. The pilot fired them all with one button on the control stick inside the plane. When he pushed that button, there were eight .50-caliber machine guns that started firing at the target. Now he had to aim the plane; he didn't aim the guns. And when you dove on your target, he would press that button and open up those .50-caliber machine guns. Then George Wallace, our engineer, he had two .50s up on the top turret. He also could fire forward. And Ed Stevenson, the tail gunner, fired two twin .50s in the tail area, and I had a .50 on each side of the radio compartment. If we were attacked by fighters, we would call out, "One o'clock high!" and we would know what direction the plane was coming in.

Our job was mainly to blow up bridges, ammunition depots, anything that looked suspicious. We actually blew up some Shinto shrines because they were storing ammunition in some of them. We weren't supposed to, but we knew what the Japanese were doing, so of course we felt that we had to do it.

We carried fragmentary—or frag—bombs. When these bombs exploded, they would blow into hundreds of pieces. There were parachutes on those bombs, so coming in at low level, maybe fifty feet off the ground, to drop those bombs, the momentum would carry the bomb forward. The parachutes would slow down the bomb so when it hit the target, we would be out of there and it wouldn't blow our tail off.

I guess we were considered pretty fortunate coming in at low level. The Japanese Zeros, the fighter planes, wouldn't dive on us because when they finally realized how low we were, they didn't have time to pull out and they would crash. So they wouldn't attack us at that low level. And the antiaircraft batteries wouldn't fire on us, because they would be shooting the buildings around them. So like I say, we were pretty fortunate in that we didn't get a lot of fire except coming from ground personnel: machine-gun fire, rifle fire, and things like that.

We would come home with bullet holes in our plane, and there wasn't too much there to protect you, just a thin sheet of aluminum. That was the way that it was. You just prayed that that bullet coming through didn't have your name on it.

There were a number of our planes that would get shot down. They would hit the engines, and of course, the guys would crash. At that low level, you couldn't bail out with a parachute. That was the chance you took—that you wouldn't get shot down.

While we were in Ie Shima, there were so many fellows who were going home that there weren't enough replacements coming in to keep up the four squadrons, so the 345th dissolved, and we transferred to the 38th Bomb Group over in Okinawa. We weren't flying on missions every day, but it would be a day or two out of the week. It would depend on how many planes came back and how many crews were available at the time.

While we were on Okinawa, Japan finally surrendered. The B-29s carried the atomic bomb to Japan, and once they had gotten a taste of those

Operation Iceberg: The Battle for Okinawa

The eighty-two-day battle for the southern Japanese island of Okinawa was the largest, bloodiest, and last of the major Pacific conflicts between the Allies and Japan. Located 360 miles from the main islands and 1,000 miles from Tokyo, Okinawa was a critical prize. Stretching 65 miles long and ranging from 3 to 20 miles wide, it contained rugged cliffs and ridges into which the Japanese had carved a network of interconnecting tunnels and fortified defensive pillboxes. With multiple airfields, harbors, and its proximity to China, the Philippines, and supply lines, Okinawa was an asset that the Japanese could ill afford to lose. The Americans saw it as a staging platform from which to bomb and, if necessary, invade Japan.

Code-named Operation Iceberg, the attack started on April 1, 1945. On this Easter Sunday, 100,000 U.S. soldiers and marines were ready aboard 1,300 ships, including 40 carriers, 18 battleships, and 200 destroyers. Invading the island's west side, the first wave of 60,000 troops quickly fanned out. Surprisingly, although Japan had 100,000 troops on the island, they met no resistance and quickly occupied the northern four-fifths of the island.

atomic bombs, they changed their minds quickly. Some people thought that was an awful thing Harry Truman did to allow that to happen, but it saved many lives of our people, because the war came to an end then.

We came home on the SS *Falcon,* a Liberty ship. The boys had a crap game going on that lasted the whole time from when the ship left Japan to Seattle. One guy won thousands of dollars and ended up hiring a guy to guard him while he slept. When we got to Seattle and stepped off the boat, they gave us a pint of ice-cold milk. All we had was powdered milk overseas. Now I don't particularly care for white milk, but that white milk really tasted good, and it was ice cold. It was just something I always remembered.

From Seattle they loaded us on a train to Chicago, where we changed over

Then they moved south, where Japanese troops offered fanatical resistance to the death at spots like Sugar Loaf Hill and Conical Hill. Fighting hand-to-hand and bayonet-to-bayonet, U.S. troops began counting gains by yards. The American commander, Lt. Gen. Simon Bolivar Buckner, rejected the marines' suggestion to mount an amphibious landing to the enemy's rear, instead ordering a bloody frontal attack.

American casualties were staggering. They exceeded 49,000, with 12,500 killed (more than 7,000 on land and 4,900 at sea) and 36,600 wounded, the worst of all Pacific battles. A total of 1,465 kamikaze flights attacked the naval fleet, damaging 368 ships and sinking 34. The Allies lost 763 aircraft. Japan's losses, too, were enormous: 109,000 troops killed and 24,000 sealed in caves and presumed dead, as well as 100,000 Okinawan civilians killed. Japan lost 8,000 planes and 16 ships. Its battleship *Yamato,* the largest warship ever built, was sunk en route to Okinawa.

Buckner was killed by enemy fire. When the cause was lost, the Japanese commander, Lt. Gen. Mitsuru Ushijima, committed ritual suicide. All of this took place over 450 square miles—an area about the size of Los Angeles. Considered together with the Japanese culture's deep-rooted belief that surrender was dishonorable, the cost of taking Okinawa weighed heavily in President Harry Truman's decision to use the atomic bomb to end the war. ★

to another train and ended up at Fort Dix, New Jersey. I was discharged there at Fort Dix, and they let me come home. So by the grace of God, here I am.

AFTER THE WAR . . .

Robert Book took advantage of the GI Bill and learned the shoe-rebuilding trade. He opened a business in Quarryville and now does some part-time repair work at home. He and his wife, Fay, have been married for more than fifty years and have four children.

☆ Lester Weldon ☆

New Bloomfield, Pennsylvania

Lester Weldon was drafted into the army in 1942.
He was a machine gunner in the 3rd Infantry Division.
During his time in combat, Weldon earned
five Purple Hearts and four Bronze Stars.

I was working for a company in West Virginia at the time of Pearl Harbor, and I worked until the week before I was drafted in 1942. I did my training at Camp Wheeler, Georgia, close to Macon. They taught us how to kill people. That's what we learned.

I went overseas in January of 1944. Went to Italy. I was in the front lines at Anzio and saw a lot of dead bodies; a lot of dead and wounded people, that's about it. I was there two weeks until I got wounded the first time. It was my first battle against the Germans, and I was one of the first ones to get wounded. I was hit in both legs with shrapnel. There were probably fifty-some people lying around me on the battlefield. I laid there for four or five hours, and no one came to take me out, so I crawled out. I dug my fingers into the dirt, grabbed on to clumps of grass, and crawled out. As I was trying to get out, a tank shot at me twice, but he missed me.

Finally I got out, and got back to the hospital the next morning, and when I woke up after leaving the operating room, the Germans were shelling the hospital. That night they put me on a hospital ship and took me back to Naples Hospital, and while I was there, they bombed that hospital!

I was in the hospital six weeks. I got out and went back to Anzio again, and I was there three and a half weeks until I got hit again. This time I got hit in the head with shrapnel, so I was back in the hospital for another five or six weeks. The day I got back to Anzio was the day they made the break-through to Rome. All of us who were coming back from the hospital were given the job of carrying the wounded back. That was a full-time job all day long, just carrying the wounded. We didn't carry back any of the dead, just the wounded. We would get up to where the front lines were, where they made the breakthrough, and there were hundreds and hundreds of dead bodies laying all over the place. We had to walk through these bodies that were lying so close together. They died right where they were hit.

We got shot at quite often. One time I walked out of the woods to ask a guy where a wounded man was who we were looking for. About that time a tank fired at me, and I jumped into a hole on top of two other men. The last shell they fired landed right where I had been standing, right on the edge of the hole. I did that job for two weeks, until we got to Rome. When we got to Rome, it was declared an open city, so there was no fighting at all. In Rome they gave us two weeks to rest up and recuperate. After that I went back to my own company. I was a machine gunner in the machine-gun squad in the infantry.

When we left Rome, we ended up training to land in France. We got into Rome on June 4 and we practiced until August 15. Then we landed in southern France, in the Mediterranean area.

When the ship was going into shore, it hit a mine in the water, and we lost thirty-two men before we got off the boat. There were whole areas 300 to 400 yards up the beach just covered with mines. As soon as we got out of the minefields, a mortar came in and landed right beside me. Five of us got hit there. I was probably hurt less than the rest of them, but the mortar actually landed right beside me and I got hit in the neck. The rest got hit pretty bad, but I didn't. The medic patched me up and I kept on going. That was the third time I was hit.

Once we landed in France, we were on the front lines for over three months before we got relief. We were moving forward all the time, fighting continually the whole way. It was terrible. Every day it seemed like we lost men, and some days, maybe a week or more, we wouldn't even see the Germans; maybe we'd just get a glimpse of them. Yet we kept losing men. The Germans would set up roadblocks and empty their guns at us and take off, and we would lose several men. The artillery would come in and we would have to dig foxholes. I sat in a foxhole for several days before I got a chance to move, and that was the only rest I got. But we kept moving.

All of our fighting in the 3rd Division was in the mountainous area of France, Germany, and Austria, and when we got up to the middle part of France, I got hit again. That was the fourth time I got hit. The closer we got to Germany, the tougher the fighting was.

We had two machine guns in our company. One would be in the front with the lead platoon, and the other would be in the reserve. One day in France, when my squad was in reserve, the shooting started and I jumped into a ditch beside another man. Just as I landed in the ditch, he got shot in the head. I yelled for a medic, and the medic came and I took off through the woods to where most of the shooting was. I stopped and looked around and saw a man to my left, and just as I looked at him, a little black hole appeared in his forehead. About that time a shell exploded in the trees. I went over and saw that both of my gunners had been shot.

When the fighting was over and we started counting heads, we had thirty-three men left in the company. There were four platoons in a company, and thirty-two men in a platoon, and we only had thirty-three men left in the whole company. There were five men in my squad, and I only had one man left.

The Germans kept attacking and attacking us, and we were almost out of ammunition. We were sitting in a little area—about an acre of ground—and the Germans were surrounding us on three sides. If they had known we were almost out of ammunition, they could have taken us any time, but fortunately God was with us, because they stopped attacking.

We sat there for a week, and then we got quite a few replacements, all new recruits. Normally you have five sergeants and four corporals in a platoon, but now there were only four men left, so the captain asked me to take over the rifle platoon. At the time, I was still a private, but I took over the platoon, and when we left there, I was the one to lead the first attack. We went down over the mountain and captured some of the Germans at the foot of the mountain.

Now it was getting toward winter. It was cold and miserable, and everybody had trench feet. The conditions were really rough. We got into the low land and toward the Rhine River, the German border, and the Germans were fighting hard. They were fighting for every inch of ground. We lost a lot of men. I probably saw thousands of dead people, thousands of wounded people. It just seemed like we were losing men all the time, day in and day out.

It was rough in the winter because of the snow, and a couple times we were surprised by the Germans. One time there was a foot of snow on the ground, and we came on these German foxholes. We didn't see any signs of Germans, so we settled in for a nice quiet evening. That was the only time I remember them bringing fresh baked bread to us. I had it all laid out there in the foxhole, and after a bit we heard the German tanks in the woods about a half mile away. They started up and started coming toward us. When I looked out of the hole, all I could see was a streak of machine-gun fire going across the valley in front of me. We sat there awhile, and then the other guy in the hole with me stood up and looked around and said, "Let's come on, everybody is gone." We jumped out of the hole, but all we could see was a streak of machine-gun fire, so we took off running. We left everything, left all the groceries, the bedrolls, everything. I just grabbed my gun and ammunition and took off.

The next thing I remember, it was night, and we had crossed the river and met up with our lieutenant and the other guys in the machine-gun squad. All at once the lieutenant said, "What are you retreating for? No one gave the orders to retreat." So we turned around and went back across the river. As soon as we got across the river, we saw a man way out in the distance in the dark. Well, we didn't know where the rest of the Americans or the Germans were. We didn't know anything, so we were pretty jumpy.

We debated what to do about this man we saw coming toward us, and I said, "Shoot a burst at him and see what happens." We shot a burst at him and he started yelling. That's how we figured out that he was one of our own men. I'm sure glad I didn't hit him, because I was the one who gave the order to shoot.

We had eight or nine men with us, and we walked down along the river a little ways and found some foxholes and crawled into them. That night we just about froze to death, because there was a foot of snow on the ground and it was really cold. I took the first watch on the machine gun until around midnight. Everyone took turns on watch. I laid down and shivered myself to sleep.

In the morning when I woke up, it sounded like all hell broke loose, because shells were exploding everywhere. I jumped out and went over to the other holes, and nobody was around. Everybody was gone and I was there by myself, so I took off along the river. I didn't see anybody until I got up to a footbridge. Just as I got there, a shell landed in the water right beside the bridge. I went across the bridge, and while I was running, I could feel the breeze off the artillery shells that went by my head. I felt the breeze on my face, that's how close it was, and I just kept running. There were hundreds of men there, and they were all running, and I was toward the back end of them. I thought I would never make it to the woods, but finally I got there.

It was pretty terrible, because no one knew what to do or what was going on, but finally we got the company together, as small as it was—there wasn't many of them left—but we got the company and pulled back to a little town and spent the night there.

That was just the way it was all winter long, every day. When we did get a break, it was only for a week. We would get a week off to get new replacements in and take a couple of days of training. And every time we started out, we knew it was going to be another river crossing, another fortification, another town or something to take. We would have a full company of men at the beginning, but after the first day's attack, we would probably lose a third of the men. And that's the way it went the whole time, until finally we crossed the border into Germany.

We went through Germany into Austria, and the day the war ended we were at Salzburg, Austria. We stayed there a couple of days, then they moved us back out into the mountains and down toward the east, because a lot of the Germans didn't know the war was over. So we were trying to round up the Germans, going into fortifications, castles, and places where the German officers were staying. But a week after the war ended, I got notice that I was being sent home, and two weeks after the war ended, I was on my way home.

AFTER THE WAR . . .

Lester Weldon went into the flooring business and eventually started his own business. He then went on to build and remodel homes until he was seventy-six years old. Weldon and his wife of more than forty-six years raised four daughters and one son. She passed away in 1994.

☆ Edward Ovecka ☆
Lebanon, Pennsylvania

••

Edward Ovecka was an aircraft sheet metal worker
for the Army Air Forces. His primary responsibility
was to repair aircraft. He was in Pearl Harbor on
the day of the bombing and was wounded.

••

I did my training at Wheeler Field in Hawaii, and my assignment was two
years in Hawaii. I enlisted that way, but it never worked out that way.
Actually, I spent six and a half years on one enlistment. When I left Lebanon,
I didn't expect to come back. But here I am.

I was an aircraft sheet metal worker. I learned whatever it would take to
patch an airplane up. They even told us how to patch an airplane up with
tin cans if we had to. Whatever had to be done in the metal part of it, I did
it. I did everything down to building the potty pots for them.

We were the first ones at Hickam Field, Hawaii. We had to wait until
everything was built. After the barracks and the hangars were built, we did-
n't have an eating area, so they set up tents where we got our food. But we
were the first ones there.

One day a B-24 came into our area. It was being sent to a place where

The B-29 Superfortress:
The Plane That Dropped the Atomic Bomb

Designed to enable the United States to bomb Germany from the American mainland, the B-29 Superfortress bomber instead was used exclusively in the Pacific against Japan. In the end, it was the plane that forever changed the nature of warfare, ending World War II by dropping the atomic bomb.

Early in the war, when the fate of England was wavering, American military planners feared that it would fall to the Nazis. That meant that America would have to wage war on Germany from across the Atlantic. A transatlantic round-trip was out of the question for B-17s or B-24s, so Gen. Henry H. "Hap" Arnold, then acting commander of the Army Air Forces, named a committee to begin to plan for a long-range heavy bomber. One member was Charles A. Lindbergh, who, having toured German air bases and aircraft plants, believed that the Allies would quickly fall behind if they didn't press for advances in aviation technology. The panel's recommendations laid the groundwork for Arnold to promote development of a very-long-range (VLR) bomber.

Already contemplating such a plane, the Boeing Aircraft Company designed what it called Model 345, which it submitted to the government in May 1940. One year later Boeing received a contract to build 250 B-29s; after Pearl Harbor, the quantity grew rapidly to 500 and then to 1,500.

Able to fly at 357 miles per hour, the four-engine B-29 measured 99 feet long and had a wingspan of 141 feet. With a pressurized cabin (the first of any U.S. bomber), its crew of eleven—pilot, copilot, bombardier, navigator, flight engineer, radio operator, radar operator, central fire control gunner, left gunner, right gunner, and tail gunner—could fly at nearly 34,000 feet. Its range varied from 3,250 to 5,725 miles. The price tag was $639,000.

The program was nearly canceled when, after initial test flights starting in late 1942, a prototype XB-29 crashed in Seattle on Feb-

New B-29s on a parking apron at a Boeing plant in Wichita. FRANKLIN D. ROO-
SEVELT LIBRARY, HYDE PARK, NEW YORK

ruary 18, 1943. Minutes after taking off from Boeing Field, the plane
developed an engine fire; attempting to land, it smashed into a meat-
packing plant. All eleven crewmen died, as did nineteen people in the
factory. The crash couldn't be covered up, but the model of the plane
was kept secret. After this, even President Franklin D. Roosevelt, who
had approved the B-29 program, questioned it.

Boeing wanted to abort the project, but Arnold, now commanding
general of the Army Air Forces, investigated, finding that the problem
lay in the construction of the engines, not in the plane's airworthiness.
He insisted on repayment of $200 million in development fees if Boe-
ing withdrew. Boeing grudgingly agreed to build the plane, but Army
Air Forces took over all aspects of development and testing.

On April 15 the first production B-29 emerged from Boeing's
Wichita, Kansas, plant. Soon production was in high gear. On March
10, 1944, Army Air Forces personnel and some 600 of Boeing's
workers at that facility began what they called the "Battle of
Kansas"—working for four weeks around the clock outdoors (B-29s
(continued on page 206)

(continued from page 205)
were too big to fit existing hangars) in a bitter plains winter to ensure that 150 B-29s were ready for delivery on time. They made their goal, and 98 B-29s flew their first combat mission on June 5, from India, in Operation Matterhorn, against a railroad yard in Japanese-occupied Thailand. It was a 2,261-mile round-trip, the longest Allied bombing run to date in World War II.

In all, 3,898 B-29s were built, mostly at Boeing's plants in Renton, Washington, and Wichita, with smaller quantities built at the Glenn L. Martin Company's plant in Omaha and Bell Aircraft Corporation's plant in Marietta, Georgia. At first the B-29s attacked Japan from bases in China. But as the Allies won more and more Pacific Islands from the Japanese, the battle plan changed. The goal of the invasion of the Mariana Islands—principally Saipan, Tinian, and Guam—in mid-1944 was to secure a foothold from which to strike Japan, which lay 1,400 miles west and just within the reach of the B-29s. Superfortress raids against Japan began flying from Saipan on November 24 of that year.

After first concentrating solely on conventional high-explosives bombing of core defense industries, the AAF added another tactic in March 1945, dropping incendiary bombs to set off firestorms, which would destroy feeder industries while also incurring civilian casualties. Sorties of as many as 472 B-29s destroyed large sections of Tokyo, Kawasaki, Kobe, Nagoya, Osaka, and Yokohama, killing more than 100,000 civilians.

they might need guns, but this plane didn't have any mounted guns. There were .50-caliber guns lying on the floor of the plane, and my job was mounting them. So the old man—I say the old man; he was my boss—picked me and another guy by the name of John Mann, and we took the job. We started Saturday morning and worked all day until 6:00 P.M., and then he came in and said, "Hey guys, this plane doesn't have to go out until tomorrow at noon. Why don't you knock off? Your efficiency is getting low and you need a break." So we took off.

I cleaned up and went into Honolulu. It looked like it had snowed. The navy was in town, and they were already half crocked, drunk, and laying in

As the secret Manhattan Project to develop the atomic bomb proceeded, plans were developed to modify B-29s to carry and drop the device. Harry S. Truman, who succeeded to the presidency after FDR died on April 12, 1945, foresaw that an invasion of Japan would cost 500,000 to 1 million casualties, and decided that using nuclear weapons would end the war and save American lives. A test detonation, code-named Trinity and conducted on July 16, 1945, at Alamogordo, New Mexico, was declared successful. The same day, one of two bombs intended for Japan, the uranium-armed "Little Boy," was shipped to Tinian for final assembly. It was soon followed by the plutonium-armed "Fat Man."

On August 6, Col. Paul W. Tibbets Jr., a veteran of both B-17 combat in Germany and North Africa and the testing of the B-29, piloted a B-29 named Enola Gay on the historic mission over Hiroshima. When the "Little Boy" bomb was dropped, more than 75,000 people died. Japan ignored an Allied ultimatum, and three days later, a B-29 named Bockscar, piloted by Maj. Charles W. Sweeney, dropped the "Fat Man" bomb over Nagasaki, killing 35,000 people. On August 15, VJ Day, Japan unconditionally surrendered. B-29s embarked on mercy missions, dropping food and medical supplies to Allied POWs in Japan.

The B-29 fleet had one wartime duty remaining. When Japanese diplomats signed the formal surrender papers on the deck of the USS *Missouri* on September 2, a vast formation of 500 Superfortresses flew overhead at low altitude as a show of force. ★

the gutters. The MPs would pick them up and throw them in the paddy wagon and take them back. It was so crowded I couldn't even get a beer, so I turned around and took a cab back.

I got up the next morning and went to church at 6:00. I walked up Hangar Avenue about 6:50 to go to work, and it was like a morgue. No aircraft engines running, nothing. We were completely at ease. I was in the hangar about five minutes, didn't even have the doors up, when the first bomb went off. It blew up the plane I was working on. One of my buddies was lying there. He had black hair like I had, but it was all red from blood. I picked him up to get him out of there. I looked at him and his eyeballs turned white, and I thought, "That's the way you die." I never saw anybody die, so how did I know? So I put him down and went outside.

When I got out of there, I got strafed by a plane and caught one in the side. So I got down on my hands and knees and crawled. They kept on strafing, and I could see the bullets go *pop, pop, pop,* coming right at me like in the movies. Then I caught another one, but the only thing it did was cut a groove into my side. I had a lot of holes in me, but the only ones that were real bad were on the bottom of my foot. I never realized that one I got in

Transatlantic Troop Transport

To send millions of American forces to Europe, the military had to use everything that floated. Ships of every size and type were converted to carry troops, from tankers and freighters to the luxury liners *Queen Elizabeth* and *Queen Mary.* On such large ships, thousands of soldiers from widely diverse branches of service were packed into cramped quarters. In July 1943 the *Queen Mary,* built to carry about 2,200 passengers, made a crossing from New York to Gourock (Glasgow), Scotland, with 15,740 troops and a crew of 943, for a total manifest of 16,683.

Despite the danger of torpedoes from German submarines, such ships often traveled alone, because they were fast enough to outrun the subs. Although they were capable of top speed, all ships were slowed by the need to take a zigzag course to evade targeting by subs. Most voyages across the 3,000-mile-wide North Atlantic lasted a week to ten days; some took as long as fifteen days.

Slower transports needed protection. Sometimes they were shadowed by aircraft that could spot subs and drop depth charges, but early in the war, a plane's range was limited to a few hundred miles from each coast, leaving a vulnerable "air gap" in between. Some troop ships traveled in convoys, together with freighters, tankers, and aircraft carriers, and protected by escorting destroyers—often consisting of thirty to sixty ships spread out over a five-by-eight-mile area.

Most departing troops sailed from New York Harbor, with others embarking from Boston or the Newport News–Norfolk area of Vir-

the side also got me in the heart. I never knew it until sixty years later. They found it when they did my bypass. I have a piece of metal in the muscle part of my heart. It doesn't bother me. In fact, the doctor who did the bypass said he should take it out, and I said, "No, it's been in there that long, don't cut around my heart."

From there on, I was lying in the field watching the whole show go on. They were flying right past me. I could have killed them with a .22. It was weird. It was just like being in a movie.

---

ginia. Most arrived at Southampton, Liverpool, or Gourock in the United Kingdom. Others headed for Casablanca, French Morocco, or, after D-Day, Marseilles, Cherbourg, or Le Havre, France. Upon arrival, most soldiers were sent to bases to be organized for action, but some loaded in the United States and went directly into combat from the ship they'd traveled on, such as an amphibious assault on Sicily in 1943.

Officers fared better on these ships than enlisted men, who might sleep in shifts in six-high bunks in lower decks. Evacuation drills were held daily, and passengers were instructed to always wear a life jacket by day and sleep in their clothing at night, prepared to bail out. Meals were served twice a day, but for some soldiers, even that was too much in rough seas. The choppy North Atlantic made thousands of men seasick.

With no military duties during the idle time, entertainment consisted of twenty-four-hour gambling at games of craps, poker, or bridge. The presence of any nurses aboard helped brighten morale. On rare occasions, movie stars and singers were onboard to entertain the troops. In 1945 the USS *West Point* sailed from Virginia to Naples, Italy, with comedian Red Skelton, a Special Services private, aboard. He told jokes to the fresh troops on the outbound trip and helped cheer the wounded on the return trip.

As the war wound down, the military devised Operation Magic Carpet to return some 8 million soldiers from the European and Pacific Theaters. Many Liberty and Victory freighters were converted to troop use, and in all, more than 700 ships, including army, navy, Coast Guard, and British vessels, did the job. Even the aircraft carrier USS *Enterprise* got into the act, ferrying soldiers home from Europe in December 1945. ★

I figured I was going to die. I could see all my bones in the bottom of my foot, and all the meat was shot away from it. You know, when you get hit like that, you don't bleed right away, so I tied myself off so I wouldn't bleed to death. I never belonged to the Boy Scouts, I just did what I thought I should and I tied it off.

I saw a torpedo bomber come in and thought he was going to dive into the Hawaiian Air Depot Hangar. The hangar had a big high side. He was coming right at it, and when he was ready, he released his bomb. The bomb was as long as the bottom of his aircraft. It went in, broke the glass, and all of a sudden *Vroom!* When that went off, he peeled right away over the top, and off he went. All of a sudden there was one big explosion, and I looked back. I could see between the hangars down into Pearl Harbor. It was the biggest explosion of all the bombing. I saw when it went up, but I didn't realize it was that ship until I got into the hospital. They told me that the *Arizona* went up and they killed so many people.

I hate to tell you this; I'm glad I didn't see it, but I was told. A friend of mine who was a very good mechanic had both of his arms and legs shot off. He just lay there until all the blood was out of him. He died that way, right along the hangar. Another one of my friends ran right past me while he was on fire. He had a uniform on like me. He wasn't supposed to be working that day, but he came in. But he made it, he lived.

Then I got lucky. My commanding officer, Lieutenant Colonel Reily, picked me and a few other guys up. He had a 1936 Buick with leather seats. We only had to go a little ways to the aid station; they already had it set up by the time I got there. When I got to the hospital, it was like going into a butcher shop. They had the intestines there, arms and legs that they chopped off. I figured that's where my foot was going. I got shot around 8:00 A.M., and I didn't get operated on until about 8:00 that night. Luckily a doctor who was on vacation in Hawaii volunteered his services. He was an osteopathic surgeon, and he worked on my foot. That's the reason I still have my foot. He told me, "Don't let them cut that off!"

We were the first ones back from Hawaii. We came back on the *Monterey.* It was a luxury liner, and they converted it into a hospital boat. We had an escort of two or three destroyers with us, and they had to zigzag in front of us because they didn't know if the Japs were out there and were going to throw a torpedo at us. Then I went to the Presidio in California at Letterman General Hospital, and they performed the operation on me.

I spent ten months in the hospital, and my foot would not heal completely. I had a spot about as big as the end of my thumb. It would break open as soon as I would walk on it. The scar tissue was preventing the blood from going in there to heal it. So they sent me to Fitzsimmons General in Denver, and that's where they performed another operation. They took that scar tissue out and moved the flesh over the hole to give me a little padding so I could walk on it. Ever since that, I have the pain. But you get used to it.

AFTER THE WAR . . .

Edward Ovecka was discharged from the military in 1945. He went on to work for Bethlehem Steel as a draftsman for twenty-eight years and retired at the age of fifty-five. He has been married for more than sixty years, and he and his wife have one son.

☆ Morris Goltz ☆

Warwick, Pennsylvania

Morris Goltz was a medic with the 26th Infantry Division.
He followed Gen. George Patton through northern France,
Germany, Luxembourg, Belgium, Austria, and Czechoslovakia.
Goltz has a Purple Heart for the wounds he received
during hand-to-hand combat with an SS soldier.

I was born July 1, 1919, in a little town called Ladischune in the Ukraine. At the time I was born, the Cossacks were hiding out in the hills, taking out revenge on the population, even though my father had fought with the Russians in World War I with the Allies against Germany.

When I was one and a half years old and had just learned how to walk, the Cossacks rode into this little town and ordered all the women, mainly Jewish women, and their children to stand out on the road. My mother had a rope that she tied around her waist and around my waist. The Cossacks lined all the women up on this dirt road and got on their horses, drew their sabers, and galloped and trampled and hacked all these women and children to death. You could imagine all the screams, but my mother was phenomenal. She showed no fear, and by a miracle, we survived.

At that time it was very difficult to get out of Russia, and it is a long story how we escaped to Romania. We were in a horse-drawn hay wagon hiding in the hay. The different guards would stop and stab their sabers into the hay. But luckily we got out and came to America in 1923. I was about three and a half years old.

I wanted to save money to go to college in 1936, but there were very few jobs available. I was very fortunate to find a coal-mining job in the Frackville and Shenandoah area of Pennsylvania. I made quite a bit of money then, and went to Temple University School of Podiatry, studying to be a foot doctor. I graduated in June 1941, six months before Pearl Harbor.

In December 1941, when the Japs bombed Pearl Harbor, President Roosevelt declared war against Japan and Germany. The United States needed everything. We had no guns, no ships, no bullets, no nothing. Three schools were opened up, and I attended one school that taught you to become a burner or a ship fitter or a welder. I asked the instructor what paid the most, and he said a burner. So I graduated as an acetylene gas burner and got a job working for Sun Ship Building Company in Sharon Hill, Pennsylvania, and I soon learned why burners made all this extra money.

It was a very dangerous job. We had to stand up on these little eight-inch planks, high above the waves, and they only had a little railing. You had to hold on to the rail with one hand and burn with the other. A lot of guys would slip and fall. I had a few narrow escapes. I worked there for about a year, until one day I was working in the pump room down in the bottom of a ship, when lo and behold, a welder up above me dropped a piece of a bulkhead that came crashing down through the ship and, luckily, just glanced off my head. We wore thick plastic helmets, but it broke the helmet and drove some of the plastic into my skull, and I was knocked out. That was the end, I figured. After that, I quit.

Shortly after that, my draft number came up and I joined the army. I took basic training in Fort Jackson, South Carolina, and after completion I went to a port of debarkation, which was Camp Shanks, New York. I was shipped to Europe, and on the way across the Atlantic, one of the ships in our convoy was torpedoed by a German U-boat.

We arrived toward the end of D-Day, landing at Utah Beach. Shortly thereafter I was assigned to a mine-clearing team, even though I was a medic and didn't have any training in mine clearing. One of the guys told me, "Don't worry about it; we will teach you in a couple of minutes." We used this tool that looked like a waffle iron with a long stick. We went over the different areas, and when it clicked, we dug our knife into the ground and had to dismantle the mines.

We were in Carteret, France, where we cleared over 7,000 mines. Most of them were what they called "bouncing Betties." They were shaped like a flowerpot, and they had three or four iron rods sticking out. They were a horrible type of mine, because when you stepped on it, it didn't explode right away; it bounced up and exploded about waist-high. They created horrible wounds to the poor guy that stepped on it, and of course, it got a lot of the guys around it, too.

We were assigned to General Patton's 3rd Army, and our first job was to relieve the 4th Armored Division in a town between Nancy, France, and the German border. I fought in four major battles. There was northern France, Rhineland, the Battle of the Bulge—Ardennes—and then there was Central Europe. During combat, I was wounded on four different occasions, but they weren't that serious. I had shrapnel in my left calf one time, and I had a severed finger from a mortar barrage that, believe it or not, I sewed up myself. And I did a pretty good job.

I had two other injuries. One day in 1945 in Czechoslovakia, I was captured by an SS officer. I was on patrol with my buddy Pattrick, and we lost contact with our patrol. All of a sudden the Nazi officer pulled up behind Pattrick, and he had him. I turned around, and he had me too. He made us drop all our weapons in a bush nearby, and he was walking us to what we call a prisoner collecting point. He walked us to the end of a cliff and suddenly stabbed Pattrick and pushed him over. Then he turned around and pointed his rifle and fired a shot at me. It went through my jacket and missed me. I went to throw a block into him, and that's when he caught me in the upper jaw and swung at my head with his rifle. He cracked my head, and the rifle actually snapped when it hit a tree. He was on top of me and got in a lot of stab wounds. By some miracle Pattrick, who had landed on a ledge, crawled back and tackled the guy. I got his knife away and hit him one hard shot. It went through his upper shoulder and into his neck, and cut his jugular vein. He got up and took about ten steps and dropped dead. I got my Purple Heart for that.

Another time I was captured in a town called Sarre-Union, France. Our 101st Regiment had just taken the town. Our captain gave me a lousy job. He wanted me to get in this jeep with our liaison sergeant and make sure we found a nice place for our aid station. We had just taken this town, and the sergeant let me out in front of a building. I was scared to death and told him, "Please make sure you don't get knocked off before you get back and tell them where I'm at."

I was in this building, a little one-room schoolhouse, when the Germans counterattacked. All of a sudden a Tiger tank came down the road and blew out the whole front of the schoolhouse I was in, and I was knocked unconscious. When I came to, I had a concussion. These three Germans had me captured, but they only had me for about fifteen minutes when our 104th Regiment, that was fighting close by, suddenly turned around and attacked them to retake the town. The three Germans who had just captured me for about fifteen minutes then surrendered to me.

I have had a lot of "back flashes" from the war when, for some reason, thoughts would come back of some experiences I had during the war. Different psychiatrists told us we should try to forget about the war when we got home, and most of the World War II veterans came home and wouldn't tell their experiences to their children and grandchildren, figuring that they could forget. But it didn't work that way. The more you tried to keep it out of your mind, the more it came in. I'll tell you a couple more of my back flashes.

One time we were in Metz, and our 101st Regiment was ordered by Patton to capture the last fort in Metz, which was the largest fort. It was called Fort Jeanne d'Arc. I was one of the four fortunate guys that watched the German commander of the fort come out with a white flag. They rode up in a German jeep and surrendered. Shortly thereafter, a couple buddies and I went into the fort. We weren't supposed to loot, but we thought we would grab some interesting souvenirs. We were walking along one of the hallways, and one of my buddies said to me, "Hey Sergeant, you are now a general in the Kraut army!" Believe it or not, there was a plaque on one of the doors to an office, and it had the name of a high-ranking German officer, and he had the same name as I have, spelled the same way.

So I sat behind this officer's desk and put my muddy boots on top of his desk and was blowing cigar smoke circles, when all of a sudden the door banged open and there was a GI with his M-1 pointing at me. Suddenly he said, "I can't believe it's you!" By some miracle he was my uncle Ben's wife's brother, Sammy, who was with the 80th Infantry Division. He was on the other side of the fort, not aware the Germans had surrendered. We used to tell the story to our kids and family for years later on.

There's another back flash I had forgotten about for quite a while: Every once in a while after a battle, we would go to a rest area for a day or so to replace our dead and our wounded. We had this fellow named Doucette, who was a litter bearer. He came up to me—he was sort of a sad-sack-looking type of a guy—and he had to go to the bathroom. Fortunately there was a little outhouse there. One of our other guys said, "I got to go, too. Wait for me." So the other guy went and we waited for a while, and there was a shelling going on and he didn't come out. Finally we said to Doucette, "You can go out and use the outhouse." He went out and he came back, and his hands were shaking and he couldn't talk. We went out, and lo and behold, the first guy that had gone in was sitting down on the toilet in the outhouse, when a big hunk of shrapnel went through and decapitated him. His head was on the ground and he was still sitting there.

Another interesting back flash that I had was when I was running under a shelling and finally crawled into a German house. All of a sudden I heard the cry, "Medic!" I crawled out the front door, and there beside a tree was one of the infantry guys who had been hit. I crawled over and looked at him and told him he had a "million-dollar wound." I used to say that no matter how bad a guy was hit. I would always say, "Oh man, you're lucky, you got a million-dollar wound. You are getting the hell out of this war. I wish I could trade places with you."

There were a lot of times you could be hit and you could be dying, and you would never know it. You would be talking, never knowing how serious the wound was. But this guy just had a simple arm wound, and I patched him up, put a little sulfa on it, and gave him a shot of morphine. I was just through patching him up and there was another shelling, and he hollered, "Mama!" and blood rushed out of his mouth and he died. I couldn't figure it out. I looked him all over and noticed that a piece of shrapnel in the second shelling had hit his thigh and ricocheted up through toward his hips, and evidently chopped up some of his insides and he died. It was just one of those things.

AFTER THE WAR . . .

Morris Goltz practiced as a foot specialist for sixteen years, and then went into the real estate business for seventeen years. He and his wife raised a daughter together.

☆ Murray Friedman ☆
York, Pennsylvania

....

Murray Friedman was in the Army Air Forces and was
combat pilot trained as both a navigator and a bombardier.
He flew a variety of missions that included D-Day.

....

I was at Penn State in the middle of my sophomore year when I took the aviation cadets' exam and was notified that I passed it. A few weeks later I was called up to active duty. I started out in New Cumberland and then went down to Miami, then to Memphis, Tennessee, for classification. Then from there I was sent to Santa Ana, California, for pretraining.

I went to Kirtland Field in Albuquerque, New Mexico, for bombardier training with a class called 43-11. We competed with the other bombardier schools, there were about ten of them, and we were first—we won the championship. As a matter of fact, I was number one and, as a result, became an instructor. After a month or so they sent me to navigation school, because they wanted to experiment whether a bombardier could be both a navigator and a bombardier. It worked out well, because it saved my crew on one or more occasions.

From there I was sent overseas; my air base was below Norwich, England. I was with a B-24 Liberator Bomb Group. I can't tell you how many groups were there, but there were a lot of groups. The main problem was in substituting losses. There were a lot of losses. I have a photograph of me with a group of six men—six survivors after one raid. There were twenty of us living in a barracks together, and there were six survivors. So we decided that we should go out and take our picture right away.

They told us that the crew I was assigned to would be broken up for the first mission, and that I would fly with an experienced crew for a break-in mission. I was told it would be rather short. It turned out to be the longest mission I was on: eight and a half hours, all the way to Leipzig, to Czechoslovakia, and back. It was a long day. They gave us Hershey bars for every

The Point System

As World War II was playing out its closing chapters, American leaders realized that they needed an orderly system for both redeploying and demobilizing a military force that numbered well into the millions. The Adjusted Service Rating (ASR)—commonly known as the Point System—became that method, awarding points for length of service, marital status, and battle credits.

Proposed by Gen. George C. Marshall and modified by Secretary of War Henry L. Stimson, the system became effective on May 10, 1945, and redeployment, or R-Day, was May 12. The ASR determined who would be sent home first, who would remain to occupy Europe, and who would be sent to the Pacific Theater. Enlisted men everywhere became preoccupied with the intricacies of the system and hounded company clerks to update and correct their scores.

The target scores were 85 for enlisted men (44 for enlisted women). Those with a sum of 85 or more points qualified to be sent home and discharged. Others would continue to serve until their score increased or until the target number was lowered.

Points were assigned as follows, all dating from September 16, 1940:
• 1 point for each month of service (12 points per year).

mission. If they gave you one bar, it was a so-called easy mission. If they gave you two bars, you had better watch out. So the first mission was a two-bar mission, and we sure got the experience we needed.

After the first mission, I came back and the maintenance man asked if I enjoyed it, and if I had any problems. I said, "Not really," and he said, "Let me show you something." About six inches to a foot away from my head was a hole, and he reached into where the hole was and pulled out a piece of flak. It had the number eight stamped in it. So the number eight is my lucky number.

From there we went on the typical raids, the big cities in Germany: Berlin, Augsburg, Munich, Kiel, and a group of others. And each one was a different experience.

- 1 point for each month served overseas (also 12 points per year).
- 5 points for each combat award, such as the Distinguished Service Cross, Distinguished Service Medal, Distinguished Flying Cross, Purple Heart, Silver Star, Bronze Star, Navy Cross, Legion of Merit, or Soldier's Medal.
- 12 points for each child under eighteen years, up to three children.

Men who had won the Medal of Honor were eligible for immediate release on their request, as were married women in the Women's Army Corp whose husbands had been separated from the military and returned to civilian life. Personnel whose scores did not reach the thresholds were held for service in Europe or sent to the Pacific. Those holding essential jobs—radar operators, cryptographers, Signal Corps personnel, and translators—were exempted from the Point System and were required to remain in the service until later.

For others the target score was higher: Colonels through majors needed 100 points to be discharged, and medical officers needed 120 points. The plan went into effect on about four days' notice. The military began processing and sending home tens of thousands, then hundreds of thousands of personnel each month. In November 1945 the War Department dropped the target score to 70 points or 51 months' service for officers, and 55 points or 4 years' service for enlisted men. A month later the requirements were lowered again. ★

By the time we started flying, it was early spring 1944, and the German Air Force had been pretty well beaten up. They still came at you and you had problems with them, but it was not what the earlier missions were experiencing. At that time, they said that if you survived 20 or 30 percent of the missions, you were lucky. I was luckier—we could survive 35 to 40 percent.

There was no such thing as a usual mission. If it was a big raid such as Berlin, there might have been 1,000 planes. A thousand planes carried nine or ten men each, so that would give you an idea how many people were involved.

It really was remarkable how it was orchestrated. Each base took off and formed its own formation. They didn't all fly in one clump; they flew maybe in a thirty- or forty-mile stream. There were three or four squadrons at an air base and they formed a group—ours was the 93rd Bombardment Group—and each group had a leader plane, and each leader plane was a different color. It was kind of wild. And after you formed on this leader, the other leaders all got together and peeled off, and away you went.

The biggest problem we had was dodging flak. Flak was artillery put up by the Germans. The conversation always was that the Germans started manufacturing these guns right after World War I, they had so many of them, and every little town had at least half a dozen guns. But when you went to one of the big cities, they might have had 1,000, and they put up patterns and tried to guess where you were in the sky, and they were built pretty accurate. I think that most of our losses came from the flak. My plane was hit many times with small pieces. If it was hit with a larger piece, you were doomed. So I don't know, we may have had 100 pieces hit us here and there.

I don't think we were ever scared. We were too busy to be scared—everybody was doing something. Some of the people didn't have as much to do all the time, like the gunners, for example. The only time they really worked was when we were attacked by the German fighters. But the officers were flying the airplane, navigating, bombing—they were always doing something.

Everybody expected D-Day to come for weeks; there were rumors floating all around the place. If I remember correctly, they got us up at 2:00 or 3:00 in the morning for a special briefing. We knew what was coming. During the briefing, they said, "Now don't tell anybody where you are going. This is a big secret." By the time we got out to the airplane, everybody knew where we were going—the maintenance people, the mechanics—they all wanted to come along. There were people offering money if we would take them along. This was true all over England. So we decided to take an extra person or two. One was a flight surgeon; we figured he would come in handy. Another one was the senior maintenance man. We just made room for them and they came along.

When we started to take off, things were pretty dark out. We tried to follow our lead plane, and other people tried to follow their lead planes. We wound up with other airplanes in our group following the lead of our plane, but somehow or another we got into a formation. We flew directly over the North Sea and directly over the beachheads. Our target was to secure a railroad bridge and a highway crossroad so that the German troops up in this peninsula could not come back to help the other Germans. And it worked out very well.

After hitting that target, I believe it was called Carentan, I remember we turned to the right and headed back to England, and that was the end of D-Day for us. By 9:00 in the morning I was taking a shower. Those other poor kids down on the ground, they suffered so much. Our hats were really off to them.

Our losses were nothing. The Germans were completely held down. I don't know how many airplanes flew over that beachhead, and we had fighter planes to help keep the enemy away from us. I think it was a very well-organized mission, both in the air, on the ground, and at sea.

I returned to the United States in October 1944 and was assigned to Atlantic City. I remember the doctor saying, "How do you feel?" And I said, "Pretty good." He said, "Suppose I told you we were going to send you over to Japan to fly combat again?" "I'd say go to Hell!" And he said, "Fit for duty! That's the answer we were looking for."

But I didn't have to go to Japan. I became a combat instructor at Mountain Home Air Force Base in Idaho—that air base is still in existence today—and I stayed there until the war ended.

AFTER THE WAR . . .

Murray Friedman graduated in 1947 from Penn State with a degree in business administration. He was employed as a CPA, and then was called up for duty again during the Korean War. Later he worked for the attorney general in Harrisburg, and then started his own firm called Seligman, Friedman and Company, P.C.

☆ Harry Tillman ☆
Oreland, Pennsylvania

∙∙

Harry Tillman was a marine stationed in the South Pacific. He also spent time in Okinawa, where he was critically wounded.

∙∙

I enlisted and was assigned to Parris Island, South Carolina, and then from there it was on to New River, North Carolina, now called Camp Lejeune. I went overseas in June 1942. We had to zigzag across the ocean because of submarines, and we made a practice landing on the Fiji Islands. We had to stay there overnight because a couple of our landing boats were wrecked on the coral. While we were there, some of the men caught a big boar and cooked it. We ate it that night.

When we set sail, we didn't know where we were going and weren't told until about a day before we landed on Guadalcanal. There was actually a small group of islands together: Guadalcanal, Tulagi Island, and Florida Island. I was among the first to land on Guadalcanal on August 7, 1942, at 6:00 A.M. At first there was no opposition, but the marines that landed on Florida and Tulagi Island did meet some resistance when they first went in. We landed at Guadalcanal to secure the airport so our planes could take off.

We didn't get hit until August 21, during the Battle of the Tenaru River.

We were in foxholes all along the river. The Japanese landed about three miles below us and were marching up. The battle took place at nighttime, and you couldn't see in front of you. You just had to know that somebody was out there in front of you and you had to shoot.

They were firing at us and we were firing at them, and we didn't know how we made out until morning. At dawn we looked over to the other side of the small river and saw all the bodies lying there. Quite a number of our men got wounded, but we killed an awful lot of Japanese in that battle.

After that we moved inland and secured the airport. We put a ring around the airport so our planes were able to get in there. There were great crew planes there and a wonderful group of fighter pilots. They did a tremendous job on the Japanese Navy and the Japanese fighter planes.

Every once in a while we would engage in some fighting. We would go out into the jungle and hunt Japanese who would run away from the airport. We were bombed quite a bit by an airplane that came over every night. We called the plane a "one-lung Charlie." He would come over and drop one bomb on us and take off. We were also shelled by the Japanese ships and bombed by the Japanese Air Corps.

One time when we were walking through the jungle, we had to go up a very high hill. At the top, it was so beautiful; we had a view of what an island really looks like. Then we captured a couple of Japanese and brought them back in for interrogation.

We had other small battles throughout our time on Guadalcanal, and we were there until just before Christmas, when the army came in and took over for us. We had secured the island, and all the Japanese that we could have possibly gotten, we did.

We left there by ship and went to Espiritu Santos, an island that was owned by the French government. There was a naval station there and all the warships were there, either getting repaired or preparing for more battles. We had about two weeks of rest and relaxation there, and we got our first ditty bag from the Red Cross, that contained a lot of little goodies. One thing that it contained was raisins, and the men all gathered those raisins up and made booze out of it.

After we left there we went to Melbourne, Australia. There we got replacements and started to train again. We actually went out on His Majesty's Ship to train and make landings. The first night we slept in hammocks on the ship. Somebody had cut the ropes on the hammocks about halfway through, and all during the night you could hear *thump . . . thump . . . thump*. The hammocks were all breaking, and the guys would come down on the deck. We were all mad at that.

My buddy and I caught malaria, and we were put in the hospital. I had picked up the bug in Guadalcanal, but I didn't know I had it. We were in the hospital for about three weeks, and our outfit had packed up and sailed off for another invasion. So they sent us back by ship to the States, where we spent another year and a half.

Then in 1945 I was sent to Okinawa as a replacement. On the way there, we docked in Pearl Harbor. I said, "Oh, this is going to be great—we are going to be able to go out and see Pearl Harbor," but the captain said that nobody would get leave because he thought some of the guys would jump ship and take off. So we didn't get any liberty at all. Then we zigzagged across the ocean and landed in Okinawa at the end of May 1945. The original landing on Okinawa was April 1, April Fools Day. I came in about the middle of May, and the fighting was very fierce.

We had some rain, and when it rained, the mud got so thick we had trucks stuck in it halfway up the body of the truck; they just couldn't move. And when it rained at night, and if we weren't fighting in a battle, we would go into these caves that turned out to be burial caves. There were jars of people who had been cut up and put in the caves. I don't know whether it was better out in the rain or in there putting up with the smell, but it was pretty horrible. Some of them had been in there for years, and of course, they were just nothing but bones, but some of them were fairly new.

When we moved again, we landed in Naha, the biggest city in Okinawa. Then we moved up to the northern part of the island, where we met fierce fighting. During one of the battles, I was up on a little knoll and saw a hole that looked like a cavity where the Japanese would hide a gun. I dropped a grenade down in it. I didn't even hear it go off. The next thing I know, I got hit like an NFL linebacker would hit me with a flying tackle. I had gotten shot in my left leg and the bleeding was fierce. From my old Boy Scout knowledge, I took a handkerchief and wrapped it around my leg, and put a stick in it to make a tourniquet. Then the medics came and picked me up and carried me back to the temporary first aid. They gave me a shot of morphine and bandaged up my leg as best they could.

In the hospital they doped you up so you didn't feel anything right away, but they didn't want to give you too much dope, because you would become an addict. When I woke up, I saw something sticking through my leg like a little wooden skewer. They had the wood tucked in the wound and had gauze around it, but I was in terrible, unbearable pain. My wife wonders how I can stand so much pain now. Well I did all this in the Second World War, and I went through all that pain there.

The base hospital was something like you would see in "M★A★S★H": It was tents and things like that. That's where they operated on me and did what they could on my left leg. Then they put a cast all the way up to my hip, put me on a stretcher, and then onto a small plane like a Piper Cub to transport me to another part of the island.

From there we went on board the USS *Solace,* a hospital ship. A hospital ship, according to rules of war, has to be lit up, so we were all lit up so we looked like a Christmas tree. On board the ship, they changed my cast, which was from my toe to my hip—changed it about three times because the blood eased down through. And for everybody who had a wound where they had a cast on it, it would bleed through the cast and the smell was horrible. But I got used to it. I don't know how other men made out, but I got used to the smell. I had to.

When we came back, I was put on a hospital train and went to the Charleston, South Carolina, Naval Base, and that's where they did most of the doctoring. As my leg was improving, they measured me for a brace that was made in Philadelphia. I wore the brace, which was fastened on either side of my shoe all the way up to either side of my knee, because I had the "drop foot." When you walk with a drop foot, you drag your foot and fall. It's not a brace you would see today, but I wore it for about five years after I got out of the service. The only time I would take it off was to go to bed, and all the rest of the time I would wear the brace.

Around January 15, 1946, I was recuperating, and they sent me up to Asbury Park, where each marine, sailor, or whatever, was assigned to their own room with their own bath. This was a classy hotel, and the bathtub was heart-shaped. When I was able to walk, I was able to take the train and come home on weekends. Then on February 19, 1946, I was finally discharged from the Marine Corps.

AFTER THE WAR . . .

Harry Tillman got married and went to work in his grandfather's china repair shop. He and his wife had a son. Tillman later worked in refrigeration for thirty years. Following the death of his first wife, Tillman remarried.

☆ WORLD WAR II TIMELINE ☆

1931		Japan invades Manchuria (northern mainland China).
1933	January 30 March 20	Adolf Hitler becomes chancellor of Germany. Nazis establish first concentration camp at Dachau.
1935	March 16	Germany begins to rearm.
1938	March 12 November 9	Germany annexes Austria. *Kristallnacht,* when Nazis carry out coordinated attack on synagogues and Jewish businesses and residences throughout Germany and Austria.
1939	March 15 April 7 August 23 September 1 November 30	Germany annexes Czechoslovakia. Italy invades Albania. Germany and Russia sign a secret nonaggression pact in which they agree to carve up Poland. Germany invades Poland. Russia invades Finland, which surrenders in March 1940.
1940	March 18	Italian dictator Benito Mussolini meets Hitler and formally joins forces with him as part of the Axis powers.

	May 10	In Operation *Sichelschnitt* (Sickle Stroke), Germany invades Holland, Belgium, Luxembourg, and, on May 12, France.
	May 13	Newly installed British prime minister Winston Churchill makes his "I have nothing to offer but blood, toil, tears, and sweat" speech.
	May 27	Allied retreat of 300,000 troops from Europe begins at Dunkirk, France.
	June 14	Paris falls to the Germans.
	June 18	Churchill gives his "This was our finest hour" speech.
	June 22	France surrenders to Germany.
	July 10	Battle of Britain begins; aerial siege by Luftwaffe lasts three and a half months.
	October 28	Italy invades Greece.
	December 9	British troops begin rout of Italians seeking to occupy North Africa.
1941	March 31	Germany lands troops in North Africa to aid retreating Italians.
	April 6	Germany invades Yugoslavia.
	June 22	Germany begins invasion of Russia.
	September 1	Germany orders Jews to wear yellow Stars of David for identification.
	December 7	Japan mounts a sneak aerial attack on U.S. naval forces at Pearl Harbor, Hawaii.
	December 8	President Roosevelt asks for, and Congress grants, a declaration of war.
	December 10	Japan begins invasion of Philippines.
	December 11	Nazi Germany and Italy declare war on the U.S.
	December 26	Churchill addresses a joint session of Congress, the first British prime minister ever to do so.
1942	February 15	Under Japanese siege, British surrender Allied control of Malaya and Singapore.
	March 8	Burma falls to Japanese control.
	April 9	U.S. forces on Philippines surrender; Bataan Death March follows.

April 18	Doolittle's raiders bomb Tokyo.
June 4	At the Battle of Midway, U.S. successfully defends its strategic hold on the Pacific island of that name.
June 7	Japan invades the Aleutian Islands in Alaska.
June 21	Germans attack and take Tobruk in Libya, North Africa, from the British.
August 7	Second Battles of Guadalcanal (six-month series of battles between U.S. and Japan) begin in Pacific; U.S. prevails.
October 23	Battle of el-Alamein begins; British force retreat of Germans and Italians threatening Egypt and Suez Canal.
November 8	In Operation Torch, Allies invade Morocco and Algeria in Northwest Africa.

1943	January 10	Soviet Army begins counteroffensive to relieve Stalingrad.
	January 14	Roosevelt and Churchill meet in Casablanca to discuss strategy.
	January 27	U.S. begins daylight bombing of Germany.
	April 19	Jews in Warsaw Ghetto conduct unsuccessful uprising against Nazi SS occupation.
	May 12	Axis forces (Germany and Italy) in North Africa surrender to Allies.
	July 10	Allies invade Sicily.
	July 25	Mussolini is forced to resign and goes into hiding.
	September 3	Allies begin invasion of Italy but face fifteen-month battle for control of the country.
	September 8	Italian government announces surrender, but German troops occupy Italy to hold it.
	September 9	Allies conduct amphibious invasion of Italy at Salerno and enter Naples.
	December 24	Gen. Dwight D. Eisenhower is named supreme commander of Allied forces in preparation for D-Day.

1944	January 22	Allies invade Italy at Anzio Beach.
	January 27	The 900-day Siege of Leningrad fully ended as the Soviet Army breaks the German blockade of the city.
	June 5	Rome is liberated.
	June 6	D–Day: Operation Overlord begins, with the successful Allied invasion of the Nazi–held French coast of Normandy.
	June 22	Russians begin Operation Bagration, an offensive against Germany.
	August 15	From the Mediterranean, the Allies invade southern France.
	August 25	Paris is liberated.
	September 17	Operation Market Garden, an unsuccessful Allied attempt to break into Germany from France, is launched.
	October 2	Allied forces enter Germany.
	December 16	Germans launch Battle of the Bulge, attacking westward through the Ardennes Forest of Belgium, but are driven back within a month.
	December 22	Germans demand surrender of surrounded U.S. 101st Airborne; U.S. general Anthony McAuliffe replies, "Nuts!"
1945	January 9	U.S. begins invasion of Philippines.
	January 26	Auschwitz concentration camp is liberated.
	February 4	Conference of Allied leaders at Yalta begins.
	February 19	U.S. begins invasion of Iwo Jima.
	April 1	U.S. begins invasion of Okinawa, eighty-two-day battle that becomes the last great conflict of the war.
	April 12	U.S. president Franklin D. Roosevelt dies of a stroke at age sixty-three; Vice President Harry Truman succeeds him.
	April 21	Red Army reaches edge of Berlin.
	April 28	Mussolini is captured by Italian partisans and executed.

April 30	With Allied troops surrounding Berlin, Hitler commits suicide in his bunker.
May 7	Germany signs unconditional surrender.
May 9	VE Day declared.
June 30	U.S. troops liberate Philippines.
July 17	Potsdam Conference of Allied leaders in Berlin meets to draw up map of postwar Europe.
August 6	U.S. B-29 bomber Enola Gay drops world's first atomic bomb on Hiroshima.
August 9	U.S. B-29 bomber Bockscar drops atomic bomb on Nagasaki.
August 15	VJ Day declared.
September 2	Japan signs formal terms of unconditional surrender aboard USS *Missouri*.
November 20	Nuremburg war crimes trials begin.
December 21	Gen. George S. Patton dies.

☆ ADDITIONAL MAPS ☆

THE EUROPEAN THEATER
1942–1945

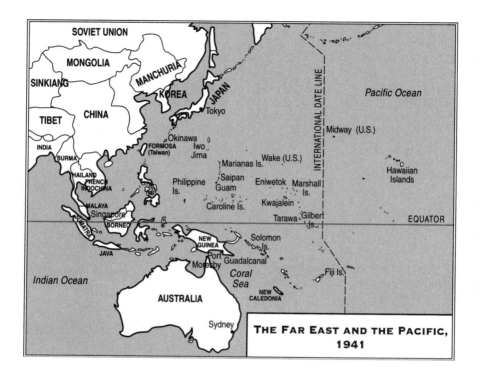

THE FAR EAST AND THE PACIFIC, 1941

☆ BIBLIOGRAPHY ☆

PUBLISHED SOURCES

Ambrose, Stephen E. *Eisenhower: Soldier, General of the Army, President-Elect, 1890–1952.* New York: Simon and Schuster, 1983.

Army Times. *Warrior: The Story of General George S. Patton.* New York: G. P. Putnam's Sons, 1967.

Blair, Clay. *Ridgway's Paratroopers: The American Airborne in World War II.* Garden City, NY: Dial Press, 1985.

Dupuy, Col. R. Ernest. *World War II: A Compact History.* New York: Hawthorn Books, 1969.

Eisenhower, David. *Eisenhower at War, 1943–1945.* New York: Random House, 1986.

Eisenhower Foundation. *D-Day: The Normandy Invasion in Retrospect.* Lawrence, KS: University Press of Kansas, 1971.

Gilbert, Martin. *The Second World War: A Complete History.* New York: Henry Holt and Company, 1989.

MacDonald, Charles B. *A Time for Trumpets: The Untold Story of the Battle of the Bulge.* New York: William Morrow and Co., 1985.

Perret, Geoffrey. *Winged Victory: The Army Air Forces in World War II.* New York: Random House, 1993.

Pimlott, John. *B-29 Superfortress.* London: Bison Books, 1980.

Ray, John. *The Illustrated History of WWII.* London: Weidenfeld and Nicholson, 1999, 2003.

Snyder, Louis L. *The War: A Concise History, 1939–1945.* New York: Simon and Schuster, 1960.

Stenger, Charles A. *American Prisoners of War in WWI, WWII, Vietnam, Persian Gulf, Somalia, Bosnia, Kosovo, and Afghanistan: Statistical Data Concerning Numbers Captured, Repatriated, and Still Alive as of January 1, 2003.* Prepared for the Department of Veterans Affairs Advisory Committee on Prisoners of War.

Whiting, Charles. *Patton.* New York: Ballantine Books, 1970.

————. *Year by Year: 75 Years of Boeing History.* Seattle: Boeing, 1991.

WEBSITES

Airborne Warfare, including Paratroopers

xoomer.virgilio.it/webyankee/stosil8.htm

www.ww2-airborne.us/18corps/101abn/101_overview.html

home.att.net/~C.C.Jordan/

www.grunts.net/army/82abn.html

www.grunts.net/army/101abn.html

Aircraft, Military

General

www.daveswarbirds.com/usplanes/

www.csd.uwo.ca/~pettypi/elevon/baugher_us/

www.fighter-planes.com/

www.ghostsquadron-ggw.org/base/base.cfm

B-17

www.wpafb.af.mil/museum/air_power/ap16.htm

www.b17.org/

www.memphisbelle.com/

www.centennialofflight.gov/essay/Air_Power/B-17_29/AP28.htm

B-24

www.wpafb.af.mil/museum/research/bombers/b2-45.htm

www.b24.net/index.html

www.b24.net/ (Click on "The Search" for the story of Jim Marsteller of New Park, Pennsylvania, who researched the final, fatal B-24 mission flown by his uncle, York County native Everette "Jim" Morris of Fawn Grove, Pennsylvania. The plane was shot down over the Black Forest of Germany.)

life.csu.edu.au/~dspennem/MILARCH/Virtual_B-24s.html

www.cafb29b24.org/diamondlil.shtml

home.att.net/~jbaugher2/b24_37.html

B-25

www.airforcehistory.hq.af.mil/planes/b25.html

history1900s.about.com/library/prm/bljimmydoolittle1.htm

www.cv6.org/1942/doolittle/doolittle.htm

www.history.navy.mil/photos/events/wwii-pac/misc-42/doolt-p.htm

B-29

www.centennialofflight.gov/essay/Air_Power/B-17_29/AP28.htm

www.cafb29b24.org/fifi.shtml

www.boeing.com/history/boeing/chr2_war_2.html

www.strategic-air-command.com/aircraft/B-29/b29-history.htm

home.att.net/~jbaugher2/b29_9.html

BT-13

www.natlcapsq.org/our_BT-13.htm

P-51

www.p51.mustangsmustangs.com/p51.shtml

www.airforcehistory.hq.af.mil/planes/p51.html

cpcug.org/user/billb/hankeny/index.html

nasaui.ited.uidaho.edu/nasaspark/safety/history/rollsroyce.htm

Air-Sea Rescue, Goldfish Club, and Mae West vest

www.nobadlie.com/asr.htm

www.303rdbga.com/goldfish.html

www.geocities.com/b24gunr2000/Goldfish_Club.html

Anzio

www.army.mil/cmh-pg/books/wwii/anziobeach/anzio-fm.htm

Battle of Britain

news.bbc.co.uk/onthisday/hi/dates/stories/july/10/newsid_3516000/
3516193.stm

Battle of the Bulge

www.army.mil/cmh-pg/books/wwii/7-8/7-8_cont.htm

www.battleofthebulge.org

www.worldwar2history.info/Bulge/

China-Burma-India Theater

www.army.mil/cmh-pg/books/wwii/marauders/marauders-fw.htm

www.wwiilectureinstitute.com/stories/eisenberg.htm

D-Day

www.army.mil/cmh-pg/brochures/normandy/nor-pam.htm

www.army.mil/cmh-pg/books/wwii/7-4/7-4_cont.htm

www.army.mil/cmh-pg/books/wwii/100-11/100-11.htm

Eisenhower, Gen. Dwight D.

www.skylighters.org/quotations/quots3.html

www.newsmax.com/archives/articles/2004/5/29/114229.shtml

www.historynet.com/mhq/blmacarthur/

Holocaust

www.archives.gov/exhibit_hall/american_originals/depress.html

history.acusd.edu/gen/WW2Timeline/camps.html

Liberty Ships

www.fiu.edu/~thompsop/liberty/photos/liberty_summary.html

Luftwaffe

www.spartacus.schoolnet.co.uk/GERluftwaffe.htm

Malmedy Massacre

www.scrapbookpages.com/DachauScrapbook/DachauTrials/
MalmedyMassacre02.html

www.us-israel.org/jsource/ww2/Malmedy.html

Okinawa

www.army.mil/cmh-pg/books/wwii/okinawa/index.htm

Patton, Gen. George S., Jr.

members.ozemail.com.au/~mickay/patton.htm

www.brainyquote.com/quotes/authors/g/gen_george_s_patton.html

Pearl Harbor

www.history.navy.mil/faqs/faq66-1.htm

Prisoners of War

www.b24.net/index.html

www.house.gov/honda/POW_articles/RL30606.pdf

☆ RESOURCES ☆
for Further Study and Visitation

Military-administered facilities are closed on all federal holidays. Check websites or phone ahead to verify days and hours of operation. Some archive sites with limited capacity require researchers to make an appointment a few days before their visit. Also, verify any security procedures that may be necessary before visiting museums housed on military bases or any military-administered archives.

ARCHIVES AND MILITARY LIBRARIES

Air Force Historical Research Agency
600 Chennault Circle, Bldg. 1405
Maxwell AFB, AL 36112-6424
334-953-2395
www.au.af.mil/au/afhra/

Air Force History Support Office
1190 Air Force Pentagon
Washington, DC 20330-1190
202-404-2167
www.airforcehistory.hq.af.mil/

Marine Corps Air-Ground Museum
(no longer open for public visitation but remains open to researchers
as a library and archive)
2014 Anderson Ave.
Quantico, VA 22134-5002
703-784-2607
hqinet001.hqmc.usmc.mil/HD/Home_Page.htm

Marine Corps Historical Center
1254 Charles Morris St. SE
Washington Navy Yard, DC 20374-5040
202-433-0731
hqinet001.hqmc.usmc.mil/HD/Home_Page.htm

Naval Historical Center
805 Kidder Breese St. SE
Washington Navy Yard, DC 20374-5060
202-433-4882 museum
202-433-4132 library
www.history.navy.mil/

U.S. Air Force Museum
1100 Spaatz St.
Wright-Patterson AFB, OH 45433
937-255-3286
www.wpafb.af.mil/museum/

U.S. Army Center of Military History
Collins Hall, Building 35
103 Third Ave.
Fort Lesley J. McNair, DC 20319-5058
202-685-4042
www.army.mil/cmh-pg/

U.S. Army Military History Institute and
U.S. Army Heritage and Education Center
22 Ashburn Drive
Carlisle, PA 17013-5008
717-245-3971
carlisle-www.army.mil/usamhi/

U.S. Coast Guard Historian's Office
2100 2nd Street, SW
Washington, DC 20593
202-267-0948
www.uscg.mil/hq/g-cp/history/collect.html

The Veterans History Project
American Folklife Center
Library of Congress
101 Independence Ave., SE
Washington, DC 20540-4615
202-707-4916
www.loc.gov/vets/

MILITARY MUSEUMS

Commemorative Air Force (formerly Confederate Air Force)
P.O. Box 62000
Midland, TX 79711-2000
432-563-1000
www.commemorativeairforce.org/

Commemorative Air Force, Inc., B-29/B-24 Squadron
P.O. Box 61945
Midland, TX 79711-1945
www.cafb29b24.org/index.shtml

82nd Airborne Division War Memorial Museum
Department of the Army Airborne and
Special Operations Museum
Fort Bragg
100 Bragg Blvd.
Fayetteville, NC 28301
910-432-3443
www.bragg.army.mil/new18abn/museums.htm

Le Mémorial de Caen
Esplanade Eisenhower
Caen, France
Phone: 00 33 (0)2 31 06 06 47
www.memorial-caen.fr/portail_gb/hp/hp.asp

National D-Day Museum
945 Magazine St.
New Orleans, LA 70130
504-527-6012
ddaymuseum.org/

National World War II Memorial, Washington, DC
Info: 2300 Clarendon Blvd., Suite 501
Arlington, VA 22201
800-639-4992
www.wwiimemorial.com/

Normandy American Cemetery and Memorial
American Battle Monuments Commission
Courthouse Plaza II, Suite 500
2300 Clarendon Blvd.
Arlington, VA 22201
703-696-6897
www.abmc.gov/no.htm

Pennsylvania Military Museum

P.O. Box 160A
Boalsburg, PA 16827
814-466-6263
www.psu.edu/dept/aerospace/museum/
World War II shrine: www.psu.edu/dept/aerospace/museum/shrine2.html

U.S. Army Heritage Museum

22 Ashburn Dr.
Carlisle, PA 17013-5008
717-245-4364
www.carlisle.army.mil/ahec/

U.S. Coast Guard Museum

c/o U.S. Coast Guard Academy
15 Mohegan Ave.
New London, CT 06320-8511
860-444-8511
www.uscg.mil/hq/g-cp/museum/MuseumIndex.html

Wings of Liberation Museum Park

Museumpark Bevrijdende Vleugels
Sonseweg 39, 5681 BH
Best, The Netherlands
Postbox 89, 5680 AB Best
Phone: 0499-329722
www.wingsofliberation.nl/index-uk.html
Formerly a temporary exhibition in 1984, commemorating fortieth
anniversary of Operation Market-Garden. Became a permanent museum
in 1997.

ADDITIONAL WEB RESOURCES

General World War II History

For 1941: www.decades.com/Timeline/n/954.htm

For 1942: www.decades.com/Timeline/n/955.htm

For 1943: www.decades.com/Timeline/n/956.htm

For 1944: www.decades.com/Timeline/n/957.htm

For 1945: www.decades.com/Timeline/n/958.htm

Glossary of World War II Terms

worldwariihistory.info/on/

Overviews of World War II History

worldwariihistory.info/WWII/

www.worldwar2history.info/

U.S. Army Awards and Medals

www.perscom.army.mil/tagd/tioh/Awards/Ribbons/
OrderofPrecedence.htm

☆ INDEX ☆

☆ ABOUT THE AUTHORS ☆

Brian Lockman, president and chief executive officer of the Pennsylvania Cable Network, is host of the weekly television series "PA Books," as well as host of the PCN Call-in Program. He joined PCN in 1994, after sixteen years at C-SPAN, where he served as vice president of operations. He is the son of Felix Lockman, who served in Burma during World War II with the 1st Air Commandos and is featured in this book. A native of Norwood, Pennsylvania, and a graduate of Temple University, Brian lives with his wife, Nancy, and their two daughters near Harrisburg, Pennsylvania. He is the editor of one previous book, *PCN Tours: A Companion to the Popular Television Series,* published in 2003.

Dan Cupper, a historian and author, has written ten books on railroad, highway, and Pennsylvania history topics. A native of Lewistown, Pennsylvania, he is the son of Ralph C. Cupper, a World War II combat-decorated veteran, who as an eighteen-year-old with the army's 7th Infantry Division, 32nd Infantry Regiment, won a Purple Heart after taking a bullet during the invasion of Okinawa in the spring of 1945. Dan and his wife, Shirley, live in suburban Harrisburg, Pennsylvania.